Goin' Crazy with Sam Peckinpah and All Our Friends

Goin' Crazy with Sam Peckinpa

and All Our Friends

Max Evans
as told to **Robert Nott**

University of New Mexico Press · Albuquerque

First paperback printing 2023
ISBN 978-0-8263-6502-6 (paper)

Library of Congress Cataloging-in-Publication Data
Evans, Max, 1924–2020
  Goin' crazy with Sam Peckinpah and all our friends / Max Evans with Robert Nott.
    pages cm
  Includes index.
  ISBN 978-0-8263-3587-6 (hardback) — ISBN 978-0-8263-3588-3 (electronic)
  1. Peckinpah, Sam, 1925–1984. 2. Peckinpah, Sam, 1925–1984—Friends and associates.
3. Motion picture producers and directors—United States—Biography. 4. Evans, Max,
1924– —Friends and associates. I. Nott, Robert, 1960– II. Title.

Cover photograph courtesy Dan Faris.

Designed by Lisa Tremaine
The text is composed in Century Oldstyle; display type is American Typewriter.

Contents

Acknowledgments

A book like this would never get completed if not for the contribution of a lot of people—most of whom knew and loved Sam Peckinpah, which means they probably wanted to punch him in the nose at least once.

Fern Lea Peter (Peckinpah) patiently and repeatedly gave her time over the phone to recall her relationship with her brother. David Peckinpah's widow, Sandy, helpfully reconstructed the life of her late husband for a vital chapter. A number of actors helped us out along the way too. Among them: L. Q. Jones, who will likely outlive us all, allowed us to build an entire chapter around his relationship with Sam. Morgan Woodward shared his memories of meeting Sam, and actor Seymour Cassel graciously agreed to a phone interview to discuss the ill-fated trip to Colombia that he took with Sam. He's lucky he got out alive. Thanks to Bo Hopkins, who said Sam gave him his real start with a prime role in 1969's *The Wild Bunch*. And a special thank-you to the still-beautiful actress, author, and activist Ali MacGraw, who provided commentary and support.

David Weddle, Garner Simmons, and Jeff Slater—all of whom have written important works on Sam's life and films—provided moral support and gave permission to quote from their works. Garner also gave us permission to use many of the photos he took of Sam on various film sets. Peckinpah historian Dan Faris donated the great and rare cover shot for this book—thank you, Dan! Noted Peckinpah documentary filmmaker Mike Siegal offered photos and support as well. We also received helpful written reviews of the manuscript from film historians Jeff Berg and Richard Gaughran, and one anonymous reader.

We must give a nod to Chalo González, who deserves more credit for his work with Sam and more literary space in his own book.

Katy Haber, Sam's mistress and right arm through eight years and eight films and his costar through a good part of this memoir, helped us throughout with photos, anecdotes, and connections to others who knew Sam. We cannot thank her enough.

To my wife Pat, who always reviews my work with an eye toward making it better, and who gave this book an exceptional first read before we submitted it to University of New Mexico Press. And many thanks to Santa Fe author Johnny D. Boggs, who sat in on the initial discussion of this project and who provided moral support and protection of the manuscript throughout its development.

From the press we have enjoyed the enthusiastic and sharp-eyed support of editor John Byram, marketing and sales manager Katherine White, and ace copyeditor Nicole Wayland. People like that just don't get thanked enough. We thank them all.

There are no doubt countless others whose names will regretfully come to me after publication. And then there are scores of Sam's noted and unknown friends, enemies, and associates whom I have somehow outlived and who thus cannot sue me. Regards to you all.

—Ol' Max Evans
Albuquerque, New Mexico
April 2014

Introduction

Sam Peckinpah once tried to drown Max Evans. Evans responded by breaking Sam's ankle, though in truth Max was aiming for Sam's neck. When Max told me he wanted to title his memoir of Sam *Goin' Crazy with Sam Peckinpah and All Our Friends*, I asked Max why Sam seemed to drive everyone around him insane—except for Max, who survived it all.

"I was crazy before I met Sam Peckinpah," Max explained.

Maybe I was crazy to accept Max's offer to cowrite his memoir on the late, sometimes great, often mad film director, but I knew I couldn't say no. I had always respected Peckinpah's talent. After working with Max on this book, I came to like Peckinpah, flaws and all.

This is an "as told to" reflection that allows Max Evans full voice, an extremely personal look at a man who dragged his personal demons with him wherever he went and who was capable of great generosity and cruel indifference. Max told me that Sam was "the greatest goddamned paradox in the art world." He may be right.

I can see why the two men liked and admired each other. Max had been a cowboy, a soldier, a smuggler, a painter, and, most importantly, a storyteller. Sam had been a would-be cowboy, a soldier, a would-be smuggler, a director, and, most importantly, a storyteller. They were roughly the same age when they met up early in 1962, and they both achieved success in their respective fields—Peckinpah in film, Evans in literature—within a few years of each other. Perhaps Sam filled the void that the death of Big Boy Hittson—a close personal friend of Max's—created for Max after Big Boy was shot dead by his younger brother in the late 1940s in the beautiful Hi-Lo Country of northeast New Mexico. "Black things hovered around him like an invisible spray—felt but never quite seen," Max wrote of Big Boy in his novel *The Hi-Lo Country*. The same could be said of Sam Peckinpah. Not surprisingly, it was this book that brought Sam and Max together after the director read it and decided he wanted to option the rights and make it into a film. Sam never quite pulled it off before his death in December 1984, but British director Stephen Frears did bring the book to the screen in 1998.

Max's story of his friendship with Sam starts in 1962 and ends with the release of that film in 1998. Along the way, you'll run into an ensemble of likable lunatics who passed—often as if moving through a revolving door—through Sam's and Max's lives, including Lee Marvin, Brian Keith, L. Q. Jones, James Coburn, Burt Lancaster, Ali MacGraw, Steve McQueen, Joel McCrea, Dale Robertson, Stuart Whitman, and a still renowned French actress who appears here in the nude, I am happy to report. You'll also encounter con men, hit men, ladies of the evening, and people whom no one should ever get to know.

Max was born in Ropes, Texas, in 1924. Not long afterward, his mother and father, Hazel and W. B., founded a town called Humble City in New Mexico's far southeastern Lea County. He left here for the Hi-Lo Country of northeastern New Mexico when he was about twelve years old. An infantry veteran of World War II combat, he tackled a number of career options before comfortably settling in as a writer with the 1960 publication of his breakthrough novel, *The Rounders* (later made into a motion picture starring Henry Fonda and Glenn Ford). Among his other works are: *Bluefeather Fellini, War and Music: A Medley of Love*, and the acclaimed novellas *My Pardner* and *The One-Eyed Sky*. He weaved in and out of Hollywood from the early 1960s into the 1990s optioning—or trying to option—his many works. In the late 1960s he moved to Albuquerque, New Mexico, which is where I first met him in the spring of 2002, after the publication of his memoir *Madam Millie*, which chronicled the life of Mildred Clark Cusey, who ran a string of bordellos in New Mexico, Kansas, Wyoming, and Alaska (among other sites). At that time, Max told me, "I'm nailed as a Western writer, but I would rather be known as a writer of the West."

That was another connection between Max and Sam. Peckinpah often said he did not want to be known only as a director of Western films. Of his 1970 movie *The Ballad of Cable Hogue*, Peckinpah told journalist Stephen Farber, "It's about people in the West—not a Western." Yet of Peckinpah's fourteen films, seven can be classified as Westerns. That grouping includes three classics—*Ride the High Country, The Wild Bunch*, and *Junior Bonner*—as well as the underrated *The Ballad of Cable Hogue* and the unfortunate misfires *The Deadly Companions* and *Major Dundee*. I would include *Pat Garrett and Billy the Kid* in this latter group, but I must note that Max considers it a brilliant misfire.

As with Evans, Peckinpah's familial roots can be traced west. His ancestors worked as sheepherders, loggers, lawyers, and judges, and he spent many early happy days on his Grandfather Denver's expansive ranch outside of Fresno, California. Like Evans, Sam served in the military in World War II, as a marine stationed in China, where he saw little (or perhaps no) action. His postwar direction led him into theater, and then television, before he landed work as an assistant to director Don Siegel, as a dialogue director, and as an occasional actor (you can spot him playing a bank teller in the 1955 Joel McCrea Western *Wichita*) for independent producer Walter Wanger at Allied Artists. Though Peckinpah claimed he loathed writing (a point echoed by Max Evans), he first broke through the film business as the scriptwriter for such television shows as *Broken Arrow, The Rifleman*, and *Gunsmoke* before writing and directing the short-lived series, *The Westerner*, starring Brian Keith.

In 1961 Peckinpah made his first feature film, the low-budget *The Deadly Companions*. It was the first of many productions in which Peckinpah would run up against producers who he believed were trying to extinguish his creative lights. That same year, he shot his first masterpiece, *Ride the High Country* (released in 1962), about a pair of aged lawmen—played by Joel McCrea and Randolph Scott—who head off on one last adventure to reclaim their integrity before the Old West recedes into the sunset. Though the picture was not a commercial success (it did much better at the box office in Europe than in America), it put Peckinpah on the map.

Disappointing misadventures followed, including the troubled production history of *Major Dundee* (and another battle with a producer), being fired from *The Cincinnati Kid* (more battles with producers), being fired from *Villa Rides!* (fighting not just producers but star Yul Brynner), and becoming, as Peckinpah himself put it, "persona non gratis" in Hollywood. But some fine television work, including the once-obscure drama *Noon Wine* (now finally being recognized with revival screenings), bought Peckinpah a second chance. Just as he started the decade with a brilliant Western, he would end it with another—the groundbreaking *The Wild Bunch*. That film focuses on a band of old-time outlaws trying to pull off one last haul before the New West—in the form of automobiles, airplanes, and political upheaval—swallows them up. Due to the movie's success and notoriety, even today many film historians believe that Peckinpah invented both slow-motion filming and screen violence. "I think violence is ugly," Peckinpah told interviewer Joe Medjuck in 1969, shortly after *The Wild Bunch* was released. "But if we don't recognize violence, that we are all violent people—we all are, every one of us standing around here—we're dead."

Making movies became an endurance race for Peckinpah (those are his words). So did friendship. Over the years, his erratic behavior—fueled in part by whiskey, tequila, and, later, cocaine—drove away most of his professional colleagues and personal companions. Max, like actor James Coburn, was one of the few to stick by Sam until the end. When Max ran into Coburn at the Taos Talking Pictures Festival in New Mexico in 1995, he said to the actor, "I don't know how we survived Sam." It took Coburn a few hours to contemplate this before he responded, "I don't know how Sam survived us."

Peckinpah died at the end of 1984 at the age of fifty-nine. He looks fifty-nine in photos taken during his fiftieth birthday party in the mid-1970s, actually. He lived hard, and the people around him often took the fall with him, causing a lot of pain.

Somehow Max managed to get through it unscathed. In Evans's comic novel *The Great Wedding*, Max wrote of the antics of the two protagonists, "All hell and things that were more fun broke loose." That's why, in my view, Max and Sam stayed friends. All hell was always breaking loose, and they both thought it was fun.

"I don't know how we got away with some of this shit," Max once told me of his exploits with Sam. I don't know how they did it either—I'm just glad they did.

—Robert Nott
Santa Fe, New Mexico
January 2014

1. The Madman of Film and His Legacy

The first I heard about the death of Sam Peckinpah was from the editor of *Impact* magazine, a Sunday supplement of the *Albuquerque Journal*. I didn't believe it.

About three weeks prior to that, I had visited Sam at his now-famed trailer house at Paradise Cove, Malibu, California. My last living image of him was still with me: eyes dark as a bat cave, disguising both his eternal torment and his special sense of ridiculous fun as they bid the world good-bye.

The editor, sensing my disbelief in Sam's departure to another dimension, adamantly insisted that the Associated Press, Reuters, and every other news service confirmed Sam was deceased. Now I believed.

The shock to myself and my wife, Pat, was erased to a degree by the editor's request that I write a five thousand–word story in twenty-four hours to make the lead for the next *Impact*. I did it. The magazine changed my title, "Sam Peckinpah, A Remembrance," to "Me 'n Sam." It has been reprinted through the years since in several hardbound anthologies under my title. I liked the story then, and I still do. The immediate call to action had erased the pain and disbelief. You see, I'd been busy on a book, and the instant-news world had passed me by. It still mostly does even as I scribble these words.

About five years later, I decided to write a very personal memoir.

I had written the very first book ever published on Sam. It was mostly about making a film with him, *The Ballad of Cable Hogue* (1970). It was called *Sam Peckinpah, Master of Violence: Being the Account of the Making of a Movie and Other Sundry Things*. Ironically, that was a mad, mad, mad, mad shoot. It was also the gentlest of all his films, and he told me often it was his personal favorite. He never said it was his best—simply his favorite.

1

Now I had witnessed screenwriter Garner Simmons struggling for years to get a book written about Sam that involved the completeness of this complex man and his works up to date. Garner was very often forced to wait here and there just to get in a few words with Sam when Sam was talking business or simply visiting with less talented people. I felt a great deal of compassion for Garner, and I admired his courage to continue under often-embarrassing circumstances. Garner was quietly tough and dedicated. He put out the first book of substance of Sam's life's work. That 1982 book, *Peckinpah: A Portrait in Montage*, still holds up and has been widely quoted over the years and around the world.

Once I decided to do a very personal book on some of the truly wild-ass times I had with Sam and our mutual friends, I went to the one person left who had known him the longest—Sam's sister, Fern Lea Peter. She and her husband, Walter Peter, had been there during the best of times at Sam's "Birdhouse" on Zuma Beach and, later, his Broad Beach house. They'd been there afterward when he was being crucified by the press and rancored ex-associates. Fern Lea warred with Sam on many matters, but she was a trusted confidante when he needed it most.

As I was prepared to take my first notes, I felt Fern Lea's hesitation. I was puzzled by this holding back as we had, since the first time we met, been close friends. So, out of respect, I stopped my inquiries with her and moved on to other projects. I soon found out that the family had given the authorized book rights to David Weddle. He is the son of James Weddle, who was Walter Peter's best friend. Pat and I met David for the first time the day and night of Sam's memorial service. He drove a bunch of Sam's closest friends to everything. He was a bright, extremely polite young man, and I could only wish him the best. I volunteered to help him in any way I could. He had some experience writing for *Variety* and other newspapers and magazines, but this was his first book, titled *If They Move . . . Kill 'Em! The Life and Times of Sam Peckinpah* (1994). Weddle's fine book was an initial success and is quoted more than any other of the many books done on Sam since. I liked it very much, with only one regret: Grove Press had Weddle cut about one hundred pages to make the book more "manageable." I felt then, as I do today, that as fine a work as it is, it would have been a true biographical masterpiece if he had been allowed to keep his total vision.

David has gone on to create other works. One—a story about his father and the demons left over from combat in World War II—is as fine a piece of long nonfiction newspaper writing as we will ever read. He has had a very successful career as a television writer and producer, including his work on the original *CSI*. He bought (but no longer lives in) Sam's old trailer in Paradise Cove. Weddle's biography of Sam stands out among the great masses of words on the singular Sam Peckinpah.

Yet after reading Weddle's book, Garner Simmons's book on Sam, plus Paul Seydor's in-depth masterpiece of a review of *The Wild Bunch*, I felt that there were things that only I (and a very few others) knew about him. So, knowing I might not live long enough to write it down in the traditional way, I chanced dictating it. That involved being lucky enough to find and choose the one person who was patient enough to take it all down, skilled enough to put it in form by connecting pieces of Sam's history, and a true lover and student of film—a tall order, indeed. Somehow the essence of the mostly unknown multiple unbalanced paradoxes of Sam Peckinpah's soul came along in writer Robert Nott. He loves films and the people who make them and inhabit them. I'd read his fine biography of film actor John Garfield and his *The Films of Randolph Scott*, so it was a simple choice. I asked him to consider all aspects before deciding whether to commit. He did. Then he accepted. And we did it. I feel it worked out, but you, the reader, must judge for yourself.

2. Everybody Wanted to Meet Sam Peckinpah—Until They Met Him

I had already lived several lives of bullshit when I first met Sam Peckinpah. It was sometime in 1962, around the time of the release of *Ride the High Country*, though I hadn't seen that film yet. I was living in Taos when a young MCA agent, Peter Field, called me from Hollywood and said, "Great news: the hottest young director in Hollywood wants to fly you out here to have lunch with him. He's interested in *The Hi-Lo Country*. Mr. Peckinpah said, 'I want to meet the son of a bitch who did this book.'" That book was based on my own experience working as a rancher in the beautiful loneliness of the Hi-Lo Country of northeastern New Mexico in the 1940s. I didn't know who the hell this agent was talking about, although I had seen the short-lived television series *The Westerner* and was deeply impressed with it. When this agent mentioned that Sam had made *The Westerner*, I knew he was the real rock.

I went out west on the Super Chief to meet Sam for lunch at the Polynesian, which was then near Warner Bros. I checked into a hotel, called a cab, and was at the restaurant by noon. Sam was there with a young couple and one of his agents. He summarily dismissed the young couple. We started drinking and talking. We started out with martinis and changed over to scotch. We were really hitting it off. The agent got crocked relatively fast and retreated. Sam was a really good drinker when he made up his mind to hold his drinks. I discovered that whenever Sam met people, he'd usually have a drink with them, and then decide if he liked them within two or three drinks. In his youth, before he got on the cocaine, he expected a guy to be a good drinker. And you can tell if a guy can hold his liquor within three drinks.

We talked about the similarities in our backgrounds, being outdoors when we were young. He spent childhood summers on his grandfather's ranch. He was impacted by the fact that his grandfather, father, and uncle were all judges. I also had a grandfather who was a judge and a rancher. Even coming from a family like that, Sam was basically an outlaw. It seemed like that was the happiest part of that first meeting, us remembering being back there on the ranch. He had been involved with riding and branding, but he wasn't horse crazy. He wasn't more afraid of them than anyone else, mind you. He just understood that they were bigger and tougher than he was. We ended the night by getting thrown out at closing time, somewhere around two o'clock. To meet a new friend like that and know that it is working right away is one of the great pleasures in life.

Sam told his agent to draw up some papers on *The Hi-Lo Country* to make it into a movie. He fell in love with my work. He would option five or six of my stories over and over again. Alan "Killer" Keller, who for a while worked as an actor and had been a champion rodeo performer before becoming Sam's stunt man and bodyguard, told me later that Sam once said to him in frustration, "I'm never gonna get any of Max's work done unless I finance them myself. So I'm gonna option 'em all and nail 'em to the wall so nobody else can make 'em either." This obsession would cause some complications later.

I didn't know he was interested in optioning *The Rounders* until much later. He optioned a lot of my other stories, including *The One-Eyed Sky, My Pardner, The Great Wedding*, and "Big Shad's Bridge," which was my only semi–shoot 'em up. We'd write the contract on bar napkins and sign 'em, Sam and me, and he would almost always give me cash. Sometimes, when I later bought them back, he insisted I pay him in cash! We both lost track of who owned the rights to *The Hi-Lo Country* over the years. Every time he optioned that book, it just got more complex. Once we had four or five lawyers trying to figure it all out. Sam first optioned that book for $75,000. It hit the front page of the trades the next morning, and I was a hero by one o'clock—a rich hero. Except I was about $86,000 in debt from the price of copper dropping in half in 120 days and thus breaking my mining company. I was working to pay off that debt so we actually had little of that option money to pleasantly spend.

Sam had just divorced Marie, his first wife, with whom he had found common relevance in the world of California State University, Fresno. Sam was born in Fresno. His heart and soul remained there in the mountains nearby and showed up in all of his Western films. Sam was partially raised on his grandfather Church Peckinpah's ranch. Nearby was an old mining town called Coarse Gold (which would serve as a setting in Sam's first major film, *Ride the High Country*). Church, a politician and rancher, was really tough on Sam and Sam's older brother, Denver. He taught them that hunting was first designed for the meat and not just for sport. He took them on rides into the mountains and taught them to observe all elements of nature and to never, ever leave an animal wounded. It must be tracked down until it—or you—died. The hunter must make sure to kill it and bring back the meat to eat. I was also taught to be a meat hunter growing up in southeastern New Mexico, so the very soul of our blood experienced the same attitude toward nature and animals and hunting before either of us was ten years old.

Sam and Denver went to a little school in North Fork, California, a small town near Fresno, where at least one-third of the pupils were Indians. The other two-thirds were mostly black, though there were some white kids and Hispanics, too. When Denver and Sam went to this school, they told everyone they were Indian, and people believed them because they had such dark eyes and they spelled their last name differently. They had already changed the spelling of their family name— Peckinpaugh, which is German/Dutch—to Peckinpah. I have no idea why they did this, but it lasted forever. By the time I moved to Glorieta Mesa in New Mexico (I was almost twelve), I had already spent a lot of time with my Cherokee/Choctaw grandmother, who was a medicine woman, so we had that Indian background in common, too.

Here's an incident he told me about at that first meeting: The young Peckinpah brothers were hunting on horseback, in single file, in the mountains with their grandfather for grouse. Grandfather Church carried a .30-30 rifle; Sam wondered why they hadn't brought shotguns. All of a sudden, the lead horse stopped and Grandfather Church took his rifle out of the scabbard, turned his horse sideways, so not to hurt its ears, and fired, shooting a grouse out of a nearby tree. Then he turned to the boys and said, "You're not being observant. You would have rode right under him without noticing. Always observe everything around you: every rock, every crevice, every tree, and every branch." This experience led to the famous phrase, "If they move, kill 'em," used in *The Wild Bunch* and again as the title of David Weddle's biography of Sam. It may explain Sam's obsession with every button on every Mexican uniform being just right in *The Wild Bunch*, and with the details of everyone's job on the set, be it the stars or the cameraman or the gaffer. He was obsessed with these details, and it can all be explained here with his experiences in those mountains with his grandfather. It was a wild and magical time for him.

Every opportunity Sam and Denver got, they would spend time on their grandfather's ranch. At that time—the 1930s—the old-time miners, lumberjacks, and horseback cowboys of the West were still around, and they were men Sam got to know. It was a West in transition, and that's what Sam showed in every Western he made. I think that's one reason why Sam's modern non-Western films, with the possible exception of *The Getaway*, didn't work too well. Sam lost his soul with those modern-day films. Sam's Westerns were films about transition, and transition creates friction. That's what my *Hi-Lo Country* is about. So we had that in common, too: we were both deeply affected by that transition. To me, the West really changed forever when they began making pickup trucks by the thousands after World War II. That was my transition, which inhabited most of my own written works.

Sam later told me about the first screening of *Ride the High Country*. He had worked his soul out on that film, putting his father into the characters of Joel McCrea and Randolph Scott. He and producer Richard Lyons were both damn proud of that film. With great struggle and very little money (about $825,000), Sam had made a classic in the span of about a month's shooting schedule.

Lyons set up a screening on the MGM lot with two or three studio executives present. Right smack dab in the middle of this screening, one of those executives fell asleep and started snoring. That's what he thought of his film: it was a snooze. A Hollywood in transition didn't understand a Western movie about the topic.

MGM threw it away on a double bill. Wouldn't that make any hot-blooded, passionate film director bitter? Sam was sometimes justified in his hatred for producers. He liked Dick Lyons, Daniel Melnick, Martin Baum, Phil Feldman (most of the time), and Ken Hyman because they treated him with respect. But he got totally double-crossed on his first film *The Deadly Companions* (1961). They nonsensically butchered that film.

Ride the High Country had been a sacrifice and risk for both McCrea and Scott to make. They could have been out dealing real estate and making hundreds of times the money—which they both enjoyed doing! They didn't know this film was going to come out a brilliant piece of work. But the picture opened in Paris, and within two days people were lining up around several blocks outside the theater. The European critics went crazy for it; MGM's man in France called the studio to tell them what a phenomenon it was over there. It won first prize at the Belgium Film Festival (beating out Fellini's *8 1/2*), and MGM brought it back to the United States for a run.

I met Sam right in the middle of all this. And our friendship helped me and hurt me over the next two decades. That son of a bitch was an amazing mix of almost unearthly dimensions.

I do not know why Sam liked having me around. If he was having a meeting, whether it was with a lawyer or an agent or a studio executive, and if I was in town, he wanted me there. I had an undeserved reputation as someone who could lay out a guy with a right hook. My busted face belies this. But he would have me sit in on these meetings for no other reason in the world than me dismembering these guys' minds. It was like he was having his hit man join in on the dealing. I think I gave him a little safety net in some way. Intellectually, I gave him a comforting feeling, because we could talk about coyotes, mountain lions, how to stake out a deer, and reading the classics, all at the same time. That gave him a comfort that Hollywood never gave him. As for my reputation as a tough guy, I thought it was rather ridiculous as I was of average weight and build, and I didn't like most of those studio people he was meeting with anyway. I would have liked to have a legitimate excuse to whack one of them. And I almost did, once.

There have been a lot of stories of how Sam got fired from *The Cincinnati Kid* (1965). I'm going to tell it just as he told me.

I was staying at the Sportsman's Lodge in the Valley. He called and said, "I'd like you to come over to Metro (MGM). I need you. I've got to give up my offices here at four o'clock." I told him I didn't have a car, and he said, "Grab a cab! You've got to get here by a certain time or I can't get you through the gate."

My attitude was sort of like Bogart's in *Casablanca*: "Of all the gin joints, in all the towns, in all the world, she walks into mine," only it was, "Of all the lousy people Sam knows in the world, why did he have to call me?"

I took a cab to Metro, got through the gate, and went to his office, which was in the first building on the left. Sam was there alone, which was unusual—he usually had a secretary or somebody around helping him. He always seemed afraid of being alone. He took a few things out of a desk drawer and put them in a little box, but I think this was all an act for me. Never forget, Sam was a helluva actor. In fact, he was so good that people were unaware of this skill. I didn't ask him what was going on. I just waited.

Finally, he said, "Two suits are coming here to tell me how sorry they are and they are going to see that I leave here by four o'clock. What are we going to do to them?"

I said, "I don't know. Why?"

Here's what he told me: "I wanted to shoot a nude scene with Ann-Margret and they told me no. So I talked to a few members of the crew and Ann-Margret and we agreed to come over here at night and shoot it. And they caught me and fired me. They hired Norman Jewison to replace me!"

Sam never held it against Norman, who followed this film with many more of high quality, including *The Russians Are Coming, the Russians Are Coming* and *In the Heat of the Night*.

Sam named the two suits, but I didn't know who they were. "I want to scare the shit out of them," he said.

I said, "Why don't we tell 'em we're going to use the bedeezers on 'em?" Bedeezers are used to castrate cattle without any bleeding. They sever the testicle cords without breaking the skin. I explained this to Sam, and he loved it. He got a big grin on his face, seeing the possibilities here, and he began plotting. Sam would set it up for the suits, telling them I just bought him a new set of bedeezers and explaining their use, and when the time was right, I would simply open a desk drawer and say, "Here they are, Sam—let's get 'em!"

As scheduled, the two men showed up. And they were in well-tailored suits. One came in, and one hung in the doorway with a sense of caution. Maybe he was the smarter one. Sam started explaining to them what bedeezers were. I went along with the act. At just the right moment, I jerked open the drawer and said, "Here they are, Sam!" And the guy in the office turned and damn near ran over the other guy in the doorway. They fled down this narrow hallway with us chasing them, laughing— and without bedeezers. They ran into an office, locked the door, and I swear I heard them moving furniture against it from inside.

I turned to Sam and said, "Let's grab your box and get out of here. The cops are on their way."

We zoomed out of there and jumped into Sam's car. He gunned the engine like they were coming after us. They weren't. Anyway, I didn't hear sirens.

Shakespeare *and* Freud would have a hard time explaining the plot devices behind all this nonsense. See, Sam hadn't figured out how to get his final vengeance against the studio, so he called me. I later thought about why I went along with it all—it had to be the thrill of the unknown.

Sam was having so much fun replaying the whole scene as he drove me back to the Sportsman's Lodge that he didn't even thank me. He wasn't a man to thank you anyway. He was a man who would give you anything, and then take it back from you the very next day.

Professionally, he helped me stay afloat. He enjoyed rewriting scripts, but he could not sit down and write one by himself. When he was black-balled in Hollywood, he took a lot of scripts under the table for the money. There was a group of producers who would hire Sam to work on scripts uncredited. That violated Writers Guild guidelines, but it paid the bills. They paid cash. He got no credit. He was a wonderful rewrite man. And he would get more work than he could handle, and he'd call me to help on some of them. As far as I know, I was the only one he did ask. I would always try to insert tragicomedy, which was my specialty. It was a helluva way for a man like Sam to survive, writing scripts under the table for inferior movies. We wrote five or six of them together, and I swore to him that I would never tell anyone the titles, and I haven't. Only two or three were ever made.

I hadn't fully caught on to the endless parade of ironies that made up Sam Peckinpah. Before the start of a project, he would go through the idea of stealing scenes from films he admired. Sam's motto was, "If you steal, steal from the best." In one of those inimitable turns of fate, he would rapidly become the one stolen from.

My wife, Pat, and my two daughters and I spent the 1964–1965 school year in California, staying in Studio City. Every weekend we were invited to Malibu to Sam's Birdhouse (the invitation was practically mandatory). He, his sister Fern Lea, his brother-in-law Walter Peter, and their kids, our kids, Sam's kids, and his other invited guests would have wild-ass parties. Sam always roasted a pig on a rotisserie outside in front of the house. You were expected to go out there and visit with him while he poured beer over that pig.

It was then that I had an idea for a TV series, *The Horse Traders.* I wrote down a five thousand–word outline and asked Sam if he'd like to see it. To my surprise, he stood up and read the whole damn thing while he kept barbecuing. Then he said, "I'll give you $5,000 for this if you work on the script with me." He gave me a check for $5,000, and it turned out to be good! One thing I respected about Sam was he never pulled that old director/producer thing where he bullshitted you about a project. If he liked something, he would pay you. And he didn't say, like 99 percent of them do, "Don't worry, I can get this made." If he liked it, he bought it, and he never promised you something he couldn't deliver. He bought *The Hi-Lo Country* over and over again, for instance, but he could never get it made.

The Horse Traders was about two old-time cowboys in the 1950s West who manage to buy a gasoline service station. But they were idiots at business. It was a funny idea. I wrote the first draft; Sam ended up doing some wonderful rewriting on it. I accepted about 80 percent of his rewrites because he was right. He knew how to tighten up a script and make it flow; he knew where the commercial breaks were supposed to be. Still, in actual creation, he could have never in a million years come up with that idea.

I was with MCA at the time. The agencies were just beginning to package "deals" putting together the directors, writers, producers, and stars, and these agencies would take 10 percent off the top for packaging the whole damn thing. This was the beginning of packaging deals in one agency, which have since become common practice.

My agent, Robert Goldfarb—a wonderful reader, no bombastic bullshit about that man at all; he was honest and thorough—worked with the agency and CBS to get it going. He called me up one day and said,

"If you can get Sam on board, we've got a deal with CBS." The three big networks, including CBS, were all-powerful in those days before cable television. Jennings Lang, a big-shot producer within the CBS hierarchy and a client of MCA, had approved *The Horse Traders*.

I called Sam. He was tickled. And he called my agent, and he called his agent, who said everything was OK—until Sam found out that MCA was going to take 10 percent off the top. And then he threw a screaming, cussing fit and blew the whole deal. It took us some months to get this going, and it took Sam about a day to blow it out of sight.

He tried to get me to act in his films. I can't remember which part he wanted me for in *Major Dundee* (1965), but I turned him down. I was writing a book. At that time I discovered Sam had a tremendous respect for novelists. I think he secretly might have wanted to be one himself.

At one time Sam had a plain little ol' trailer near the ocean in Paradise Cove, Malibu. I was staying there with him at this time when Pat called. She told me, "You've got five or six days to write a novella for *South Dakota Review*." That publication was founded and edited (brilliantly) by John R. Milton, who took a lot of chances and published stuff nobody else would publish. Sam went out and bought me an old standard typewriter, and I wrote my most reprinted story, "Candles in the Bottom of the Pool," at that trailer. Sam was very gracious that way. He had total respect for my craft. He'd be in the kitchen fixin' me something to eat while I wrote. He always had some Heineken on hand, though I never drank while I was working, which he also surprisingly respected.

He gave my family his house in Malibu so I'd have a place to write while he went to Mexico to film *Dundee*. Later, when he made *The Wild Bunch*, he wanted me to play the role that L. Q. Jones ended up playing. He also wanted Don Hammond, who owned Maria's Mexican Kitchen in Santa Fe for years, to play the Strother Martin part in that film. I knew we couldn't do the job. Sam could sometimes get strange and wonderful performances out of amateurs, but thank God he didn't try with us. L. Q. and Strother turned out to be two of the finest character actors in the world and served as the backbone of many Peckinpah films. He later tricked me into appearing as a stagecoach shotgun guard in *The Ballad of Cable Hogue* (1970), which I've already written about in my book *Sam Peckinpah, Master of Violence*.

Shortly after Sam optioned *The Hi-Lo Country*, I went to a private screening of the rough cut of a 1964 television show Sam was directing and had cowrote (with Bruce Geller) called *The Losers*. It starred Lee Marvin, Keenan Wynn, and Rosemary Clooney. It was about a couple of crooked cowboys in a beat-up pickup truck getting into trouble and having fun. It was a little similar to *The Rounders*, but what got me was, in the last reel, I realized Sam had lifted almost an entire chapter from *The Hi-Lo Country*, dialogue and all. He also lifted characters and scenes from some of his own works, notably *The Westerner* and *Ride the High Country*. He stole from Mack Sennett, too. He had set the whole thing up to torment me, and spent a lot of other people's money for that pleasure.

That evening I met Sam for dinner and drinks. He was already sitting at the table, and before he could speak I said, "You son of a bitch. I just saw *The Losers*, and you didn't even bother to change my dialogue."

Sam didn't flinch. He just said, "It just shows you what good taste I have. What are you drinking?"

3. The Night I Tried to Kill Sam Peckinpah

Sometimes the fun got a little out of hand. In the mid-1960s, producer Mitch Lindemann gave a copy of my 1963 novel *The Great Wedding* to Gene Kelly, the renowned dancer/choreographer/movie star. The idea was that Kelly would direct it as a stage musical before it became a movie. I thought it was a crazy idea, but Mitch had already gotten this particular project to several notable people in Hollywood, including Burt Lancaster. An appointment was set up between me and Gene Kelly for 10:30 a.m. on a particular day.

I was staying at the Sands Motel on Sunset Boulevard, but I had forgotten that I had already invited my friend, Perry Nichols, to come visit me there the day before. I had also promised to take Perry down to Malibu to meet Sam Peckinpah.

Perry Nichols was a dedicated artist from Dallas, Texas. His work still brings in considerable money at auctions. But during this time, he was struggling, though he'd already had an impressive career as a muralist, visual artist, and scenic designer for theater. He was married to the daughter of Texas wildcatter Jake Hammond, a tall, handsome, square-jawed son of a bitch who gambled over and over again, wildcatting until he hit it big—real big. Hammond was a well-known figure in the oil industry in Texas and a very prominent member of the Dallas Country Club set—which Perry Nichols was not. But Perry was forced to attend Country Club events on many occasions. Perry and I were working on a documentary, and Pat and I decided to spend a week with Perry and his wife, Diane, on the outskirts of Dallas where they had a big home. To my surprise, Diane, like Perry, was just a regular person, and she made us feel at home right away. About this time Perry had made a film on trompe l'oeil painting, an amazing work of art that would have cemented my respect for him instantly. Perry was small in stature and big of heart and talent, and so he was welcome to join me at the Sands in Hollywood.

Perry drove out west in a big old black Lincoln, the type of car that was popular with Hollywood types and within certain oil patches of Texas. I remember when he arrived at the Sands, as we walked to his car in the parking lot, he looked out at the constant parade of good-looking women walking up and down Sunset (they kept hoping someone important in Hollywood would see them), and said to me, "My God. Where do all these beautiful women come from? If I was twenty-five years younger, I'd pitch me a tent right here on the sidewalk."

We took our time driving to Sam's, stopping at the Holiday House for lunch and a preparatory drink for Perry's meeting with the madman. When we arrived at Sam's Broad Beach house, I was surprised to find him alone. That was unusual. You never knew with Sam; he'd often have somebody hidden off in a room somewhere. Perry and Sam hit it off right away; they started to have a few drinks, and we came up with the idea of returning to the Holiday House for dinner and more drinks. We did the drinks and somehow forgot about the dinner, or maybe we had the dinner and then forgot about it. What with the view of the ocean and the full turn of the moon—as well as a lot of drinks—both Sam and I were turning into idiots.

Now I had told Perry about my morning meeting with Gene Kelly the next day. He, being considerate and far more thoughtful of such business meetings than I was, kept reminding me of this appointment, and he let it slip that it was about *The Great Wedding*.

Well, Sam's mood instantly changed from one of frivolity and comradeship into a demented withdrawal from our festivities. Sam would become extremely jealous or possessive over certain matters, like property and prostitutes. He wanted to do *The Great Wedding*; in his mind, I was giving *his* story to a damned dancer. In spite of Perry's insistence that we get back to the Sands so I could rest for this critical meeting with Gene Kelly, I insisted we have one more drink for the road. Whether that one drink played a role in changing the events of the night, I'll never know. That "one more drink" has probably altered the events of the world more often than all the dictators in history.

We had our nightcap and left the Holiday House, walking by its pool on our way to the parking lot. It was late at night, and all the swimmers were gone. Suddenly, I felt myself being propelled into that watery body by a push—by Sam. I can't swim. I'm a sinker. But when it comes to survival, I have been a very fast thinker, so as I proceeded to sink to the bottom, I had the presence of mind to hold my breath and prepare to make one helluva jump from the bottom. I had my boots on, which weighed me down. I finally hit the bottom. Then I gave every ounce of energy and probably prayers left in me to push up. Somehow I reached the surface, where I got my hands on the edge of the pool. To my astonishment, Sam kicked one of my hands loose from the edge. It was hell for me to hold on with one hand—185 pounds of soaking-wet drunk. About this time I realized, from experience, that the dunking had ripped the cartilage from my rib. That was of little matter at the moment. If I went down again, I'd be certain to stay down.

To my wonder, Perry had grabbed Sam around the waist with both of his arms and jerked him away from the edge of the pool. I managed to pull myself out of the pool, disgorging some of the water that had replaced the air in my lungs, and crawled onto the wet cement like a beached whale. I was saved—for the moment.

Sam relaxed, and Perry turned him loose. Even with my cartilage torn loose and my body full of chlorinated water and alcohol, I stumbled to Perry's car. We made it to Sam's Broad Beach house. Sam was suddenly silent the whole time. We gathered at his bar there for yet another nightcap. Though I still hadn't had the time to piece this strange tapestry of human drama together, I could feel the pain from the cartilage pulling away from my rib, and I was still having difficulty breathing air and water at the same time. Still, I told Sam I would mix up a drink for him.

There was a ceramic ashtray with two or three cigarette butts in it sitting on the bar. I poured bourbon whiskey, scotch, and another ingredient in that ashtray to make a very special cocktail for Sam. He looked at my concoction, well aware of what that ingredient was, since the ashtray was now devoid of cigarette butts. To my surprise, Sam took a slug from the ashtray martini, perhaps as an act of defiance or possibly (unlikely, but possibly) as penance for his sin.

I stared him down. "You bastard. You tried to drown me."

He said, "Yes, you son of a bitch. You're going around me and selling my book to someone else!"

I soon got the idea that he thought he owned the rights to all of my work whether he had paid me for it or not.

Once Sam acknowledged that he had tried to drown me, I decided to break his neck. But I forgot that I was still physically incapacitated and that Sam had served in the Marines. Forgetting such details at a time like this can be dangerous.

As I moved toward him to pick him up, lift him over my head, and slam him down on the floor, he kicked me square in the *huevos*. I still managed to get a hold on him, but, sadly, I could only lift him about chest-high. Nevertheless, I went to the floor with him, using all the strength I had left. Then I stepped back to survey the damage.

Sam tried to stand up, staggered back down, and screamed in pain, "You son of a bitch! You broke my leg!"

I walked over, patted him on the head, and said, "Sam, I am really sorry. I broke your leg. I meant to break your cockeyed neck."

Perry went to the phone to call the hospital for help. As with all Sam Peckinpah productions, things got screwed up somehow, with Sam instructing Perry to call others, including Walter Peter, Sam's brother-in-law, who we woke out of sleep. A woman I did not know showed up at the house to take Sam to the hospital. During the time we had to wait for her, Sam would sometimes laugh and sometimes curse at the events of the night.

The woman took Sam away, and Perry said to me, "What a damn fool he is. If he'd let me call the hospital, he would be getting treatment already."

We got into Perry's car and pulled out on to the old Malibu Highway (now known as the Pacific Coast Highway) to head back to the Sands. But Perry, showing semblance of a sound mind, said, "We can't afford to get caught driving drunk," so he pulled over behind a row of houses that faced the beach and turned the engine off.

The next thing I remember was the sunlight waking me. I was stretched out in the backseat of Perry's Lincoln. I peered over the seat to look up front, but Perry wasn't there. He had vanished. I got out of the car and stumbled along the highway, looking for signs of him, water still squishing in my boots and pain stabbing at my ribs.

All of a sudden, Perry walked out of the front door of one of the beachside houses. He hurried me into the car as he explained what had happened. He decided to sleep on the beach, so after I fell asleep in the backseat, he walked through the unlocked front door of one of those houses, went through it, went out the back door and walked down to the beach to sleep. A dog had followed him from the house and stood over him for a long time, barking furiously. The dog finally deserted him and he slept. In the morning, he awoke, walked back up the beach, through the back door of that same house, and as the dog barked, the owners woke up and began yelling at the dog just as Perry walked right out the front door to greet me! In the years to come, I came to realize that this was just another typical night and morning with Sam Peckinpah.

We got out of there and stopped at a restaurant on Sunset to have breakfast. I could not change my clothes. Every cowboy knows that if his boots are wet and he takes them off, they will shrink and he can't get them back on. I didn't have time to have my ribs treated. I had to meet Gene Kelly.

Fortunately, I had already checked out where Gene Kelly lived on Rodeo Drive in Beverly Hills, so Perry got me there on time. I knocked on the door, leaving Perry in the car (where he would grab a nap), and Gene's wife answered the door. She said Gene was waiting for me in his study. I went in. Gene was sitting at a desk. He got up to greet me. How could I explain to this great entertainer why I was in sodden clothes, water squishing around in my boots, and deeply fighting pained grimaces on my face as the rib cage battered me from within? I had a helluva lot to hide.

Kelly acted the gentleman. French Impressionist paintings hung on the walls of his large study—I remember a Monet among them—and I asked him if I could take a moment to study them. He was pleased, and somehow that put us both at ease. He asked, "How did you people come to pick me to direct this as a musical? It's a wonderful idea." We talked about the project, and about art, but at some point I didn't want to intrude anymore and felt I should get my vile presence out of his house. I bid him good-bye and returned to the car, where I found Perry getting some much-needed sleep. I woke him, and he drove back to the Sands. I have often since marveled at the control and presence of mind he demonstrated that crazy night.

Later, in Taos, I bought one of Perry's paintings, a strange wondrous work that could only come from a man with a great depth of wisdom and perfect control of his paint, his brush, and his emotions. His verbal title for it is "Dead Sea under a Dying Sun," but he told me I could call it whatever I wish. I can't top that title.

The Gene Kelly production of *The Great Wedding* never went anywhere. Several years later, he came to New Mexico to direct a comic Western, *The Cheyenne Social Club*, with Henry Fonda and James Stewart. I deliberately did not visit the set out of respect for all three men.

As for Sam, it turns out I had not broken his leg. Hospital X-rays revealed that it was a beautiful crosshair break of his ankle. He got off easy. If I hadn't broken his ankle, I'da had to shoot him.

Even now, late in a time of a life that was often misspent, I am thankful that all our future get-togethers weren't like this one, or I wouldn't be here to write about them. There would be many quiet, dedicated times of work for both of us. I don't know for sure about Sam, but I've never had a single drink during my hard-earned writing time. Never. It was the unwritten law.

However, I have never heard of a book about a writer sitting alone at his desk. It's the time between those solitary sessions that are sometimes worthy of print.

4. Bring Me the Head of Max Evans

In the late 1960s Sam moved from the Birdhouse down to Broad Beach, on the north end of Malibu. That period was probably the most joyful, and at times the most peaceful, period of Sam Peckinpah's life. As David Weddle noted in his excellent biography of Sam, *If They Move . . . Kill 'Em!*, Sam used his salary from *The Cincinnati Kid* (though he was fired from the film, he fought for, and received, close to $68,000) to purchase a beige, two-story, square-shaped house with high ceilings and equally high windows that included a master bedroom with a balcony that overlooked the beach. Sam started to host his long weekend pig roasts about that time. These Broad Beach parties started and lasted all weekend long. Broad Beach became more than just a place—it became a fiesta.

Sam's inner circle mostly stayed the same. It included Mexican guitarist Julio Corona (who had played the guitar in one episode of Sam's short-lived television series *The Westerner*), a man whom Sam respected and loved. He loved Julio's Spanish music so much that he would set up a circle of chairs around Julio and direct the audience. We knew we had to shut up and listen when Julio played—and we did. If anybody talked or got out of line, Sam "sssshhhed" them. Sometimes he would get caught up in the music and sing along. Then we'd all join in. Then Sam realized we were ruining the mood, so he'd tell us all to shut up—even though he was the one who started it!

Sometimes Begoña Palacios, Sam's second wife, joined in, hammering out flamenco rhythms on the floor with her hands. Sam's youngest daughter, Melissa—who was my favorite at that time, though I loved all his kids—was particularly enraptured with Julio's music. She later told David Weddle, "It was magical, uplifting. It made me feel very alive. His music got into your soul." She also shared that Sam once told her that "you have to grab hold of the ass of life with your teeth and never let go.

You have to embrace life; really live it instead of just exist . . . Whatever the experience is, take it to the limit. Don't let the moment go. Live it!"

I can't recall anyone from Sam's casts or crew coming to Broad Beach, although I do remember that the actress Vera Miles would sometimes show up. Sam liked her; she married Bob Jones, who worked as the assistant director of *The Ballad of Cable Hogue*. Writer Jim Silke and his beautiful wife, Lynn, were always there. Sam would invite Begoña's family from Mexico to Broad Beach. The parties began to grow in size because she kept flying in more and more of her family members from Mexico, including her uncle, the talented and fun-loving Chalo González. Each weekend, an additional two or three people were there until the house was full, the beach was full, and the bar was full—and Sam was paying for all of this. He could be an enormously generous man. I don't think people realized that. I don't think his own family had the slightest idea how generous he was to them with his time and his love in between periods of great torment.

I would say that this was the only time Sam was truly happy—aside from when he was nailing a picture and he knew he was nailing it, because directing was his main drive and love, and he'd sacrifice everything else for it.

There were times at Broad Beach where Sam would get out of line and be put under control by his brother-in-law, Walter Peter. Walter was a big man, and he'd simply pick Sam up, carry him outside, and throw him like a spear into the ocean. Sam would come up cussin' and sputterin' at Walter, and then laugh like hell. He enjoyed it. Nobody would mess with Walter—he was a gentleman, but there was a quiet strength to him. He went into the stockbroker business, and Sam helped land him some clients including Warren Oates and Jason Robards Jr.

Sam would play a lot of kid games on the beach. He'd get up on the second deck of his house and yell out, "The king is dispensing treasure today!" He'd throw coins and the kids would scatter around to pick 'em up. He loved to have water-balloon fights. He tried to get the grownups involved. Sam would intently watch the balloons that got thrown into the ocean. They'd go out fast, but then come back in toward the shore really slow, and at night the lights would play on them. I think these balloons infiltrated his creative mind; you might even say it had something to do with his obsession with slow-motion filming. During the water-balloon fights, the balloons would explode with sudden power, sending water in every direction—they'd speed up, have a grace to them, and then go away fast, like a ballet dancer. I think he was studying slow motion through those water balloons. He would also study the kids when they moved in on him to attack him; literally coming in from all sides for the kill. He learned that kids can be inherently cruel, and he used that in some of his films—mostly notably in the opening scene of *The Wild Bunch*.

Norman Powell, the son of the late actor and producer Dick Powell—who hired Sam for *The Westerner*—later told David Weddle, "They were tremendous; these fights, the kids all bombing each other and getting violent. Sam said later that this was the inspiration for using kids in the opening shoot-out of *The Wild Bunch*."

The weekends at Broad Beach were crowded, noisy, and exciting. There was a strong aroma of danger always present. Frequent visitors would have noticed that however chaotic and out of control the scene might appear, Sam was weaving casually through the mob of guests, a margarita glass in one hand and a cigarette in the other, his eyes as bright as a snake's, orchestrating the mood of the day and the action at Broad Beach. He'd try to get us either fighting or laughing. He'd invent games where people's fantasies and passions would come out. Then he'd just smile with satisfaction and walk away, knowing he had directed a successful scene. That son of a bitch was always directing.

We all spent a lot of time around Sam's barbecue bullshitting and laughing and having a lot of fun as he poured beer—Heineken—over the pig as he roasted it. In the beginning of the Broad Beach period, there was a lot of pot smoking going on. During one of these barbecues, Sam and Walter had emptied and refilled some of Fern Lea's Kool cigarettes with cannabis. She took her first puff of the devil weed from the Kool pack. Next thing you know, she suddenly shouted, "Let's get naked and go swimming!" That jarred the shit out of everybody. Her husband, Walter, simply said, "I don't think we better do that."

The pot smoking didn't last long. Sam didn't really like pot. It clouded his judgment. He would become confused, and he soon announced that pot was a great mental crippler. Sam's only nephew, the writer and director David Peckinpah, once explained this concisely: "Pot was a mellow drug, and Sam was never into mellow." Later Sam would abuse the most powerful drug ever made—cocaine—but I never saw him smoke pot again. The beatniks had been singing the praises of weed for years, and in just a few years it would permeate middle-class America, but in 1965, possession of marijuana was a dire criminal offense. There was a real fear of the FBI cracking down on you for using drugs, and a fear that you'd be put behind bars. Remember, this was only a few years after Robert Mitchum had been publicly arrested and jailed for smoking pot. This vision of the FBI descending on his Broad Beach home made Sam nervous of keeping his stash anywhere in the house, so he buried it out on the beach. To everyone's dismay, thanks to the wind and the waves, it became lost forever.

I think it's time to explain what Fern Lea meant to Sam. She was among the few rocks he depended on through his speedy, fateful life. At times—rare times by this period—when Fern Lea and Sam were alone, he would confess his doubts to her, such as his fear that he would never make another picture or, intuitively, with great sadness, reveal to her that he knew he would not live very long. Fern Lea shared most of Sam's wild life from childhood on, and after all the joyous adventure and fun of the early days, these confidential revelations had to be hard for her to assimilate. Years later, she said he once called her to tell her about a threesome he enjoyed with two women. She was not amused and began telling him he was disgusting. But her husband, Walter Peter, said, "Let him talk. It helps him, and it's not hurting you."

Sam hit on a lot of women. I knew he was always staring at Pat, and at Silke's wife, Lynn. They were both strikingly beautiful women. He made a pass at Pat once, and when she turned him down, that was that. He never intimated that he made a pass at Lynn, but he'd make gestures and movements to let her know he was interested in her.

Lynn later put it this way: "Sam was incredibly attractive to women. It was his authority. He had a lot of heart and, of course, charm. He was sexually attractive, and he was putting out that sexual attraction. Sam was a gentleman, really, who could do outrageous things. He once leaned over and bit my fanny while I was doing the dishes. He once told my twelve-year-old son, Todd, 'Your mom is the only woman who can keep me in line.' In fact, Sam kept himself in line. Jim was his friend, and Sam would never do anything to betray that particular friendship." Lynn continued,

He had a sense of honor that was very strong. I wasn't privy to the times that he broke it. He flirted outrageously with me, but it was all out front for everyone to see. It was a wonderful flattery, really. Women could easily fall in love with Sam. I loved him, but I didn't fall in love with him. Later, when he became a world-famous director, women fell all over him. I think it was pretty confusing to Sam— "What do they really want from me?"—so he was pretty rough on a lot of women.

We were sitting at a table alone once having a drink. Jim was off somewhere, and so was his wife, Begoña. Sam looked at me, reached over, and gave me a kiss. I said, 'I love you, Sam.' He looked scared and embarrassed. I laughed because I didn't mean it as anything other than 'I love you,' and I made him blush. It was funny.

Sam was a searcher. He was like my father . . . a very private man. He hid his emotions because they could be maudlin; they were so deep. He drank because it was hard for him to deal with his emotions. Sam was an Irish drinker; my father drank that way, too, and when he'd drink he could say things he wouldn't have otherwise said. I think if you knew Sam too well, too long, too intimately, he'd be frightened. That's when I think the big trouble began between him and Begoña. It's kind of a dichotomy to try to explain it, but that's what Sam was—a mystery.

Then, Lynn was through talking, and she stared off into a space only she knew.

Sometimes the booze-fueled rush took a hairpin turn into the dark side at Broad Beach, and the exultant dream world that Sam conjured up there transformed into a nightmare. I had, over the years, tried to invite my local New Mexico friends to experience a little bit of Hollywood, but it always turned out badly because they expected too many star experiences—too many, and too soon. So I became hesitant about inviting any of them out. But in the year that Pat and I spent living in Studio

City, I decided to take a chance and invited a couple of close friends out. One was Buddy Ayres, who became a millionaire dealing with oil leases out of the Bureau of Land Management. He once bought a painting from me when I really needed the cash, and he bought Pat's best painting, *The Blue Nun*. The other friend was Don Hammond, whom I had been through a lot of successful barroom brawls with—though not with each other. He was born on a small ranch near the cattle town of Wagon Mound in north central New Mexico, known by many as the Hi-Lo Country. Shortly after finishing high school, he joined the United States Marine Corps and fought in the Pacific Islands campaign during World War II. Surviving that adventure, he returned to New Mexico and became a state trooper. He was both respected and feared as his tendency to be physically impatient with suspects often caused concern. They wished him well when he left to become the only bodyguard for the newly elected governor of New Mexico, John Burroughs. On his days off, Don was known to celebrate by studying the emptying of bourbon bottles and busting the nose of anyone who interfered with his research. So, naturally, when Burroughs left office, Don was appointed state liquor director, serving the state from experience.

In the mid-1960s Don bought the popular Maria's Mexican Kitchen, still a mainstay in Santa Fe. After several years of dispensing hot food and cold libations there, he sold it and became Sergeant at Arms for the New Mexico state legislature, eventually winding up his eventful life as head of security at the state capitol, fondly known as the Roundhouse. He had a marvelous sense of humor, and, like both Sam and me, Don could laugh at anything, including himself. He was actually at Maria's Mexican Kitchen when I first introduced him to Sam, and I knew then that he would become one of the many odd friends I would share with Sam.

I asked Sam if I could bring Buddy and Don to Broad Beach one night. My intentions were honorable and well thought out. But it turned out much differently than I imagined. Since I had been drinking a mix of red wine and scotch all day long, I was already a bit out of it when we got to Broad Beach. So I will quote Fern Lea and Walter Peter as they related the event to David Weddle many years later.

Fern Lea recounted: "We got there that evening, and Max Evans and his wife, Pat, were there with friends from New Mexico—two couples. One of the two friends had been a bodyguard for the governor of the state and the other had hit it big in the oil patch. Max got absolutely plastered. I knew the vibes were wrong. It was the worst feeling in the world. Where Max's friends were, I wasn't. They scared me."

Walter later told me that I fell asleep drunk on a stool in the kitchen and hit my head on the stove on the way down.

As Walter told Weddle,

That big bodyguard [Hammond] must have been jealous. He said, "I'm going to kill that son of a bitch" [Evans]. Max had been drinking red wine, he was half-asleep, and this bodyguard says he's going to kill him. Sam looked at me, and I said, "No, you're not going to do that. First of all, he can't defend himself. If you've got a beef, at least have the decency to wait until Max can defend himself."

This guy said, "No, fuck no."

I said, "Well, pal, then you're going to have to go through me."

Sam was standing behind me and had a coke bottle in his hand. He later told me, "If you went down I was gonna hit the son of a bitch in the head." But that ended it. The guy backed down—thank God.

Walter went on to tell Weddle:

Warren Oates was there that night. His wife, Teddy, got there quite late. She was introduced to Max. Her first comment to him was, "I heard a lot about you. I don't think you're so fuckin' good." As the party went on, she was getting frickassed [plastered]. Warren had been smoking pot all afternoon. He went out on the beach to clear his head. Teddy approached him and said, "Who the fuck was that broad you were with?"

Warren said, "What broad? Knock this shit off."

She kept riding him all night long. Later, when they were inside sitting on the couch, Warren gave her the back of his hand—whack!—and she fell right on the floor.

And that was the end of Walter's tale.

Now, when I heard about this later from Walter I was surprised, because if ever there was a gentleman in Hollywood, it was Warren Oates. Violence wasn't part of his life; he saved his violence for the screen. Peckinpah connoisseurs are aware that Warren Oates was one of the very few protégés of Sam's creative life—he appeared in Sam's best two Westerns, both classics: *Ride the High Country* and *The Wild Bunch*, and later starred in *Bring Me the Head of Alfredo Garcia*. I was really sorry to hear about Warren's troubles with his wife, because later on we went to a couple of parties at their house and she treated me real nice. But she couldn't make it with Warren. She expected too much from him.

One night in 1965 Warren called me to say he was playing the lead in the play *One Flew over the Cuckoo's Nest* on Santa Monica Boulevard. He said Sam was coming, and he sure hoped I would come, too. Pat and I did. Sam sat with us and said he'd buy us all dinner afterward—us and Warren and Sam and Sam's date, Doris, who later ended up with Jason Robards Jr. She and Sam didn't look like they were dating, actually. They just looked like friends. We had enjoyed Warren in the play and were anxious to get to dinner to talk about the play with him. After Pat and I had given our heartfelt praise to Warren for his performance, Sam waited a couple of minutes and just tore Warren's head off, telling him what he was doing wrong. I thought about whacking Sam in the mouth. His comments must have hurt Warren terribly. It took me a long time to realize that Sam was not doing this out of meanness. He was regimenting Warren for *The Wild Bunch*. Sam was not tutoring Warren for plays. He was tutoring Warren for film. There was always a pro and a con—and a con and a pro—to everything Sam did, but there was no way to read that brilliantly chaotic mind of tumbling-mad genius.

Some years later, after *The Wild Bunch* had made both Sam and Warren immortal in the film world, I took a nostalgic trip down Sunset Boulevard to see whether my beloved Sands Motel and Bar was still there. It was gone, though the little restaurant that had been attached to the hotel was still there. Out of curiosity, I walked into the restaurant, foolishly expecting the same waitresses to be there serving. There was one beautiful surprise waiting for me: Warren Oates was sitting at the counter with his coffee, a huge breakfast plate in front of him, and he was reading a newspaper.

I sat down next to him and was drawn to what he was so intently studying in the newspaper—it was the stock-market page. Walter Peter, being a stockbroker, inherited many of Sam's friends as his clients, including Warren Oates. He helped make Warren a millionaire after the latter's emotionally and financially disastrous divorce from Teddy in 1966. Well, Warren and I had a helluva laugh about the erratic and sometimes wondrous turn of events that occurred for him. I was suddenly very happy for Warren Oates. It was a special moment: such a contrast from the only time he hit a woman in his life to him sitting there studying the stock market in my old Hollywood habitat.

The restaurant was soon gone, by the way. Years later, director Stephen Frears, screenwriter Walon Green, and I went down to a little restaurant that was across the street from the old Sands to supposedly meet actor Johnny Depp, who had been an early oddball casting choice to play the part of Little Boy in Frears's film version of my novel *The Hi-Lo Country*. We sat there for about an hour drinking iced tea. Depp never showed up. But while we waited, I was trying to explain how I used to have so many adventures across the street in the old Sands. I can't remember what went up in place of the Sands. I haven't returned there to this day.

As for Don Hammond, despite his attempt to kill me at Sam's party, we remained good friends the rest of his life. But I never invited him back to Hollywood, and Sam never asked about him.

5. Did You Hear the Phone?

Film historians may disagree with me, but I believe that *Major Dundee* was the worst experience of Sam Peckinpah's filmic life. Pat, our two daughters, and I were staying at his so-called Birdhouse in Malibu while he shot the picture in Durango and Mexico City early in 1964. Back in the states, the reports were coming in, and we were all getting worried about the film. I could tell even before Sam left for Mexico that he felt he was going to make an epic, something wondrous.

Charlton Heston's autobiography, *In the Arena*, suggests that while Heston saw the film as a Civil War drama, Sam wanted to do a character study of a General Custer–type figure (Heston as Dundee), and Columbia Pictures wanted an old-fashioned cavalry-versus-Apaches saga. Over the nearly three-month shoot, Sam fired about fifteen crew members, insulted Heston by calling the actor a liar in front of everyone (in response, Heston tried to kill Sam by running his horse at the director and swinging at him with his sword—he wanted to cut Sam's head off!), and fought with studio executives from Columbia.

At one point, Sam invited Columbia producer Jerry Bressler over to talk about their differences. He set Bressler up. Sam had his friend and driver, Emilio Fernández—who was rumored to have killed a lot of people in Mexico—take him to the airport to meet Bressler. Once Bressler and Sam met in the airport, Sam jerked Bressler's trousers down, pulled them off, and left the poor man standing there with no pants. I'm sure Bressler had polka-dotted shorts on. Sam was very cunning about his vengeance—not only cunning, but colorful.

But in the end, the studio won out. It cut about twenty-seven minutes of footage out of *Dundee* and threatened to fire Sam. Heston, recovered from his run-in with Sam, offered to give up his salary if they kept Sam on and returned the missing footage. Sam stayed on, but the film was slowly destroyed. The rumor is that Jerry Bressler burned the original negative. There was no real repair job on *Dundee* when it was released in its restored version—the repair job was put together with outtakes. The original was gone, and Sam knew it was gone. The hurt was so damn deep, he never got over it. Who would?

Sam came back to California. He insisted that we stay at the Birdhouse for at least a month more. He didn't complain to us about the tragedy of *Dundee* for a very long time. He was in a good mood most of the time—and then he wouldn't be. I remember Sam's kids had Barbie dolls. He asked if our twins had them, and Pat said you couldn't buy Barbie dolls in Taos yet. About an hour later, Sam took off for town, to Beverly Hills or Burbank. He was gone for a couple of hours. We thought he was going to a meeting for some film project. Damned if he didn't come back with two boxes of Barbie dolls for our girls, Charlotte and Sheryl. Pat and the girls loved him from that day on.

Not many people know that Sam Peckinpah was a mystic, though Fern Lea, his only sister, said once that only she and I knew about it. About ten days after his return from the *Major Dundee* shoot, he asked me to go into town with him to meet some industry people for a business lunch at a place that was called either the Steak 'n' Ale or the Scotch 'n' Sirloin. We were driving down Highway 101. He was driving a Corvette at the time. A car was coming straight at us in our lane, but it was quite a ways off. Then a phone in Sam's car rang, and then again—except there was no phone in the car. Lord. And just at that time the car coming at us went right through us—head on.

Sam looked at me and said, "Did you hear the phone?"

"Yeah."

"Twice?"

"Yeah."

"Did you see what just happened?"

"Yeah."

It was a miraculous metaphysical phenomenon. We were sober. It happened. I don't care what anybody else thinks.

Sam expected his friends to know what he was thinking. After that phone incident, he would often say to me, in a crowd or during one of his business luncheons, "Did you hear the phone?" to tip me off that he wanted something to change. Sometimes I would catch on; sometimes not. If he was in a business meeting with some industry people he didn't like, and he wanted it to end, and I was there, he would turn to me and say, "Did you hear the phone?" and I was expected to find a reason to end the meeting there and then.

Not long afterward, while Pat, the girls, and I were still living in Studio City, the four of us were going down to Sam's Broad Beach house for another mandatory weekend. Pat was carefully driving the twins and me from Studio City, where we lived, to Broad Beach. The road down to Broad Beach was a narrow pavement drive with what I would call "land waves" up and down along its surface to the front or back of the houses along Broad Beach. There was only one dangerous spot on this Broad Beach road, right at the bottom of the last of the "land waves," just before the turn parallel to the beach. As Pat navigated the car at this point, a phone rang in our car three times, so loudly it shocked the hell out of all of us.

There was no phone in our car. The twins stood up in the back seat and peered over the front to double-check, wide-eyed—they wanted validation. Pat slowed to a stop as we hit the turn. Just then a huge car came our way at a great, reckless speed, missing us by about six inches. We were all stunned and thankfully silent as Pat stopped our Buick sedan. That phone sound saved our nice little family from becoming a pile of hamburger meat—and we were thankful. Without any doubt, we were still alive because of that nonexistent ringing phone.

We didn't talk about it at all that day—except for when Pat and I decided not to bring it up to the girls again since it was something we could not explain. We were justified in this silence as the twins slowly adjusted to similar "happenings" as they grew up. Varied beyond-the-norm incidents became a part of natural life for them over the years.

I told Sam about the incident. He wasn't surprised. "The ringing is saving us for something, huh?" he said with a smile. "We better get after it."

And we did.

Sam was a mystic. Here are several examples of this. They can be accepted or not.

One morning in the mid-1970s, we were alone at his trailer in Paradise Cove, talking about some story around ten o'clock in the morning. He hadn't had any dope or a drink. He said, "Let's take a walk down to the beach." We started walking down the trail that led from the trailer park to the beach in those days. As we walked past the trailer houses to the trail, I looked over and saw a little woman walking on the other side of Sam. She was about five feet tall, maybe even shorter. She wore a turned-up derby-type hat—like the kind you'd see people wearing in Peru. Sam started talking to her in Spanish. And to my surprise—that I wasn't surprised—we went along that trail, and she moved like a young girl. We made our way down to the beach, and while there were a few people around, nobody was near us.

All of a sudden, she stopped, and I understood her saying to Sam, "Don't ever forget—the world is held together by hexagonals." I looked off for a moment at the wet, wispy clouds over the ocean, and when I looked back, she was gone. Sam and I kept walking, but we didn't say a word for about a mile.

We went back to his trailer, sat on the porch, and had a smoke. Sam said, "Well, I wonder what we'll see next," and then went inside to get a Heineken. You would think in his drunkenness and occasional mad behavior that he would sometimes break through and tell people about these experiences, but he never did.

A few years before Sam died in 1984, Begoña came to the trailer with her daughter Lupita, who was about four or five years old, while I was there. Sam and Begoña had to go somewhere and asked if I would watch Lupita. Between Sam's trailer and the neighbor's trailer next to it was a small flower garden. I sat on the back porch watching Lupita as she played with toys. She only spoke Spanish. She kept talking to me as if I understood her. She kept going back to one small flower in that garden, touching it, nurturing it, and it bloomed right in front of my eyes in about sixty minutes, with a yellow bloom. She must have become known as a bruja later.

By this time, Begoña no longer treated me with the same kindness she had in the earlier days. I don't know why. She sort of ignored me in the later years. But when she and Sam got back that day, I told them the story about the flower, and Sam said to her, in Spanish, "Ol' Max is a bruja." She looked over at me and turned into another person over the next day and a half. She was friendly and warm and kind and tried to get me drunk. It may have been that one sentence Sam said to her, or it may have been the flower that bloomed in just an hour or so. It may have been that I took care of their little girl. I'll never know.

Right after Begoña had left to go back to Mexico, Sam and I were sitting and talking in his trailer at Paradise Cove. We weren't drinking. All of a sudden, I said to him, "You know, Sam, someday all of this high-tech development and machines and projectors will be obsolete. There will be a time when all this high-tech stuff is used up, and a guy like Sam Peckinpah can just walk into a room, sit down, and conjure up an entire film in his mind. One man can be the creator and projector for a film. There will be no need for producers, directors, screenwriters—nothing but the creator."

He looked up at me with those big black eyes, and to my pleasurable surprise he said, "I'm gonna think about doing that."

Sam's brother, Denver, had a mystical story to tell me about a heart attack he had suffered. I recall a wonderful night at the Hilton in Albuquerque when Sam was in town casting for his disastrous 1978 film *Convoy*. He had a row of suites reserved at the Hilton, and while he interviewed some locals for smaller parts, Denver called to me and said, "Let's have a little chat." He said, "Max, I want to share something with you," and just like an ol' jackrabbit, my ears went straight up. We went to his room. He took a shot of bourbon—he drank it straight—and proceeded to tell me about his heart attack, and the operation, and the fact that he had died. He described to me how he left his body and was floating above the table.

The doctors were trying to bring him back to life, and he didn't want to come back. He said he was on a rock overlooking a meadow. He said, "I had no control over it. I knew I had to go back. And I did." He said that because of the experience, he had no fear of death at all. He said, "It makes life easier. I can handle this (the bourbon) and not worry about it ruining my liver."

I was really thrilled to hear that because here we were at that moment whipping down the booze just as fast as we could drink it. And yet I am sure that Denver did not know that Sam was a mystic.

When Sam and I would meet in Desert Springs, we would always hook up first at the same little bar up in Lone Pine, near where a lot of Westerns were shot. The Peckinpah brothers would go there to replenish their souls. But there was something else about Lone Pine that Sam only hinted at, something he said he would show me someday.

Now in 1970, after *Cable Hogue* was supposedly put to bed—and I say that because Sam kept cutting his films in his mind even after distribution; he never quit looking for the grouse on top of the tree—he called me when I was staying at the Mikado Best Western on Riverside and said he wanted to have dinner with me there. He drove up in a great big white Buick. We had dinner. Then he began plugging the car, trying to sell it to me. He wasn't drinking. I kept thinking, "He must really want to sell that car." He walked me out to the parking lot and offered it to me for $5,000. I said, "I don't need a car." He seemed disappointed, but then asked, "What are you doing tomorrow?"

"I'm working on a novella."

"I'll pick you up at ten o'clock," he said. "There's somewhere I've wanted to take you for a long time."

The next day, he picked me up at the Mikado in a pickup truck. I don't know where the hell he got it, though he made it known that he was staying nearby with his oldest daughter, Sharon. He never mentioned the big white Buick again.

As usual, as we left Hollywood for the desert, he said, "I can feel the shit falling off me." You could see it—the color returned to his face, and he looked like a whole different human being. We stopped at the same old familiar bar where he bought a fifth of bourbon, a fifth of vodka, and a fifth of scotch. I drank scotch.

Then off we went, and the next thing I knew he was turning off into the mountains. We drove and drove and drove down this little country road into some little canyon. I saw a couple of deer cross the road—this was early fall, about mid-September—but I said to myself, "We're not going hunting." All of a sudden, he turned a corner in the canyon and we drove up to an old wooden building. A little ol' truck was parked outside of it. I noticed that there were two burros in a nearby pen. A burly old man came to the door of the cabin and calmly said, "I've been expecting you, Sam." He had a trimmed beard but everything else about him was rugged, although he seemed clean. He said, "Y'all come in!"

Sam said, "I got your dinner here, Nabasco." And he pulled out the fifth of bourbon.

We all went in and sat down. There were various pieces of old antique furniture in the cabin and a bear rug hanging on one wall. But it was all clean. Sam and Nabasco began visiting and talking about certain people, people I had never heard of before. It turns out Nabasco knew both Sam and Denver.

We had a big toast—Sam (vodka), Nabasco (bourbon), and me (scotch). We started visiting about hunting, about deer, big game, and random and fun tales. We told stories—no politics, no films, no Hollywood. I felt like I had run into a couple of cowboys in a line camp.

Nabasco and Sam seemed very comfortable with each other. Nabasco said, "You haven't brought anyone up here to meet me in at least ten years."

Sam, pointing at me, said, "Nobody would understand except this guy here!"

All of a sudden, this whole building—which was made up of two or three rooms—began vibrating with a noise: music. At first I thought, "Nabasco's got a radio or a record player that went on automatically." But it wasn't anything like that. It sounded like ancient music, the first music there ever was. I felt that this was music from a time before people (now that I think of it, this experience may have become part of my most recent novel, *War and Music*). It got louder and louder and began to have a rhythm to it. Then it seemed like classical music, and then like a medley of classical turning into jazz. Then the building stopped shaking. Sam and this old man were just sitting there listening. Nobody spoke. The music seemed to last an hour, but it was probably only five minutes. It seemed odd to me that it seemed to last forever—I felt as if I was in a "forever" time.

And then it stopped. That old man looked at Sam—he didn't look at me—and he said, "That hasn't visited in a long time, Sam."

I thought, "Am I supposed to chime in here?" but I kept my damn mouth shut.

They began drinking and visiting again; they seemed pleased and relaxed. Nabasco cooked us some venison and potatoes on an old wood stove. He had fruit—peaches—in jars. There was a spring out back where he had built a trough to catch water for the house. No more was spoken of the music. He asked me about being in the mining business.

He had once been a miner, I assumed, though I later found out he had come to America from the Bosque region of Spain as a sheepman.

We stayed until about dark, and then Sam said, "We have to go." He used me as an excuse and told Nabasco, "Max here is working on an outdoor story."

As we drove back down that canyon, I was kind of in a daze. We weren't talking. About halfway down, Sam said to me, "We've known Nabasco all our lives."

Then he said, "It happened."

"The music?" I asked.

"Yeah. I was hoping it would happen. I go up here about two or three times a year. I don't tell anyone, except Denver."

He drove me back to the Mikado, had one drink with me in the bar, and said, "I gotta go. My daughter is expecting me."

He left me there thinking I'd had one helluva day. The music was just a small part of the mysticism that Sam possessed—or possesses.

Of the many highlights of my adventure with Sam Peckinpah, this is one that is indelible. I can still see the canyon, and the landscape where the meadow opened up, and the cabin, and the pen with the burros. I can smell the trees and feel the open air. But I have no answer regarding the music—it's just another Peckinpah enigma.

I never saw Nabasco again. One time later, after Sam had yet another wreck on one of his films, he said to me, "I wish we had time to go up and see Nabasco." Some years later, when both Peckinpahs were in Albuquerque working on *Convoy*, I thought about asking about Nabasco, but in some way I thought I might be infringing upon something private between Denver and Sam, so I didn't do it.

After Sam and Denver were both gone a few years later, I asked Fern Lea about Nabasco. She told me some sheepmen had imported him up there from the Basque country of Spain to help with the sheep. He became a hunting guide and would take Sam, Denver, and sometimes Walter Peter on hunting trips up there. She could not remember his real name, but his nickname was Nabasco. She said last she heard Nabasco had died of a heart attack, probably not long after we had visited him.

I never saw that old white Buick of Sam's again. I bet Sam sold it. I often wondered if he thought I'd buy that car if he took me to the mountains to meet Nabasco.

In 1989 I was staying in the Sands Motel, researching Sam's life and interviewing people, including Katy Haber, Sam's mistress and right arm on several pictures. One night I was lying in bed, exhausted, trying to read. A mosquito came by my face. I could hear it, but I could not see it. I could not get rid of that little pest—it wasn't there, but it was there! I kept thinking, "Am I nuts? Am I drunk?" It wasn't the latter for sure—not a drop in days.

I called Katy. I said, "Katy, there's a goddamned mosquito right in my face, right in my ear, but I can't see it."

She said, "It's that son of a bitch Sam. He does that a lot."

I took her at her word and said, "Sam, you get out of this room right now." And it was gone. That was the last semi-mystical experience I had with Sam Peckinpah—and he'd been dead for about five years.

6. How Lee Marvin Won His Oscar

I had always admired the few films I saw Lee Marvin in, but I was not quite a personal fan until I saw his work in Sam's 1964 television production *The Losers* with Keenan Wynn. Sam called me one night when I was staying at the Sands Motel and asked me to go see a screening of a rough cut of *The Losers* at Four Star. He said we would meet later at the Sands to discuss it. I went to the screening and, as related in a previous chapter, told Sam he had lifted material for the show directly from my novel *The Hi-Lo Country*. *The Losers* was my least favorite thing I ever saw Sam do. I thought it had too much slapstick in it, and not enough raw humor that came from the totality of the characters. Sam said, "We're gonna wrap this thing up in a few days. I want you to come to the wrap party."

Around 1960 I had met artist Hugh Cabot III at the Sagebrush Inn in Taos. He was from the Boston Cabots, and there was a famous saying, "The Lowells only speak to the Cabots, and the Cabots only speak to God." Maybe so, but the Sagebrush Inn lounge was so small you were bound to speak to whoever you encountered. I went in there one night to visit with the bartender, who made out like he was bartending just to research a book, and it was fun to talk with him. *The Rounders* had just been published and the bartender started asking me about that book.

Sitting at a nearby table was a young, slender, aristocratic sort of kid and a good-looking woman. It was Hugh Cabot with a woman who was the female Bronco-riding champion of the world or something like that. Unbeknownst to me, she had brought Hugh there that night to dump him. She was one of his wives—the first one, I believe. He was married at least eight times. This woman's family were cow ranchers down in the Big Bend country of Texas. She had four big, tough brothers. Besides being a little mad, Hugh had a lot of guts to marry into her family. Anyway, they had all decided to get rid of him, though I didn't learn that until the next morning.

Hugh called the bartender over, and they spoke. The bartender told him something, and then I got invited over to his table. He and the woman had both read *The Rounders*, and Hugh swore that was why they were there. They were going to look me up and talk about the book, she agreed. I was flattered and pleased. The woman kept buying us drinks. Hugh passed out. She went back to their room, gathered up all his clothes—except for one pair of pants and a shirt—and took off for her home in the Big Bend Country, leaving Hugh Cabot broke, stuck, hungover, with only a single change of clothes, and with nowhere to go.

The next day he called me. I let him stay with me until he decided to leave, which was a few weeks later. He started drawing, and drifted back to Boston, and got married again to a Bethlehem Steel heiress. They held the reception at La Fonda Hotel in Santa Fe, and he invited me by to meet her. She was a small, fragile, lovely girl named Elizabeth. He told me, "Elizabeth loves your book *The Mountain of Gold*"—which he had illustrated, by the way—"more than any other book. She wants to meet you."

Now Hugh was crazier than a loon in those days, and his wife would be soon. She was trying to give me money. Not right there, but she said, "I've got to go back east and adjust a trust fund, and with your permission I will set you up with your own trust fund so you can write with freedom." I was terribly embarrassed, but the manner in which she said this made it clear that it was all settled. But I had to head back out to Hollywood for some meetings regarding *The Great Wedding*, and I soon forgot about the Cabots.

Then while I was at the Sands, I got a call from Hugh Cabot. He said, "I'm sorry to tell you this, but Elizabeth died." She had committed suicide.

As embarrassed as I was about the entire affair, I was suddenly sorry I wasn't going to get the trust fund money.

Hugh said he wanted to fly out west and see me and help with *The Great Wedding*. He said he had money. He flew in wearing a Brooks Brothers suit and looking 100 percent like any blue-blooded Cabot should. He said to me, "I've got $86,000 out there in my suitcase." I didn't ask him where he got it. I just knew I had some debts, and I had to pay my hotel bill, and I began scheming to get my mitts on some of the money. I said to myself, "By God, I've gotta figure out how to get some of this money—not all, just some." The old survivor instinct from living various lives was kicking in.

Hugh told me he was going to Mexico to see his new home and studio there, courtesy of Bethlehem Steel. It turns out Bethlehem Steel had set it up for him to go to Mexico to live for up to ten years. First, he had a suite reserved at the Reforma Hotel in Mexico City where he planned to entertain bullfighters and various women. I knew I had to make my move before he got away, because that money would disappear like magic ink. I decided I would sell him a portion of the rights to *The Great Wedding*.

Now the next night was Sam's wrap party for *The Losers*, and it turned out Hugh Cabot was interested in meeting Lee Marvin. I figured I'd take Hugh to the wrap party, and that would clinch it.

They were still shooting the last scene when we arrived. The party was set up with really long tables full of food and drinks. Everybody was drinking, and I heard that Lee was already drunk. I kept waiting for Sam to introduce me to him, but it never happened.

After a couple of hours of partying, I heard this terrible crashing noise. It was Lee Marvin. He had taken this table full of whiskey bottles and overturned it. Then he headed off across the parking lot to his car, singing as loudly as a braying donkey.

"I want to meet Lee Marvin," I said to no one in particular. And I trotted after him.

They said, "No, no, come back! He'll beat the shit out of you."

I didn't care. I ran up to him and said, "Hey, Lee, I'm Max Evans. I wrote *The Hi-Lo Country*." All the big-time actors I ever met gave me respect because I wrote that damn book. I didn't think it was *that* good. I was about half-scared and about half-ready for him to hit me. Instead he turned around, shook my hand, and said, "Where are you staying? I'll call you and we'll have a drink." I told him I was at the Sands, and he left. The entire crew—even the stunt men—were just staring at me. How the hell did I get away with that? Even Hugh Cabot was impressed.

I started plotting again. I thought of Lee in *The Great Wedding*. I told Hugh what I was doing, and he saved me the trouble of having to bring the money up. He said, "I'd like a little piece of that."

I said, "$9,000 will do the trick." I decided that an odd number like that would work—and it did. Hugh was only going to stay in town one more night, so I knew I needed another trick to get the papers signed and get the cash. The only way to do it was to find a sharp, good-looking woman to take on a date with Hugh while my agent got the papers together. I knew such a woman existed somewhere. I called Sam and explained my dilemma, not mentioning *The Great Wedding*. He told me to wait awhile and then call a number he gave me. After a while she showed, and I mean *showed*, and I could tell Hugh, upon seeing her, was falling instantly in love. She was like, as the old song said, a dream walking. We had arranged to go to a Chinese restaurant in Beverly Hills. Hugh got drunker and drunker at dinner, and then he did the dumbest thing a Cabot has ever done. He stood up to go to the bathroom, took a $100 bill out of his wallet, and stuck it down this woman's bra. She was furious—he thought she was a hooker!

My agent was due to show up around midnight, and I had to keep her there to keep Hugh there. She agreed to stay, but she wasn't happy. She said, "When it's time to leave, I'm going to go to the bathroom and I'm not coming back." (Later Sam told me she was the mistress of a very rich and famous actor who gave her several thousand dollars a month.)

My agent showed up, and I explained my plan to him. He said to me, "Nobody does this sort of thing." I said, "After 2 a.m., when this bar closes, that phrase will no longer exist." The woman left, I kept Hugh busy, somehow my agent got the papers together, and we went back to Hugh's hotel room where he counted out $9,000 in $100 bills.

Hugh woke up in the morning, got a cab to the airport, and flew to Mexico City. The first night there, he hooked up with a bullfighter who introduced him to another beautiful woman. Bethlehem Steel had set it up to send a car to take him to a morning meeting that would cement his new home with a ten-year setup there. Instead, he stumbled into that meeting with his arm around this beautiful hooker, his Brooks Brothers suit all shot to hell, lipstick all over his face, and probably smelling like forty kinds of spilled booze. Before the sun set that day, he was totally disposed. He later sent me a photo of himself dancing with a beautiful Mexican woman (it still hangs on the wall in my study). Underneath was boldly written, "The black but happy sheep of the Cabots." He never did meet Lee Marvin.

But I did, of course. Lee did call, and we met at a place called La

Taverna on Sunset Boulevard. It was just a regular bar where regular folks went, but you would see people like Casey Tibbs and Stuart Whitman in there from time to time. Now Lee didn't give many people total respect. He gave me total respect. I'd been in combat in World War II, and he really didn't have anything to do with anybody who had not been in combat, even if he enjoyed working with them. He had served in the Marines during World War II and received the Purple Heart after being wounded in action in the Pacific. For some reason, Lee thought Sam had been in combat. He hadn't, though the OSS (Office of Strategic Services) sent Sam to China, where he may have seen a little action. Sam told me once that he saw the Japanese kill some Chinese there near the end of the war, and that may have been true. One of Lee's best friends was Neville Brand, who had been in combat and won several medals for heroism. He was really crazy, but Lee loved him.

Lee would fight if somebody bothered him. Usually people didn't bother him in this bar, but one night Lee had a wreck after a night of drinking at La Taverna when this guy kept coming up to Lee and bothering him. Lee was polite at first, but eventually he got tired of the guy and said, "Don't bother me anymore." But the guy kept bugging Lee. Now there was a Hispanic guitar player in the bar that night—a musician Lee really liked. Finally Lee—who could move faster than you'd think—jumped up, grabbed the guitar from the musician, and whacked this guy over the head with it until only a little stem was left. Lee gave the Hispanic musician a check for several thousand dollars to buy a new guitar. Nobody called the cops. Lee tried to get me to go home with him after the musician had been taken care of, but I didn't accept the invitation because I had work to do on a story the next day. On the way home that night, Lee ran into a guy on a motorcycle, and settled the suit out of court, Sam later told me, for about $12,000. I later thanked many varied saints that I had not driven home with him that night. I met Lee again in this same place, La Taverna, a few months later. He drove a black Lincoln, built like a tank, in case he got in a wreck.

Lee was married to Betty Eberling then. One night, he invited me to dinner at their house in Pacific Palisades. We had about five drinks before we went over there, and that was just a tune-up in those days. We went out to his den where he had this bar and about $50,000 worth of fishing stuff—reels, nets, and such—hanging on the walls. He started serving up the drinks; about a half a glass worth of whiskey each. He liked to see if people would fall down dead-drunk while he kept going. We hardly ever talked about the war, but once in a while he would want to, but only if we were alone. Just a very little—but it seemed like a lot to me.

All of a sudden, he said, "Let's go down to Santa Monica." He knew this bar on the beach where Marines and sailors hung out, so down we went in his big black Lincoln. His wife struck me as pretty hard-nosed toward Lee. She was pretty good-looking, a tall blonde—not a real blonde, I don't think—but her humor got very biting. Once, when Lee was demonstrating how to use a bow in his house, she turned to me and said, "Look at him. He thinks what makes me crazy about him is the idea of him going out to kill some deer, bringing it here all bloody, and throwing it on the floor at my feet."

Anyway, we got down to the bar, and people were attracted to him; they treated him like he was a big star. Two or three women came up to Lee and stuck little pieces of paper with their phone numbers on 'em in his pocket. Betty noticed. Lee didn't run women; he was not a womanizer like so many of the stars I knew then. He was a one-woman guy when you get down to it. But Betty was jealous and insisted we go back home for a nightcap. We got in the car. Lee drove, Betty got in the middle, and I was on the passenger side. She put her hand on my leg. I was thrown, but I figured it out later—she was trying to make Lee jealous.

We got home. It was about four in the morning. Lee said, "I've got to go to bed because I have to get up early." He was shooting some show for Warner Bros. He said, "You two have another drink."

We did, and she kept putting Lee down. I said, "You better go to bed. I'll sleep on the couch here." She got me some blankets and a pillow, said "good night," and left. I was about to pass out and go to sleep when the whole house began to rumble. Betty was in the next room banging away on a piano! There was no way Lee could not hear this. She kept at it for God knows how long. I couldn't sleep.

Morning came, and Lee walked downstairs all shaved and looking clean—no bloodshot eyes. He was fresh and ready to go. He drove me back to the Sands and went to work at the studio. I stood there watching him drive off, wondering what the hell had happened the night before. They were on their way to a divorce, but I didn't know it.

Now despite all the pain that Sam Peckinpah had endured with the events leading up to his divorce from his first wife, Marie, he rented a house for her and the kids on Zuma Beach. I was out with Sam one night, and we decided to go over to Marie's place. She had a big table set up inside, which was strange because usually she had it set up outside on the beach. Anyway, we were outside visiting before dinner, and all of a sudden we heard two voices coming toward the house. It was Lee and Betty stumbling down the beach toward Marie's. Lee was singing again. We knew they were drunk. We all ran into the house and hid behind the furniture while Marie turned off the lights and locked the doors. Lee started beating on the door, yelling, "Hey, you sons of bitches, where are you?" He must have known we were in there, but we didn't make a sound. Eventually, he grabbed Betty and headed on down the beach. After they left, everyone stayed quiet. Sam broke the silence with, "I don't think Lee is feeling well." We all broke up laughing—Lee couldn't have been feeling better!

Lee had read *The Hi-Lo Country* and wanted to do it. Sam tried, and could never get it to work, and when Lee became a big star around 1965, Sam started going through a time when nobody wanted to hire him. It was after the *Major Dundee* fiasco. Sam was being blackballed all over town; it was worse than the McCarthy hearings and the Red Scare of the 1950s, but Sam wasn't griping. He called me and said he was going to host a dinner at a certain restaurant on Wilshire—I can't remember the name—and he wanted Pat and me to come. He said, "Some of your friends will be there."

We went in and there was a long table with a great reddish tablecloth. There were eight of us, including Lee Marvin and Robert Culp (a friend of Sam's who had turned down the James Drury role in *Ride the High Country*) and a business manager or agent or something and a wife or girlfriend or two. Lee had spotted Pat, sitting next to Sam. Like many men before him, he was obviously struck by her "different" brand of beauty. He stopped by her seat and said, "And who might this be?" smiling his most infamous smile. Sam seemed delighted to tell Lee, "This is Pat Evans—Max's wife." Lee said, "Oh," and took his seat at the long table. We then ordered some drinks, and all of a sudden Lee said, "I have to try this bit for a picture. I've been practicing. Don't worry—I'm good at it!"

And he stood up and proceeded to grab the end of the tablecloth in both hands. He was confident he could jerk that tablecloth out from the drinks, plates, and ashtrays and leave them all sitting there on the table. Like a magician on the stage, he made a little theatrical gesture and "wham!"—jerked the tablecloth off. Everything went straight up in the air, landed and broke on the floor, and everything went straight to hell. It was a majestic wreck with impressive sound effects.

Lee sat back down and said, "I haven't quite got the hang of it yet." That's all he said. He made no apology, and nobody else said anything. There was no outburst of anger or laughter. We all took it in stride. It was the first time I saw how movie stars can inspire stupidity and admiration in otherwise rational people. Never have I seen waiters move so quickly to gather up broken glass and plates, put another tablecloth on the table, reset the drinks, and turn it all back to new. They were really kowtowing to ol' Lee Marvin and the other stars at the table.

When you are with Sam Peckinpah and Lee Marvin, you stay until closing time. We did. Finally, everyone was leaving. Lee was driving a big Chrysler now. Lee followed Pat and me out on the street, and the traffic was actually picking up from the last hoorah of the closing of all the joints. We pulled into the lane with Lee right behind us, and the car died. The honking started, and then chaos. Once again, I got to witness the effect a star can have on people. Lee got out of his car, ran up to our car window, and said, "What's the matter?"

"I think the damn thing is out of gas," I said. We hadn't paid attention.

Lee talked some nearby motorists into getting out of their car to push our car into a nearby parking lot, then he got out on Wilshire and started making all sorts of traffic-cop signals. The passing cars became his squad, and like the marine sergeant that he was, he directed them. Then he said to me, "You take my car. Give me *your* keys. I'll come out sometime tomorrow with your car. Don't worry about a thing. I'll get a cab, you guys go home." And just like in the movies, a cab pulled up and Lee got into it and took off. It was almost like one of those Keystone Kops movies. Pat and I went on back to Sam's house in Malibu, although Sam stayed somewhere in town that night and for a couple more days.

The next morning, Lee pulled up in our car—all tanked up with gas— and he had two drunk sailors with him, and he was drunk as well. They came into the house, and Lee went to the cabinet where he knew Sam kept all the whiskey. Now Sam's sister, Fern Lea, had told Pat to boil some seawater and drink a teaspoon or so a day as a health tonic and to use it for cooking also. Pat did that, and poured the concoction into an empty whiskey bottle. Well, Lee saw the bottle and grabbed it and took a big swig. He then ran to the sink, spit it out, and rinsed out his mouth before he could choke to death.

Later, when everything had settled back to near normal, Lee decided to stage a one-man rooster fight. He played two roosters fighting, squat- ting on the floor and fighting like hell, and believe me, you believed him. He was magnificent. He received the greatest applause for any show he ever did in that kitchen. Our daughters heard the commotion and came to check it out. After the action had finished, Pat introduced Lee to the girls. They politely shook his hand. Charlotte said, "Oh yes, we've seen you a zillion times on TV." Sheryl nodded in agreement, and then, in unison, they abruptly turned and returned to their room to play their own games. Lee stared wordlessly after the five-and-a-half-year-olds. The show in Sam's kitchen was over. Lee and the sailors decided to find another bar and left singing. You don't get to tell many stories like that, you know—people just don't live through them.

In 1964 Lee got cast as Kid Shelleen, the drunken gunfighter in Elliot Silverstein's Western *Cat Ballou* (released in 1965), which made Jane Fonda a star. The producers were Harold Hecht and Mitch Lindemann. Well, Mitch was associate producer, actually. He had been a screen- writer but was caught up in the Red Scare of the McCarthy era, and he was a working alcoholic. Mitch knew both Burt Lancaster and Kirk Douglas—both of whom reportedly turned down the role of Kid Shel- leen before Lee took it—and later got me a job working on a film version of *The Great Wedding* for Burt Lancaster.

Mitch was a nice man, a funny man, and he once told me, "*Cat Bal- lou*'s success was an accident. Columbia Pictures stupidly tried to treat it seriously. Lee was drunk the whole time—a drunk playing a drunk, the truest son of a bitch the actor ever played in his whole life. Colum- bia screened some of the early rushes, and some of the executives were worried. I told them, 'It's funny. Shoot the whole thing as a comedy. Leave Lee alone—he's great.'" Lee verified that story to me later.

Cat Ballou was a big success, and Lee was nominated for an Academy Award for his portrayal. He also got me a job writing the sequel, *Kid Shelleen*. Mitch called me (Lee told him to call me) and said I was about the sixth or seventh guy they had hired on the deal, because none of the big-time scripters could get it right for "this little guy, Harold Hecht." Hecht *was* a little guy, about five feet tall, but he had a four-foot platform built for his desk so no matter how tall you were, you were always looking up at him. Hecht climbed down from his throne and took me over to meet Howard W. Koch, who was the head of film production over at Paramount. I don't know what the hell we were talking about or why we were there, but Koch wished me well on the script. They gave me a contract and $750 a week, but to little avail: I failed, too. It was a serious picture—Lee always said he saw Kid Shelleen as a tragic figure—but it never got made. I had hell getting my expense money paid on that one.

With the Oscar nomination for *Cat Ballou*, Lee's world suddenly changed. He had committed to making *The Professionals* for Richard Brooks, with Burt Lancaster, in Nevada. The company was headquartered in the Mint Hotel in Las Vegas. Lee was making big money at this time, and he spent it with no hesitation. He was going with Michelle Triola, a singer. They drank and had a helluva time together. He had me over to his place—a house in Malibu Beach—where I met her. I really liked Michelle; I got along with her beautifully. And Lee did, too—at that time.

Meanwhile, a petroleum engineer had looked me up in Taos. He was trying to find the right person to handle a development of property his father owned of 1,500 acres of well-watered, timber-covered foothills in the Rocky Mountains near Breckenridge, Colorado. His father didn't want the property broken down into anything less than ten-acre lots. I gave this guy a copy of my story *The One-Eyed Sky* to give to his father. His father read it, loved it, and said he wanted me to take over handling the property. I drove up to Colorado to look at it—it was a paradise. And that little story got me the deal.

I pitched it to a big-time banker I knew in Denver—Mr. B.—and we made a deal. The contracts were signed, and I reserved the right to have ten acres in my name, too. That banker was later hired to be the main lobbyist for the oil industry in Washington, D.C. I mentioned to him that I was driving out to Hollywood soon, and he insisted on driving me himself. I agreed to stay friendly and to save on expenses, and that was a mistake. He never stopped asking me questions. He was aware that I knew a lot of these Hollywood and literary people, and he was picking my brain so he could discuss books, painting, movies, and Hollywood once he got to D.C. He was driving me crazy—or, I should say, crazier than I already was.

The first night, we stopped at the cheapest hotel he could find in Utah. We went to the restaurant nearby, and there was a newspaper stand—I read the headline, "Bill Linderman, King of the Rodeo Cowboys, Killed in a Plane Crash." That was a shock to me; I had just met with Bill a few days before to discuss writing an article against using rodeo teams. Bill was afraid that the wonderful individuality of rodeo would be lost. So that was my first night on the road.

We went to bed in the same room. Another mistake. That son of a bitch snored like four rhinos. No wonder his wife left him and he couldn't keep a girlfriend.

We got out to Hollywood, and I told him we were staying at the Sands. He wanted me to introduce him to stars—especially female stars. He talked endlessly about of having an affair with some female movie star, but I didn't know many of those. I stayed at the Sands for many reasons. I had credit there, and it wasn't a total celebrity hangout.

Meanwhile, Lee's girlfriend, Michelle, was singing at Dino's Lounge. Mr. B. really wanted to meet her, and he had me over a barrel because he was paying for everything. We walked into Dino's and Michelle was singing some Italian ballad, and this guy started swooning. When she finished her set, I invited her to our table, and the guy started making goo-goo eyes at her. Here Mr. B. was trying to put the make on my friend's woman, and he knew we were going to stop in Las Vegas on the way back to see Lee. Michelle could tell what I was going through, and she handled it very well.

She said she had a favor to ask and told me I had to do it. "Lee's going to lose this job he's doing (on *The Professionals*)," she said. "He doesn't like Burt Lancaster; he called him a perverted, twisted, egotistical prick. He's been drinking on the set.

"Everyone else has forgiven Lee except Burt—and Burt owns 25 percent of the movie." If Lee got fired from that film, she explained, it might doom his chances come Oscar night.

She told me I had to find Lee and straighten him out fast. I said, "Nobody can tell him that. He'll just knock me on my ass."

"You have to," she said. "You're his friend."

She invested her soul in that statement. She was a great woman—no matter what happened between her and Lee later.

Once in Vegas, Mr. B and I went to the Mint Hotel. As we checked in, we could hear some loud voices in the bar nearby. Sure enough, Lee and Woody Strode, as well as the Japanese woman Woody was married to, and two or three other character actors from the movie were in there drinking. I went in and Lee jumped off the stool and said, "I'm taking you to the bar upstairs." The top floor had a huge bar with windows that gave a view of the entire city. We rode up in one of those outdoor elevators. We got in the bar, sat down, and ordered some drinks. I wasn't near drunk yet and neither was Lee. I could not figure out how to do what I had to do. I thought, "If I tell him this, he is going to whack me, and I'm going to go flying backward out the window down twelve floors and splatter all over Las Vegas."

I remembered Michelle's words to me. And then I did it. I said, "Lee, do not pull a Dylan Thomas on us. You hear me?"

Lee stared at me. I held my breath waiting for the blows to come. After several eternities, he suddenly smiled and said, "I hear you."

It had hit him just right. And it worked. Drunk or sober, Lee Marvin was a smart sucker. We didn't overdo it that night, and once that night was over, he stopped drinking for the rest of the picture. Michelle had used me as a possible sacrifice to save Lee Marvin's career.

In April 1966 Lee won the coveted Oscar for *Cat Ballou*. He became rich. I believe he was the first male actor to get $1 million for a picture. Nowadays, that's nothing. It sure as hell was something back then. He could get any movie he wanted produced, and he got hired to make *The Dirty Dozen* in England.

Next time I was at the Sands, he called me and invited me over to his place in Malibu to talk business. He sent Michelle out shopping with a bunch of money. Lee had a four-stool bar there, two stools on each side. He mixed up a pitcher of martinis and poured us each a drink.

He said to me, "I want to option *The Hi-Lo Country* for $75,000. But I want to make sure *The Dirty Dozen* is a success first. If it is, I'll have my agent, Meyer Mishkin, call you to work out the deal. Sam can direct. Nobody will hire him just now, so we won't mention his name until we get it all worked out. You can write the script, and produce it; Sam can do the rewrites."

We shook hands on the deal, which was made before we got drunk. But he was in a drinking mood, so he put us into a drinking contest. But he made a mistake—I had eaten a hearty breakfast in preparation for my meeting with him, and he hadn't.

Michelle walked back into the house barely able to carry two sacks of groceries. She put one sack on the table and left one sitting on the floor. Then she disappeared and left us to continue as we saw fit. She knew what was transpiring. I didn't. We kept drinking. Lee kept mixing those martinis. I was really beginning to feel them. I looked at the sack of groceries on the table. It looked like a melting sundial clock in a Salvador Dali painting. Every time I turned to look at something, I could hear the martinis sloshing around in my head. I was thinking, "He's won, he's won." But just as I was about to fall off my stool, Lee fell off his, smacking his head on the floor. I thought he was dead.

Michelle came in, checked him, and said he was OK. She asked me to help her get him to bed. She told me to take him by the arms, because if you grab his legs when he's drunk, he kicks. So we grabbed his arms and began dragging him across the kitchen floor toward the bedroom. To do so, we had to pass by a big glass double door leading out to the beach, and as we dragged him past it, he instinctively kicked and smashed all the glass out. But nobody got hurt. We put him to bed, but it was a terrible task for me to stay upright while Lee was prone.

I had inadvertently won the drinking contest, but another two or three minutes and it would have been me on the floor, and he would have never gotten to bed. I could barely make it to bed myself. Michelle pulled my cowboy boots off and guided me to the guestroom, where I spent the night.

And the next morning, again, Lee was sitting on the couch like nothing happened the night before, having a smoke. Even though he was the first to fall, he was the first to rise. Michelle made us some scrambled eggs. He didn't say anything about the broken glass door at the time, but later on, I found out that he told people that I had kicked it out while he was dragging me to bed!

Lee went to England to make *The Dirty Dozen*. Now actors and working cowboys hardly ever write letters. That's just a fact. But I sent him a short story to read, and word got back that they were doing well on the picture, though there was a little trouble with James Brown. I guess Lee and James were at dinner one night, and Brown said something about not getting paid as much as Lee because he was black, and Lee said, "Don't talk that way to me. You're sitting there with the best-looking blonde in London, and you're getting paid more than anybody else for someone with your experience." Brown had only made a few films up to that point. Lee and Brown got along fine after that.

The Dirty Dozen was a hit, but we never got around to making the deal on *The Hi-Lo Country*. Lee became a money-maker instead of a fine filmmaker, partially due to the influence in that direction by his agent and new business partner, Meyer Mishkin. Meyer had gotten Lee his first million-dollar paycheck. Meanwhile, Sam got into all sorts of jams before he finally made *The Wild Bunch*. Lee made *Point Blank* (1967), and then took a deal to make that big musical, *Paint Your Wagon* (1969), with Clint Eastwood, which I think was a tragic mistake. His agent got him into another picture, *The Klansman* (1974), with Richard Burton. You throw one human being who is susceptible to alcohol in with one of the biggest drunks of all time, and, well, they stayed drunk during the whole production. The film was a flop, and I think that affected Lee for a long time.

Lee and Michelle split. I don't know why. I liked them both very much. He may have felt a little used. He probably didn't know she helped save his career. She was responsible for him winning the Oscar and becoming rich and too damn famous. She later sued Lee for millions in a highly publicized palimony case. She claimed she was more than a wife to him; she gave her heart and soul to Lee. People called her a conniving bitch, but I don't think that this was true. The trial cost Lee a lot of money, though the judgment was only for about $100,000, and I'm sure it cost him some of his heart. I ran into Michelle one more time at a restaurant on Sunset Boulevard. She came over to say hello, and we had some laughs sharing Lee Marvin stories. She later married Dick Van Dyke and seemed happy. I sure hope so. Michelle was a fine, talented woman caught up for a time in the midst of the blessing-and-curse ride of fame.

I still remember a night in the late 1960s when Sam and Lee and I went to the Holiday House for lunch. *The Hi-Lo Country* came up—again, and as usual. I remember saying, "It's just a damn old book about some lonesome working cowboys," and they both jumped all over me. They said, "Don't put that book down; it's a grand work, we could never do anything like that . . ." I was deeply embarrassed, but it was a good time. Nobody was trying to make any deals, no girlfriends were along. We stayed until midnight, drinking. Around eleven o'clock, Sam started to get sick, so he went to the bathroom to throw up. He came back and asked Lee for the keys to his Chrysler so he could go lie down in it. Lee and I stayed until they threw us out. We walked out into the parking lot. The trunk to the Chrysler was open. We looked in, and there was Sam, curled up in the trunk around the spare tire.

Lee said softly, "He's curled up around his machine gun. He's been at his post so long, he's fallen asleep."

I don't remember saying anything.

7. The Westerner

I was sitting in the Sands talking to Cliff, the bartender, one afternoon when a woman came in to have a cocktail. She was very charming—never flirted. I was told she was the mistress of a studio head. She worked in pictures, but she didn't have to. I think she was a film technician. We became speaking friends. One day, she told me she was thinking of taking a job in New Mexico. This was in the early 1960s, when I still lived in Taos. Later, she surprised me by calling me there. She said, "I'm in Gallup working with Burt Lancaster and Brian Keith on *The Hallelujah Trail*. Brian has read *The Hi-Lo Country* and would love for you to come out and be his guest." That movie was based on a book by an old friend of mine, William Gulick. The book was good, but not the movie—though as the old cliché goes, it did have its moments.

Pat and I drove out to Gallup, and we stayed in a motel outside of town—not the famous El Rancho, but another, more modern, place. Brian was staying there, Jim Hutton was staying there, and most of the cast and crew were staying there. Burt Lancaster was not staying there, and they all joked about that. I went over to the set the next day and met Brian Keith, who was hanging out with Jim Hutton and a couple of stunt men. We were instantly tied together because of *The Hi-Lo Country*. Brian wanted to play Big Boy. He had great sympathy for Sam and was responsible for getting Sam hired on *The Deadly Companions*, the first film to get Sam all twisted around. The public still didn't have the slightest idea who Sam Peckinpah was by 1960, until film companies started to take interest in the television series *The Westerner*. Brian got nothing but adulation for that show, as short-lived as it was. The fact that it initially failed simply contributed to it receiving more fanfare and attraction than it would have had it run for ten years. Brian Keith became one of the best four or five really close friends I ever had in my life, and the best friend I had in the movie business. He was dead loyal. I remember we called Sam from Gallup once and Sam told us, "You take it easy on that Yankee boy." He was referring to Jim Hutton. I did not get to know him well, but Sam told me that Hutton was crazy for no reason. He said he was a woman abuser and a man who drank but didn't enjoy it. Unlike Jim Hutton, Brian and I would drink, and we did enjoy it.

I discovered that Brian did not want to be a celebrity. He didn't really put up with it like Lee Marvin did. He was married to a woman named Judith Landon at that point. I didn't like her. Brian had won all these combat awards for serving in the Marines, and she had them framed and hanging in the entryway of their house in Bel Air. I couldn't believe Brian would show off his medals like that. He wouldn't. It was her. One day, I went over there and noticed the medals were all gone. I said, "What happened?" and he said, "I took them out to the pier at Santa Monica and threw them into the ocean." I believed him, and never asked about it again.

His wife was something of a socialite, and he hated that. She wanted to entertain and be entertained by the elite of Hollywood. That was the exact opposite of what Brian wanted. They had adopted a boy, Michael. Brian just loved that kid. There's still a mix-up and a mystery about how that kid died. I think something hit him in the pool, some physical thing, and he just died. His death sent Brian over the hump. I stayed at the Sportsman's Lodge in the Valley sometimes, and Brian got ahold of me there once after his son died, and we started drinking. We wound up in some place with a long bar over on Melrose. I wanted to help him, but how do you deal with a man who has lost his son? How do you even go out and drink with a guy after something like that has happened? What do you say?

We were in this bar, and some son of a bitch came in, and he wanted to challenge Brian. Brian was a big man; he didn't abuse anybody, but he could handle himself. This guy kept pushing Brian. He had seen him on TV or in pictures and was challenging him to prove himself. I went down the bar and said to the bartender, "You better throw this guy out; Brian just lost his son." But before I could get back down the bar to Brian, he stepped back and hit that son-of-a-bitch bully in the throat. And just like in the movies, the guy flew up on the bar. Brian hit him again and knocked him over the bar. The guy flew over and his legs kicked some bottles over. Brian threw a hundred-dollar bill on the bar, and we left.

We forgot where we parked, and by the time we found the car, we could hear the police sirens moving in. We jumped in his car and drove off just in time, just like from a scene in one of the movies Brian had appeared in. Brian later said to me, "That's the one time they should have had a camera on a bar fight. It really made me feel good to whack that bully bastard." In a strange way, that incident cemented our friendship. By the way, that was the last time I ever knew Brian Keith to take a drink of hard liquor or any type of alcohol, except for a single beer now and then.

He and Judith got divorced. He was still doing the television series *Family Affair* (1966–1971), which made him a household name, when he went off to Hawaii to make a movie for Bernie Kowalski, *Krakatoa, East of Java* (1969), a failed picture that somehow made a ton of money. Brian met a girl there, Victoria Young. They fell in love and married in 1970. He bought a new home in Malibu. It was up on a bluff and far away from the movie colony. He had to drive a full hour and a half every day to get to and from the set of *Family Affair*, just to live away from colony people. He would drive an old station wagon into the studio for that show. *Family Affair* was a big hit, but half of that money—as well as his old castle in Bel Air—went to his ex-wife, Judith. Brian would invite me to his Malibu home, and it became a haven for me. Victoria would meet me at the front door with an oriental robe and slippers. She would cook and always join in the conversation. Brian would sometimes run movies for us, and sometimes we would tell stories of Gallup. He had a lot of time off during the making of *The Hallelujah Trail* (1965), and he would spend much of that time with the Indians in that region. I told him about my mentor, Woody Crumbo, the Potawatomi Indian from Oklahoma who became my close friend as well. My grandmother was a medicine healer, and I told Brian of my training with a great medicine man in Taos, Joseph Bernal. Like Sam, Brian was a heavy mystic, and, like Sam, Brian kept it very private.

I remember we were driving along in the Valley one day when I told him about a dream I had while I was staying over at the Sands Motel. I went to my room there one day to take a nap in the middle of the afternoon.

I closed the curtains to block out the light, but just a little sliver of light shone in. I had just stretched out on my bed when I saw a figure materialize by the window, and I thought, "I'm going nuts." It was a lady with a smile. I pinched my face and twisted my arm to be dead certain I was awake, and I sure as hell was. She slowly disappeared just as she'd come about, and I knew that my disbelief had cost me a meeting with the other world. And I told Brian this story while he was driving. He suddenly whirled that station wagon off the road and into the driveway of a little old handy store. He slammed on the brakes, and said, "Goddamn!" Once we stopped, he told me that about a month before, he stretched out in his on-set trailer to take an afternoon nap. He, too, saw a materialization. It was complete—a woman with a smile formed. He kept his cool for a while, and then lost it. She disappeared. He said he knew what it was, that there is a dual side to every human being, the male side and the female side. In rare cases, the other side will come forward with a message. He experienced the exact same thing that I had and he waited longer than I had for that message without receiving it. Still, the lack of total acceptance had cost us both a true meeting with the so-called other side.

Sam and Brian's friendship lasted for years. Sam offered Brian the role of Bishop Pike in *The Wild Bunch*. (Some Peckinpah historians note that Sam offered Brian the Ernest Borgnine part of Dutch, but that's not how I heard it.) Brian turned it down. I asked him why, and he said, "I knew the insanity that would go on down there, Max. I knew Emilio Fernández would be involved. I knew madness would occur, and I had quit drinking. To me, it was an average script, though I knew Sam would achieve greatness with it. I knew it was going to be great, but I had to give it up. I was not physically or mentally able to handle the insanity that would go on, that did go on." And he was right. His mind was too fine and extra-sensitive from the loss of his son, and it would have been destroyed by that shoot. Brian later told me, "Sam cast that part perfectly." And he did. William Holden was an alcoholic, so he fit right into the madness.

Brian was still making movies, and for some reason he got a lot of pictures that were made far away. I remember he went to Japan in 1974 to make some picture with Robert Mitchum—*The Yakuza*—and Brian would write me letters on big, yellow-papered legal pads about the experience. He'd write wonderfully descriptive letters, detailing the wild-ass antics that Mitchum would pull over there. Brian never punctuated anything. He wouldn't take the time to do that. He just had a little time, and he'd want to tell me something, so he'd write it down. He was one of the few actors I knew who wrote letters, by the way. As I've said, cowboys and actors just don't write letters. Brian's letters were always funny. He'd satirize himself and the movie industry. Once I remember he went off to make a movie in Israel with some ex–football player, Fred Dryer (*Death Before Dishonor*, 1987). Brian wrote me this long letter about traveling around Israel. Here's this heavy Roman Catholic who also believed in the Indian myth of creation coming out of the bowels of the earth, and he's in Israel where one thing puzzles him—why there's so many places where they claimed to have buried Jesus Christ. I remember he wrote, "They sure buried Jesus Christ in nice places. I don't know if I can get enough time off to visit all those wonderful places."

Now there was a Mormon film producer, Charles E. Sellier Jr., who took the story of Grizzly Adams and turned it into a big hit on TV. It was the most pretentious bunch of bullshit I ever saw. I couldn't stand it, and Brian couldn't either, but he called me to say that this producer called him to announce that NBC wanted to create a series based on the lives of the mountain men. Brian had actually made a picture in 1980 with Charlton Heston called *The Mountain Men*. It ranged from great to lousy. But this producer wanted Brian for the series, and he asked Brian, "What writer do you know who can write this?" And Brian said, "I've got the guy."

This producer called me. He was willing to put me up for a few weeks while I wrote the pilot. I stayed at the Mikado, a Japanese restaurant, bar, and hotel. Brian brought in this Mormon producer, and we had our first production meeting in this little old room at the Mikado. Brian said to us, "When I was in the Marine Corps, they threw me in the brig. I had to stand up for thirty-six hours straight, but I could read anything I wanted, so I asked for the Mormon Bible, and for thirty-six hours I read that goddamned thing." I'm not sure what this Mormon guy thought of that, but Brian was testing him by putting him on. Brian Keith had respect for anyone who truly believed in what they were doing. He did not care what it was as long as they were honest.

Brian and I came up with a pretty good first script. The producer chimed in with changes. A couple of things he was right about. Some things he was dead wrong about. One morning, this Mormon guy brought in a little pocket book that he had written about the shooting of John F. Kennedy. Brian was pissed off. He said to me, "Isn't that pitiful—the son of a bitch is trying to show you his writing credentials!"

This was in the early 1980s, and NBC had a brand new president, Brandon Tartikoff. We got a meeting with him, and there were also three NBC executives, plus Brian, plus me, and this Mormon guy. Seven people. That's a lucky number in both the Choctaw and Cherokee culture, so I thought to myself, "This is a good omen!" I was wrong.

Tartikoff said, "Basically we have to entertain the audience. I want to make this as historically accurate as we can get it. And we need to have a lucky opening."

Brian and I had gone into the old journals of the real mountain men, so Brian said, "This script is as authentic as Sam Peckinpah's *The Westerner.*"

That hit them. They knew about that series, even twenty years later. They didn't question us any further.

Still, we had to have a zillion meetings with ding-dong producers. I often felt we were close to that green light. Tartikoff kept saying it was looking good, the money was in place, NBC was talking to agents and directors, and so on.

One day, when I was back in New Mexico, I got a call from Tartikoff's second-in-command. I don't remember his name.

"We want to talk to you about the script," he said.

"And Brian, too, right?"

"No. Just you, the writer."

"I can't do that. Brian brought me into this deal."

"Max, this is standard procedure," this guy said, giving me plenty of that canned bullshit some folks hand out in Hollywood and other renowned places.

I didn't feel good about this. Something told me it would lead to a train wreck and the money wouldn't matter.

"I'm not gonna come in for a meeting unless you are going to have Brian there," I said one more time.

"We don't want an actor in on a script meeting," the guy said. That did it. I've found my actor friends to be highly sensitive, very bright people who respect a good story most of all.

I didn't go. NBC cancelled the series. In one phone call, I cost Brian Keith a fortune. He didn't gripe. And he loved to make money. But I told him about it, and he thought it was the right thing to do. I don't know why they didn't want Brian in on the meetings.

The series might have taken off, and it might have become a hit, and I might have become set for life. But I've often thought back to my mining days in northern New Mexico, when Woody Crumbo and I could have sold out our interests in a copper mine for millions and didn't. Then the price of copper dropped in half and we had no reserves. We went broke. We went into debt. And I never did regret that decision. With all that money that might have come into my hands, and with all the fun I was having in life, well, somebody would have eventually killed me.

Brian and I gave up on the series and went right on dreaming about making *My Pardner* as a movie. Brian had read a lot of my works, and he fell in love with *My Pardner*. In his heart, he believed he'd get to play ol' Boggs in the film version.

Now, every now and then I've had spells where electronic equipment breaks down on me. I spent five years writing—in long hand—my book *Bluefeather Fellini*. Pat typed it up on a computer; she didn't want me to touch the computer or even go near it for fear that it would crash! Whenever I get close to some new-fangled technology, it messes up. I've always had this affliction. It would be nice, even fun, if one had any control over it, but you don't. It may not show up for weeks and then wham!—like a sledgehammer to the head, electronic devices, phones, computers, and so on, go crazy. It ain't fun, I tell you. Not for anyone. Well, maybe for a minute and a half once in a while.

I was staying at the Sportsman's Lodge when Brian called to invite me to lunch at noon. This was around 11:45, and right after he called me the phone in my room started ringing off the hook. It was always for somebody else, or a wrong number, or an attempt to reach the main switchboard. The hotel's phone system had broken down, and I later found out that the only phone in that whole hotel that was working was the one in my room. Suddenly, people were calling me for reservations—and sometimes I took 'em! Some caught on to the fact that they were talking to either a madman or an amateur, but many did not. Brian walked into the lobby and found out what was happening. The place was going crazy. There was no explanation, and the phone company couldn't figure out what was wrong. Brian came up to my room and said, "I knew when I walked into the lobby what you had done." Brian told the manager, "That's just ol' Max." The harried manager simply went blank all over, according to Brian. I never confessed. How could I? It took days to straighten out, and no one had a real answer—not the managers, not the phone company, and certainly not ol' Max.

One time in the mid-1970s, Pat and I took the Super Chief out to Los Angeles on business. We were about to come back to New Mexico, and we stepped up on the train at the station, and the minute I stepped on the second step the lights went out in the train and confusion began to reign. A message soon came through that the entire mechanical system on the train was in disrepair. Experts were on the way. This had never happened before. Pat and I went into the bar at the station, along with all the other passengers, and I got up and called Brian and told him what had happened. He laughed his ass off.

A few months later, Brian went on *The Johnny Carson Show*. He hated doing talk shows, but he was promoting a movie or a TV show or something, and, by God, the lights went out in the NBC studio! You could hear 'em talking for a little bit, and then lights started flashing, and the announcer said, "Ladies and gentlemen, we are having technical difficulties. Stand by." Then the screen went dark all over the world.

Brian knew he had done it. He had the same uncontrollable affliction with electrical and mechanical systems that I have. The show came back on the air, and Carson made a face while pointing to his watch, like he'd lost ten minutes. And Brian said, "Ah, hell, this is nothing. I've got a friend in New Mexico who broke down the Super Chief for an hour and a half." He was too polite to mention my name on the air.

Brian's parents were actors. His father was Robert Keith, who appeared in many movies, and his mother was actress Helena Shipman. His grandparents were involved with the Keith-Orpheum theater chain, so he was raised in a theatrical environment. That background helped him a lot as an actor. He told me once, "I've overcome the fact that directors will not direct me. They are intimidated." He said they often told him, "You know better than I do what to do." He said, "I want the director to direct me even if it's his first picture." He did tell me that one thing he liked about Sam was the fact that Sam told him what he wanted from him as an actor and then let him do it. Brian was one of those actors who could take a piece of shit and make it look good. I never saw him give a bad performance. I thought his best acting work was in Norman Jewison's 1966 film *The Russians Are Coming, the Russians Are Coming*. He may have been a better actor than Lee Marvin, but he wasn't a bigger star at that time. Brian could play a subtlety that Lee couldn't master. Lee could go overboard, but he'd still be believable because his movement was so powerful and his own experience with violence came into play. To compare the two men on-screen, Lee's violence came from the earth, and Brian, who was an aerial gunner in the Marines—his violence came from the air. That may sound odd, but there's a vast difference there. Brian didn't smell the exploding guts the way Lee did. And Brian had that theatrical background, whereas Lee was a plumber who did a play or two and then just ended up in pictures. I think Brian was more focused.

Brian and Lee and Sam. All were willing to sacrifice their lives for their country. Two of them had seen terrible combat, and the third claimed to have seen atrocious acts committed. They all had an affinity for one another, they all had a respect for one another, and yet they never worked with one another after Sam hit it big. Maybe that's the reason those two actors stayed friends with Sam, because they never worked with him again. Interestingly, once Brian turned down the role of Pike Bishop in *The Wild Bunch*, Sam offered it to Lee, who also turned it down. Brian and Lee and Sam all counted on doing *The Hi-Lo Country*. None of them got to do it.

Brian had a great love for small children, and he was a sucker for those ads featuring the faces of little sad children. I think they hired kid actors for those, but he'd send money to forty of them a month and bore me to death by making me listen to the cockeyed letters they wrote him in return. But he loved children, including his own.

Brian and I often talked on the phone. And one day, in the mid-1990s, I recognized a tiny bit of weakness in his voice. I asked him to speak up, and he told me he had been diagnosed with cancer of the lung. I told him I could send him the best Indian medicine you could get your hands on. He had nothing to lose.

He was having family problems. His son had outlawed some—stole a semitruck or something like that and drove two hundred miles before the police caught him. His daughter, Daisy, was a beautiful woman; she'd been dating and done some acting, including a stint in a TV series Brian did in the late 1980s called *Heartland*.

I called him once to ask him if he had used the medicine I sent. I told him to ask Victoria to rub it on his head and chest. Then I called him again shortly after.

His voice was weak. I said, "I can't hear you, Brian."

He suddenly spoke up loud. "My daughter, Daisy, killed herself yesterday."

What do you say to someone in that situation? You're dying, and your beautiful and talented daughter commits suicide. She was still in her twenties.

Two months later, in June 1997, Brian took the same gun she used and shot himself.

Victoria called me with the news. I said, "I'm not gonna ask what I can do because I know there is nothing I can do. You were married to one of the most loving human beings on Earth."

This beautiful man's life ended in tragedy. I still think of him every day. It was a good friendship that started, indirectly, because of Sam Peckinpah. It was Sam who had given Brian a copy of my *The Hi-Lo Country*.

8. "The Role Has Already Been Cast"

In the spring of 1968—about the time he was filming *The Wild Bunch* in Mexico—Sam Peckinpah sent me the following poem, written by his only nephew, David, in all capital letters:

BILL

YOU ARE ONE OF THE LAST, OLD MAN
    YOU ARE A DYING BREED
SILVER HAIR, BROKEN TEETH, SKIN TURNED LEATHER
    FROM THE NEVADA WIND.
YOU ARE YOUR OWN BOSS
YOUR BLUE EYES ARE PALE, BUT ALIVE, AND YOUR BELLY
    SAGS FROM YEARS OF HARD WHISKEY
    YOU ARE OLD.
FINGERNAILS CRACKED AND BROKEN FROM YEARS OF
    WORK; LIPS BROKEN AND CHAPPED; GUMS PACKED
    WITH SNUFF.
    YOU ARE ONE TOUGH SON OF A BITCH.
I FIND YOU HERE IN THE DESERT, ALONE, WITH ANCIENT
    HOUSE, BEAT-UP TRUCK AND STRING OF *CABALLOS*.
    WORKING ALONE AND FREE, FEELING THE WIND AND
    THE ROUGH TONGUES OF THE HORSES.
    THIS IS YOUR COUNTRY.
I FIND YOU AT MAJORS' BAR, DRINKING WHISKEY,
    LAUGHING, AND SNORTING; TELLING THE STORIES I
    LOVE TO HEAR.
    YOU ARE MY FRIEND.

I TAKE YOU HOME, PEE SOAKING YOUR PANTS, STAINS OF
SNOOSE FROM LIPS TO SHIRT, SNORING LOUDLY.
HOME TO YOUR HORSES AND COYOTE DOG.
HOME TO SLEEP AND DREAM.
HOME—WHERE A MAN IS STILL A MAN.

David was about sixteen years old at the time, and Sam would soon orchestrate the loss of his virginity.

I first met David at Sam's Broad Beach house when David was about twelve years old. I took an instant liking to him. He seemed very grown up and respectful—that's something you can sense if you have cowboyed and mined enough. His blood was bubbling with life, his communication was intelligent. It must have been less than a year later when I received a package from Sam that, to my surprise, had David's Fresno address written on the back. Sam had asked David to send the poem to me. I was impressed with the poem, and sent it to several outlets in an effort to get it published. They all turned it down, and I'd never been turned down by John R. Milton at the *South Dakota Press*. The poem remained unpublished until now. My sense at this time is that Sam had enormous respect for his nephew, though I have related in another chapter how Sam called David's first draft of a screenplay of my story *My Pardner* a "piece of shit." Yet I knew that Sam must have had great faith in his nephew's creative talent or he would have never gone to the bother of sending me the poem.

The next time I got to visit with David was some years later, when we all went to the premiere of Sam's film *The Killer Elite* (1975) in San Francisco. Later, at the Fairmont Hotel, where we were all staying, Sam held court in his bedroom as people filed in and out to pay their respects. He was drinking *and* snorting coke. Most of that night was spent in the hotel suite's living room, away from Sam. David was there, and he latched on to me and asked a lot of questions about writing.

I felt he had a gestating creative talent that was as strong as his uncle's—and given that I had just seen *The Killer Elite*, not one of Sam's better efforts, maybe I felt David had the potential to be better than Sam. Jim Hamilton, who later helped Sam get *Cross of Iron* (1977) together, was there that night, too, and he kept joining in the conversation between David and me as if he knew everything about writing screenplays, although he had not yet written anything that was made into a picture. That kind of annoyed me, because I was trying to give David some practical tips about the writing business. It was one of the few times I wanted to chastise my friend Jim.

I ran into David again, a few years later, north of Albuquerque while Sam was shooting the bar-fight scene for *Convoy* at Rafael's. David was outside, leaning against part of an exterior door with Frank Kowalski nearby. David was wearing cowboy boots, which was unlike him. I could sense his insecurity; he was pretending to have fun that he was not having. I could tell Sam wasn't coming through for David the way he should have. He wasn't giving David the encouragement he should have either, and Denver probably felt guilty that he didn't give Sam a spanking for this neglect. David wasn't so much lost as alone.

Some years later, after Sam's death, I was staying at the Mikado in Hollywood and I got a call from David asking me to meet him regarding his screenplay for *My Pardner*. Sam had hired him to write the first draft. I read it and felt that David displayed a surprising feel for the land and the people. I told him, "You've captured the subtlety of humor in my work better than anyone Sam ever hired to write screenplays based on my books." That's when David told me that Sam told him it was a piece of shit.

I told David, "Well, Sam told that to everyone. Sam was full of shit. It's as fine a first draft as I've ever read, and I've read a lot of them."

"If you feel that way about it, let's team up and work on the screenplay," he said. He had me trapped. I said yes.

But it would be a while before we got around to starting that collaboration, because David started selling some scripts to television. He produced some of the *Beauty and the Beast* series at a time when the show was hurting. I remember thinking, "Wow, it's faltering in the ratings, and they hired him to help boost its ratings. That's a mistake." He had told me that he intended to turn the series into a work of art, and watching that last season on TV every week, I have to say I believe he did just that. He managed to turn that fairy tale into a high-class drama with sensitivity and believability. It stayed on the air quite a while and received fine reviews.

David got a shot at writing, and working as executive producer, on the 1990s cable TV series *Silk Stalkings*. It was a helluva success. It was making the production company money, it was making the sponsors money, and it was making David money. He worked on it for about five years, and I remember having a friendly cup of coffee with him in Hollywood near the end of his run with the show. He suddenly stopped talking shop, and I could tell by his silence that he wanted to tell me something. I shut up and it came out.

"I fucked up," he said. That was an enormously difficult thing for a Peckinpah to say. He went on to explain that he had become afflicted with the oldest of Hollywood diseases: quick success. He had overextended himself. "I sold out to the concept of Hollywood," he said. "I moved into an expensive home, joined all the clubs, bought a boat, have three cars in my three-car garage, and I'm mixing with the big winners. I knew this was stupid—I have already witnessed this through my uncle's destructive behavior."

David was married at this point, to Sandy. They had four children. He once told me an interesting story about Garrett, their oldest: when the boy was seven or eight years old and out shopping with David, they ran into the actress Nina Foch, who by this time was doing more teaching than acting in Hollywood. However, she remained a beautiful and respected actress and drama coach, and she was also known for her psychic abilities. After chatting with David and Garrett, she pulled David aside and told him that Garrett was special—he was extremely psychic. David had no idea to what degree, but he believed her, and when Foch asked for permission to visit Garrett at their home and be left alone with him in his room, he agreed. He later told me that she at first seemed hesitant to tell him all this, and then she just out and asked for his cooperation.

Foch told David that Garrett had a rare ability to communicate with a chosen few in a nonverbal manner. When David accepted this from her, she was wonderfully surprised, but he was excited about it all, too. I know he told his wife, Sandy, about it. I don't know how she reacted, or who else he or she may have told about this gift.

So it started. Foch and David arranged a time for her to visit on weekends and after school. Garrett and his younger brother Trevor's room was next to David's home office, so David would take Trevor away on some excuse so Foch and Garrett could be alone. Foch told David he was welcome to sit in and watch at any time, and on occasion he would. He'd watch them and told me they just sat there and never said an audible word. When he worked next to them in his office, he said he could never hear more than the occasional mumble from Garrett's room.

Now when David first called me about this, he was thrilled: he had a son who was born with a talent that David had, as did Sam. Screenwriter Jeb Rosebrook had attended a private school north of Phoenix called Orme. When it came time for David and Sandy to send Garrett off to school, they researched and chose the site carefully. You needed a certain IQ to get into Orme in those days; students had to ride and brand and ranch on the campus as well as take academic courses. Garrett was accepted there, and he excelled in everything he did, including athletics. David and Sandy were very proud of their oldest son. Then Garrett came home from break with what had been diagnosed by the school's doctor as a form of the flu. He got back home, had dinner with his family, and went up to his room to go to bed. He never woke up. It was later determined that he died of meningitis.

The son that David so worshipped—and perhaps the most gifted person he had in his entire life—had died. And soon David was slipping from his position near the top of the world. He managed to hold it together for the sake of his family—for a while. Then he started on a path of escapism. He bought a motorcycle and started riding with a gang that biked to Las Vegas, Nevada, at least twice a month for whatever damn reason. He got tattooed, and this was when he was at an age far beyond what I call a tattoo age. Bills were coming due. Fighting erupted in the household. The oldest son, Trevor, was coming of age during this turmoil. It wasn't looking good for him.

David had directed a low-budget horror film with backing from Chicago sources called *When Danger Follows You Home* (1997) starring JoBeth Williams. It came and went without leaving much of a mark. Then he got a job working as a crew member on a film in Toronto, where a great portion of the American film industry was moving in those days due to tax breaks and other incentives. It was a job way down the ranks for him, but at least it was a job. There David met a woman named Tori who worked in the film industry and he fell in love with her. In his desperation, he left Sandy, moved to Toronto, and moved in with Tori. He got a teaching job at a university and landed a job as an executive producer on a Canadian-shot sci-fi series called *Sliders* (1996–1999).

David's father, Denver, had died in the mid-1990s, but I believe that the entire Peckinpah family was, at the very least, disgusted with David's actions and therefore took Sandy's side in the matter. I said nothing. I took no sides. I stayed in touch with David, but we did not discuss his family when we talked, other than to speak of his mother, Betty, a great lady and equally fine artist. Often, when I would call Denver and he was out, Betty would speak comfortably with me about my work, and she was always insightful with her comments. We talked about other writers we enjoyed, and we talked about David. Her understanding of the creative talents embedded in her son amazed me because they were the same intuitions I had about David as well. She always thanked me for my interest in David and his work, and it often came to me, during these conversations, that David inherited powerful creative genes from both sides of his family.

But our work on *My Pardner* continued after a confusing series of events regarding the rights to the book. Katy Haber had been in England for a long time—she wouldn't admit this for years, but Sam had her deported there to get rid of her—and after Sam's demise she returned and hooked up with another Brit, Mike Segall, who worked in the film business here, and they started a film company. The first thing they wanted to option was the rights to *My Pardner*. They would pay, I think, $30,000 for the rights with the understanding that David and I would write the screenplay on a step deal—if the screenplay was accepted, he and I would be coproducers, though I wouldn't have to actually go and do anything if the story finally got made as a film.

Because Sam believed he still had the rights when he died (or at least pretended that he did), I thought we had to go to all of his children to get them to relinquish those rights. I remember that Sharon, Sam's oldest daughter, did not want to do that. But Sam's last lawyer, a man named Swindlehurst (what a name for a lawyer—but people said he was as honest as could be), went to work to help us get the rights cleared, so David and I made a run at it. Together, we wrote a pretty good script.

David ended up putting a typical Sam Peckinpah touch on the script. There is a scene where some horses break loose and people are running all over and a horse trailer crashes and . . . stuff that had nothing to do with my original story, but it had Sam written all over it. Before we could fix it, our world began going to hell. Katy and her partner couldn't get the financing, and I was told that the rights reverted to the Peckinpah kids again. I never could keep track of the rights to any of my stories when Sam Peckinpah was involved, because most of our deals were paid in cash and written on plain paper or bar napkins. Only a few made their way to a legitimate attorney's office. So there was more legal wrangling, and then there was the matter of David's personal problems.

Still, I didn't give up, and I did have a contract. The New Mexico Film Office was gaining momentum in this state under the then governor, Bill Richardson, and I got to thinking that we could get the film shot here if we could raise the money and clear up the rights. I hired a local entertainment lawyer, a woman from Serbia who had studied law at the University of New Mexico. She was tough. I told her to prepare for battle, if need be, and she did. I told David this, and I could tell it rejuvenated him. We felt good about the project again, and he admitted he got a little carried away with that one scene.

I went to the film office and met with the then director, Lisa Strout, about the project. I explained that we needed about $2 million to get the film made down in Lea County, where the story had been launched. She said the state could give us some breaks if we raised the money. I thought if everything came together it would be a wonderful opportunity for me, David, and the state. It felt right.

I got hooked up with a big state politician from the southeast whose name I won't mention, some big-oil men, and a newspaper man I knew; they all got excited about the prospect of a New Mexico–made film with the Peckinpah name attached. We all held a meeting, and I told them, "If someone will sign for just $2 million, the state will guarantee it and give us what we need to get the film made here." And this politician, in front of the newspaper man and a dozen witnesses, said, "I can do that." That's what politicians do: make promises knowing people will forget what they said a few days later. And I believed him. Knowing better, I still believed him. He was that clever.

I called David with the news, and we discussed the four or five things in the script that we needed to fix. A new life flowed into David. As with his uncle, Sam, he was revived by the hope of a new picture. David began dreaming again, as we all do in order to survive.

I met a guy here who dreamed of being a producer. He had made some commercials, but he wanted something bigger. He had some connections in the growing film industry here, and he worked to help us get it made. David—at my insistence—agreed to direct, and we were talking about casting. David wanted Peter Fonda to play the one-eyed cowboy in the story. (His father, Henry, had been in Burt Kennedy's film version of my novel *The Rounders*.) The politician kept telling me, "I'm gonna help you do this." We left the script with one of the business partners in the venture. I never found out if he read it, because we never heard from him again. Suddenly, the money part of it wasn't looking so good.

David and I kept talking back and forth about the project. He told me about the low-budget film he had made with Chicago backing some years back, and said he got those investors their money back on that film through European sales. He suddenly said, "I've got an idea. I'll get them to back it. They're dangerous but their word is good." We still didn't know about the rights. I asked David to call Sam's daughter, Sharon, and ask her to cooperate with us.

"I can't do it," he told me. "I'd rather be shot." I told him he had to do it, that I had done things I didn't want to do to get this damn thing together, and he had to play his part.

He did it. When I next called him, he told me, "She was impregnable. I couldn't get through to her. It's making me ill."

He had, just a few phone conversations back, abruptly cut off our talk with, "Forgive me. I can't talk on the phone anymore. It drains me." I knew then he was in desperate trouble.

But he rallied on. I did some researching, and looked through some papers, and it looked like I had the rights to the book now that Sam was dead. David urged me to make it happen: "The worst that can happen is they take us to court."

But we didn't have to worry about a court case, or accepting the Chicago money, or anything else, as it turned out. I read David's obituary in the trades a few days later, in April 2006. He died of a heart attack.

He was about fifty-five. I wasn't able to get any movement going on the picture at that point, and I really didn't want to anyway.

I remember one day, in the middle of talking about the project on the phone, David had stopped to say, "You know, Max, I never stopped loving Sandy and Trevor and the kids." He tried to recall the names of his other children, and his voice choked up, he stumbled, and then he went right back to talking about *My Pardner*. I didn't have a chance to respond to his comment. I'm not sure I would have anyway.

While we were working on *My Pardner*, David wrote an autobiographical story about his first sexual experience. It was twenty-six pages long. He mailed it to me and to his best friend, Garner Simmons. It is entitled *Losing It on High Street: A Saga of Sexual Awakening, Directed by Sam Peckinpah*. Both Garner and I were impressed, for despite some structural flaws, it had a raw truth to it that spoke to the dark Peckinpah passion for lust and violence. It's a powerful piece of writing that starts with this phrase: "Insanity is described in a twelve-step program as repeating the same behavior and expecting different results. I was playing poker again with Sam Peckinpah, so I guess I fit the description."

Sam was a lousy poker player and often a poor loser. After losing a hand to David one night at Sam's Malibu home, Sam hit the boy hard in the mouth, giving him a split lip. Denver, Fern Lea, and Walter all thought Sam was out of line, but in spite of David's split lip they all had a laugh as Walter gathered Sam up, dragged him kicking and screaming through the laughter, and tossed him into the Pacific Ocean. Sam sloshed ashore and strode back into the house for a shot of tequila and a change of clothes. There was no apology from Sam, and David was told not to tell his mother, Betty, of the incident. It was an unwritten law among the Peckinpah men: tell the women nothing, and damn little if pressed.

David wrote in his short story,

Denver was nine years older than Sam, as much a father to him as a brother. He was the only person Sam would listen to when his mind, filled with bats and the darkness, was swallowing him. They loved each other more than their own children but theirs was the love of survivors of a fucked-up family dynamic . . . far too complicated and private to get into.

Poker was a rite of passage in my family for both males and females, as was cribbage. We played for money and no parlor games. Guts poker: stud and low-ball. Things could get heated, but I'm the only one who ever got hit. I never knew what triggered that backhand in Malibu. I spent years looking for my own guilt in the situation and it wasn't until I had kids of my own that I realized that nothing I said or did could have justified my being hit. Sam liked to hit people. It was all part of a strange little movie in his head, one he could never cut into any shape that made sense. He played a role he loved and hated, one that he played so long and so well that he lost all track of where he left off and the character began. He played it to the end: the tough, brooding maverick director, down on his luck and surrounded by enemies, trusting no one and hiding his beautiful heart behind bullshit, blow, and booze. He was capable of extraordinary tenderness and incredible cruelty. He made the shift in a heartbeat. Anything could turn a good time into confrontation. He fed on fear and conflict. He felt nothing worthwhile came in life or art without having losses of pain and suffering.

Now Sam had a little ranch outside Ely, Nevada, where the so-called Walker River Gang—Sam, Denver, Walter, sometimes Ben Johnson and Warren Oates, and a few others—often gathered. (Sam had once ordered David to go get a gun out of his car there so Sam could shoot the cook, who refused to put some onions in a dish for Sam.) David writes of another poker game there with Sam and Denver, in which David won and Sam made it clear that he didn't like losing. David recalled:

> I was ready in that moment to kill him, and he knew it. I stepped back. Sam stepped around me to the counter, splashed bourbon in our cups and passed one to me. His eyes were little slits, his voice a gravely whisper: "Have you lost your cherry yet?"
>
> "No," I answered. It was five months past my 16th birthday and I hadn't come close.
>
> Sam clinked his tin cup against mine and said, "Tonight's the night."

David relates that there were then three legal whorehouses in Ely, all on a potholed stretch of asphalt known as High Street. He describes the bleak, icy landscape of that winter night, with the pink-and-green flashing signs up and down High Street. "Heady stuff for a horny sixteen-year-old poised on the high board of lust," David writes. "I didn't even feel like I had to throw up anymore."

Sam drove David from the ranch to Ely in his truck—well, that is, David drove, because Sam was already drunk and still drinking. On the way, David had to listen to Sam's lengthy dissertation on why whores were the only women a man could trust. Oddly enough, Sam would growl at David to slow down from time to time: "There's no more ignorant way to die than in a fucking car accident!"

The duo hit a local diner to eat first, so it was past midnight when they made their first run at a whorehouse. Sam crowed a line he had used, to similar degree, in *Major Dundee*: "Until the Apache is taken or destroyed." David's cherry would be taken, though there were complications when the truck abruptly stopped outside of town. Sam said they would walk, but David began to have second thoughts: "I felt like the guy in front of a firing squad when all the rifles jammed—maybe I could get out of this."

He couldn't. Sam marched him to the first whorehouse, the Starlite, giving David a speech telling him not to worry about contracting clap or any other sexual disease, since these girls see a doctor about once a week. "The clap's no big deal," Sam told David. "I've had it so many times I don't even get shots anymore." He told David that he simply placed his own penis in a saucer of penicillin and let the penicillin lap the disease up.

They entered the first house of flesh. The place had a jukebox, and Patsy Cline was singing "Crazy" while three girls—all clad in either bikinis or negligees—made small talk with some visiting truckers. It was not unlike a brothel scene from one of Sam's films, *Ride the High Country*. "They were carnal angels come to carry me to paradise," David noted of the trio. The woman behind the bar—a madam named Diamond with cold, flat eyes—told Sam that David was too young to be there. Sam dug into his white Levis and pulled out a handful of bills. "The barmaid was losing her attitude as Sam flirted her up, working those wadded bills like a sleight-of-hand artist," David wrote. Sam won the woman over as she toasted David with a drink: "It was terrifying. I willed my ass to stay on that cracked orange vinyl and not bolt out into the frozen night."

These are David's words:

The barmaid waved a meaty finger at the girls, and they broke off working the cheap-as-dirt truckers to join her and Sam. They huddled, and laughter started early as all three women checked me out. One of them squealed for me to stand up, she wanted to see a real live virgin. I could have crawled out of the place as laughter washed over the bar. Sam came back with a fresh drink and a tight smile. "They all want you. They want to flip coins but I said it was your choice. A man never forgets his first. Be sure she's the right one."

He nodded to the girls. They each took a step out from the bar and did a little pirouette as they introduced themselves. I couldn't take my eyes off Bonnie, a platinum blonde in a pink and black bikini. She wore white cowboy boots, a white hat, and had a set of plastic six-shooters around her waist. Sam nodded at Bonnie: "Ladies, the role has already been cast."

Her breath smelled like Listerine and Luckies. Sam made the introduction as the losers went back to the truckers. Bonnie informed the barmaid she was going off the floor and ushered us down a corridor into the girls' quarters: ten or twelve narrow rooms barely wide enough for a single bed and dresser. Towels and linens were stacked outside a couple of rooms waiting to be cleaned. Bonnie led us into her room. It was girlier than a teenager's. Stuffed animals crowded the narrow bed and spilled from shelves. There were pictures of her cats all over her walls, fighting for space with framed family photos. She wanted to know what kind of party I wanted; since it was my first time, it should be perfect. I had no clue what she was talking about. "I want to . . . have sex with you." Bonnie and Sam got a huge laugh out of that.

Bonnie then took the time to explain the usual oral and carnal sexual practices as Sam stepped out, closing the door behind him. She then set a plastic egg timer on the night table and set it for forty-five minutes.

David writes:

The seconds ticked off loudly as she drew a basin of water at the
sink as she chatted on: Was it really my first time? Was Sam really
famous? She stood in front of me, took my shaking hands and put
them on her pale, ample hips and gazed at me through layers of
eye shadow and makeup. "Pull those pistols and tell me what to do,
cowboy." I drew the little plastic pistols from the holster and told her
to strip. The bikini came off . . .

Bonnie vaulted into the saddle. I felt like Sea Biscuit being ridden
to the wire. Thank God Bonnie didn't have a crop. At one point, her
little hat flew off and landed on my head, which got her giggling. A
girl with the giggles while you're still inside can teach you lots of new
feeling. It seemed like I lasted an hour; the clock must have stopped
short. But when Bonnie felt me cross the finish line and she nimbly
dismounted to douche herself over the basin on the floor, I saw that
barely ten minutes had passed. She gave me a peck on the cheek and
said I'd make lots of girls happy with that horse.

A big round of applause went up in the bar when Bonnie led me
back in. Sam and the barmaid were talking about her part in his new
film . . . and knocking the hell out of her lone bottle of good brandy.
They both asked how I liked it. The shit-eating grin was about all
the detail they got. It was all a blur, like a ride on a roller coaster. I
remember the sensation, but damn little detail. Sam drank to us both
and tossed me my coat. "Tonight you are a man. But our work is not
done."

Sam's plan, as David related, was to take David to all three whorehouses in town— the Starlite, the Lucky 7, and the Brass Lantern—
before returning to the Starlite and starting over again. As David writes,
"The object: to keep scoring until the player can't shoot anymore. Sam
and the barmaid at the Starlite had a bet riding on it. If I could run the
full pattern twice, he'd win."

They hit the Lucky 7 next, where Sam suggested to David that he wait
for Ebony. David did: "Fast and furious, hard biting and hair pulling,
some serious dirty name-calling . . . wow. Twelve minutes and change."

Twenty minutes later, they were heading to the Brass Lantern: "Another bar, another three girls. No dialogue about me being underage this time; there wasn't a customer in the place. I can't remember who I chose. While it's true you never forget your first girl, most of those who follow are quickly lost in the fog. The pace was taking its toll. The Brass Lantern girl actually had to spend about five seconds getting me hard, and it took two positions and nearly fifteen minutes to climax."

Back to the Starlite David went. At this pace, David figured, Sam would win. David cast a guilty glance toward Bonnie, but she was involved in a conversation with a trucker and didn't notice him: "That hurt a little. The second Starlite girl was fun, but hardly the firecracker Bonnie was. I had to think about Bonnie and her gun kink to get mine off this time. And it took half an hour. I was starting to feel old." Sam kept riding David: "Until the Apache is torn off or can't get up."

It was back to the Lucky 7 for another dip and then to the Brass Lantern, as David related. The rule was: he couldn't enjoy the same girl at any place twice. This time around, he got an enthusiastic girl who he thought would tear his arm off and beat him to death with it. By the time he finished his rounds twice and got back to the Starlite, Sam was nowhere to be seen. It turns out he passed out on the floor near the couch. Diamond pointed to one last sleepy hooker at the end of the bar. "Do her and your uncle wins the money," she told David. Here's how he told it: "The tired hooker, none too thrilled about it, slid off her stool and gestured for me to follow. We were back half an hour later. She was smiling, and I had her phone number in my pocket. She wanted me to call her. She'd like to come visit me in California. I've often wondered if it was lucky or unlucky that I lost that number."

David won the bet for Sam: five dollars. Diamond told David to get Sam out of there. David got his uncle up over his shoulders in a fireman's carry. As they left the building, the flashing neon sign went out and the door slammed behind them. David carried Sam to a nearby hotel, slipping and sliding in the snow. They went down hard on the ice at one point, and would have stayed down had not a passing trucker—one of the brothel customers—saved them. He had two big dogs in his cab, so there was no room for Sam, who ended up getting thrown onto a bunch of rolls of wire in the back. Sam was feeling no pain.

"Some night, eh, kid?" the trucker asked David. He had no idea.

David and Sam spent the night in a hotel in town. A tow truck got Sam's truck up and running by noon the next day. On the way home, as David put it, Sam was quietly sipping whiskey and moving very gingerly.

"Jesus," he rasped, running his fingers along his bruised ribs. "I think someone beat the shit out of me last night."

Sam told David, "Women like fucking as much as we do. And none of them give it away. Just be sure the price is one you're willing to pay, because your cock will cost you more than any armed robber ever will."

They got back to the ranch where Denver was cooking a pot of beans and listening to Johnny Cash. This is how David finished the story:

"You get it done?" Denver asked.

"I sure did. Over and over and over and over . . ." I counted on my fingers. "And over and over."

"Congratulations, friend," Denver told me. "Your mother doesn't need to know about this."

Yet David suspects she did know.

Both Garner Simmons and I were surprised when David told us, at the time, that his agent could not find a publishing outlet for the piece. To the best of my knowledge, David only sent it to the two of us; it still has not been published in its entirety.

David's wife, Sandy, was a beautiful woman of many dimensions who could talk film, painting, writing, or whatever subject you wanted with comfortable intelligence. During the many vacations she and David had taken to New Mexico, they stayed at the Bishop's Lodge north of Santa Fe, and it was often a great pleasure for Pat and me to visit with them when they were either going or coming to Albuquerque. It was just as much a shock to me as anyone when David went what I call "temporarily crazy" after the death of his son Garrett. I know it was a puzzling blow to Sandy and the other three children, and it upset the rest of the Peckinpah clan. I offer no excuses here, only a feeble attempt at an explanation: maybe David recognized something even rarer than the creative genius of his uncle (David Samuel "Sam" Peckinpah) and the love of his own wife and his mother. The inherent and little-known depth of the mystic that ran through the Peckinpahs—Sam, Denver, and David—revealed to him through the relationship between his son and Nina Foch the need to nurture mysticism with the most fragile delicacy. Garrett's sudden death must have created such a sense of loss in David that he became lost himself and never fully recovered.

I never knew Tori—I have heard she and David married, and I have also heard that they simply lived together as a couple—and I never really spoke with her at length when she would answer the phone when I rang David, so I do not believe it is my place to comment on their relationship one way or the other. I am not sure what happened to her, or where she is today. I wish her the best.

To Sandy's credit, after David's death she held her family together and saw that all three of their children became educated and remained loved. I'm happy to report that in October 2011 Sandy married James Lawrence de Girolamo, a man she knew and dated before she met David. Her daughter, Julianne Belle Peckinpah, runs a successful clothing business in Los Angeles. Son Jackson David Peckinpah is studying law at California State University–Long Beach as of this writing. Oldest son Trevor works in the movie business alongside Garner's son Owen, and the two are collaborating on a screenplay, I am told—so the genius of film imagery within the Peckinpah family will carry on. And if so, it will be an unsolicited gift for a needy world.

"RIDE THE HIGH COUNTRY"
A Metro-Goldwyn-Mayer Picture

62/181

Among the actors Max Evans met in Hollywood during his Sam Peckinpah days was Joel McCrea, seen here with Randolph Scott in a scene from Peckinpah's first major picture, *Ride the High Country* (1962). McCrea was, in Max's view, a class act.

Max and Sam on the set of *The Ballad of Cable Hogue* (1970). It looks like Max is giving Sam direction for a change. (Courtesy Max Evans)

(*opposite*) Slim Pickens and Max onboard the stagecoach, with Jason Robards Jr. (back to camera), in *The Ballad of Cable Hogue*. The entire project was a bumpy ride, but it remained Sam's favorite of his own films. (Courtesy Max Evans)

Max got to watch this scene in which Jason Robards Jr. bathed a nude Stella Stevens in *The Ballad of Cable Hogue*. That was a good day for Max. (Courtesy Max Evans)

Max and Jason Robards Jr. on the set of *The Ballad of Cable Hogue*. Max felt Sam Peckinpah put Robards's career back on track in the late 1960s. (Courtesy Max Evans)

L. Q. Jones and Jason Robards Jr. (center) join other *Cable Hogue* cast and crew members for a drink. L. Q. was actually the only member of the ensemble who did not drink—and he never took any crap from Sam Peckinpah. (Courtesy Max Evans)

(*opposite*) Sam with his son, Matthew Peckinpah, on the set of 1970s *The Ballad of Cable Hogue*. That's Max in the background, holding his script and probably trying to remember his lines for his brief role as a shotgun guard. (Courtesy Max Evans)

"Beware of Dog" is right—Sam's brother Denver was not an easy man and probably one of the few who could put Sam Peckinpah in his place if need be. (Courtesy Max Evans)

Denver, Sam, and Max enjoying a coffee—or maybe something stronger—in the wild far from Hollywood. Here Sam truly felt free and alive. (Courtesy Max Evans)

Sam at work on an elevated camera platform. A bit of his genius always shone through even on his weakest pictures. (Courtesy Max Evans)

(*opposite*) When Sam fired a gun into the air, it either meant "action"—as in this shot on the set of *The Wild Bunch*—or he was shooting at beer bottles being thrown by Max. (Courtesy Max Evans)

Sam did have a playful side, as he displays in this shot of himself and actor Jim Norton riding mini-bicycles in the English countryside where *Straw Dogs* (1971) was filmed. (Photo by John Jay, courtesy Katy Haber's private collection)

Sam took a gamble casting Kris Kristofferson (left) as Billy the Kid in the Western *Pat Garrett and Billy the Kid* (1973). James Coburn (right) was one of the few people to stick by Sam until the end. (Courtesy Max Evans)

James Coburn (left) and Katy Haber (right) wait for something to happen—and something was always happening on the set of a Sam Peckinpah movie—on the set of *Pat Garrett and Billy the Kid*. (Courtesy Katy Haber's private collection)

(*opposite*) Katy Haber (left) was Sam Peckinpah's Girl Friday—and Saturday, Sunday, Monday, Tuesday, Wednesday, and Thursday. Here she poses with James Coburn on the set of *Pat Garrett and Billy the Kid*. (Courtesy Katy Haber's private collection)

Only a madman like Sam (center) could deal with the dangerously violent Emilio Fernández (right) *and* the sweet-natured Warren Oates (left), both of whom were cast in Sam's *Bring Me the Head of Alfredo Garcia* (1974). (Courtesy Max Evans)

(*opposite*) Warren Oates shooting it out in typical Sam Peckinpah style in *Bring Me the Head of Alfredo Garcia*. (Courtesy Max Evans)

Sam in a contemplative mood on the set of *Bring Me the Head of Alfredo Garcia*.
(Courtesy Garner Simmons)

9. The Day Clark Gable Performed *The One-Eyed Sky*

It was my great pleasure (well, most of the time) to meet a number of first-rate actors who were also fine human beings during my sojourns to Hollywood. I met most of them through Sam; others I met through efforts to get my work optioned.

Joel McCrea was one of the most authentic Western-film actors of his time. He was a cowboy in real life in the sense that he owned and ran his own ranches in both California and New Mexico. He'd made about seventy-five films before he agreed to appear as Steve Judd in Sam Peckinpah's masterpiece *Ride the High Country*, and then he pretty much rode off into the sunset to relax in the shade and tend to his home, his family, and his line of stock—which he loved.

Both Joel and Randy Scott bought huge parcels of land north of Los Angeles. I believe Randy eventually sold most of his, but Joel kept most of his intact. Rodeo star Casey Tibbs knew Joel and told me the actor lived in a cabin next to a corral with horses down the hill from a castle where his wife, actress Frances Dee, lived. That's how they stayed married. In the early 1970s I got this idea of making a documentary about McCrea, and I was curious where he thought *Ride the High Country* stood in his body of film work. So through Casey, I got his number, called him up, and asked if I could come out to see him. He knew my work, and he welcomed me down to see him. He gave me directions, and I found my way down to his place, which was in beautiful rolling-hills ranch country in Ventura County.

Sure enough, I spotted a big castle-type house on a hill, about half a mile up from the cabin. Joel met me outside and ushered me into his bunkhouse. The first thing I do when I enter someone's house is to see if they have art on the walls, because that says a lot about a person. Joel had a number of paintings of the Western artist Charles Russell, and a big ol' buffalo robe laid out on his bed. He told me that the greatest saddle bronco rider, Casey Tibbs, had that robe made and tanned for him. "It looks good and it makes me feel good," he said. To him, this bunkhouse was a great joy. It was home, but to most A-list Hollywood types it would have been crude and below them.

We had us a visit, and we got along well. He was so warm when he talked about Casey, rodeo life, and his films. He knew I was there for a reason, but I wasn't sure how to bring it up to him. He said, "Let's take a walk." We went outside, and there were some special-bred sheep nearby, and he had a couple of dogs working 'em. He was proud of those dogs. It was a beautiful day, not a lot of wind, but a lot of sun. All of a sudden, here comes this big old car down the road. Joel said, "That's my wife." The car slowed, and he walked me over to the car and introduced me to his wife, who was still a beautiful woman, even then. We shook hands through the rolled-down window. She and Joel seemed as friendly as could be, but then she said good-bye and chugged up the hill to the castle.

Joel and I walked up to within about fifty yards of that big house. I was hoping he'd invite me in there for a drink or something, but no way—it was clear that the castle was hers, and the bunkhouse was his, and never the twain would meet.

I finally said, "Well, you know damn well I had a reason for wanting to come out here. I want to ask you, what do you think of *Ride the High Country* compared to the rest of your films?"

He looked away, off at the nearby hills—not unlike the way his character, Steve Judd, does at the end of *Ride the High Country*—and he said, "That was the best part I ever had, and I came damn close to turning it down."

"Why?" I asked.

"Because Sam had a helluva reputation, even then. But then I met with Sam, and he talked about his father, and the land his family owned up in the hills, and ranching, and riding, and shooting. He opened up like that, and I agreed to do it. And we [meaning Randy and him] got the best film of our careers."

Steve Judd was symbolic of Sam's father in that film. Sam often spoke about his father with great reverence, and that carried through with Joel's performance in *Ride the High Country*. It gave that little film a big soul.

There was that something authentic about Joel: he had a visible soul. He was not corrupted by women, money, power, or fame—although I'm sure he enjoyed the results of all those blessings.

But that was not my main reason for being there. So I told him about the documentary. He listened as I gave him the outline. I wanted him to finance much of it. And then he said, in that quiet, authoritative tone of his, "I know your work. I'm pleased to meet you. I can't pay to have my own biography made on film. I hope you understand. I just can't do it."

He had all the money in the world, but he just would not finance his own documentary. It seemed to be more about his ego; he just couldn't put his own story out there like that. There was no need for further explanation, and I dropped the topic. We visited a bit more, and then I left.

That day I spent with Joel McCrea was among the most wonderful, warm, down-to-earth visits I ever had with anyone. The earth and the air felt crisp and clean; this place Joel lived in seemed pure and natural. I left feeling that there was a singular sincerity about a guy who had already had it all—and still had it all.

• • •

Morgan Woodward had become pretty well known as a character actor by the time I met him in the 1960s. L. Q. Jones was one of his friends, as was Fess Parker. L. Q. learned quickly that he was indispensable to Sam, but I couldn't figure out why he didn't introduce Morgan to Sam. I think it's because L. Q. didn't want to *not* be indispensable to Sam.

One night I met Sam at the Sands bar, and I said, "Would you be OK if I called Morgan Woodward and asked him to come have a drink with us?" Sam said OK, so I called Morgan, and he showed up about a half hour later. I introduced them, and they got along well. Sam kept bragging on him, because Morgan had just played a powerful part in the 1967 hit *Cool Hand Luke*, with Paul Newman. Sam had the memory of the best elephants that ever lived; he kept talking about parts Morgan played that I had never heard of. I got tired of it. I said, "Sam, you son of a bitch, stop bragging on him and give him a job!" But Sam never did hire him. All my buildup for Morgan was blown to hell, but it gave Morgan a great story to tell, and he still relates it with fine fervor.

Earlier in his career, when Morgan didn't have a lot of money, he managed to land a *Wagon Train* episode, and he brought his holster, gun, and blank bullets home from the set one day. There was a place near his house called the P.M. Grocery Store, and we'd buy whiskey there and go to his place to drink it. We had a private joke: "We drink P.M. in the morning!" But hell, we drank all morning, and all night. His living room was empty. He remodeled for years. The living room had a big window with a view that faced down on the Hollywood freeway. Some of his actor friends would stop by, including some New York–based actors who would come out to Los Angeles to play small parts in TV or film. I remember we stuck one of Morgan's black-and-white PR photos on the wall and started shooting at his photo with wax wads from the fake pistol he brought home. I shot ol' Morgan right in the eye just as one of his New York actor friends walked in the door! He turned around and left fast. He thought the gun was real, and we heard that he later told his friends, "Those two guys are crazy. I showed up at Morgan's house and they were sitting on the floor blasting the place apart with a pistol!"

That actor was Pat Hingle, one of the best-known character actors of that period. Back around 1960, he had fallen down an elevator shaft in his West End apartment complex and suffered great injury and pain, but he recovered and went back to work. Fess and Morgan had formally introduced me to him at a bar. I got to where I really liked the guy. He was an all-around pleasurable man, and very well read. He could play any role: he could jump from a mad old Kentucky bootlegger to the most sophisticated robber baron to a broadly comic part. Western-film fans may remember him as the judge in Clint Eastwood's *Hang 'Em High* (1968).

Around this time, I was acquainted with a film producer who made B Westerns. He fell in love with a short story I had written in the early 1970s called "Big Shad's Bridge"—the only Western I wrote that had a gunfight in it. It was set on the Rio Grande, and one writer friend of mine once told me that he thought it was a Greek tragedy because just about everybody dies at the end of it, horses and all.

Well, this B producer wanted me to fly to New York to meet his co-producers to talk about raising funds for the movie. I mentioned Pat Hingle, and this producer said, "Invite him. He would be great as Big Shad."

Hingle lived on Long Island at that time, so he drove in for the meeting. He was still stiff; he walked with a cane, but he disguised it on-screen. I remember we met at the Dallas Cowboy Café, which I think is gone now, and the maître d' was the Southern Methodist University football player Doak Walker. I never expected to find something like that in New York City. We were having the usual business martinis, and the producer was getting drunk. He said, "To have Pat Hingle play the second lead, the villain, would be great." Then here came Pat with his fancy cane, dressed in fancy clothes: Scottish attire with a cap and an ascot and heavy wool socks. He was wearing a tweed coat. He looked like he was about to go grouse hunting with Scottish royalty. And he's going to play our bad guy. He came to the table to sit with this drunken B producer and this equally drunken Z writer.

The producer wasted no time. He asked Pat if he had read my story. Pat said no, but he'd prefer to see a filmscript. This producer said, "Don't worry, Max will write the script." I didn't disavow that comment, but this was the first time I heard that idea proposed.

We drank, and we talked like it was gonna happen, but it didn't. That story got optioned several times over the years—it almost became the basis of a film starring John Wayne and Robert Blake—but that B producer never anted up the money. I remember Sam paid to option it once, writing up the contract on a bar napkin and paying me with ten one-hundred-dollar bills.

I still recall a day when I was walking on Hollywood Boulevard, which, in those days, was like a circus that never stopped. Things were not good, and I probably didn't have two dollars on me. I walked by the dopeheads, pimps, hookers, and transients along the way. And lo and behold, here comes Pat Hingle. He was staying at a medium-level hotel a little off the boulevard; a place where New York theater actors would stay when they came to Los Angeles for work.

Pat said, "How are you, Max?"

I said, "I'm fine." I was lying.

We shook hands, and he left me with a folded fifty-dollar bill in my hand. How did he read me so quickly, or get the bill out and folded so fast?

That was Pat Hingle—a gentleman all the way.

I overheard Sam remark to the cinematographer Lucien Ballard, on the desert set of *The Ballad of Cable Hogue* (1970), that he was really happy that R. G. Armstrong was going to be there the next day. Sam looked out over the set where Cable had the food laid out on the tables for the stagecoach passengers, and he said, "When R. G. gets here he'll blow that goddamned desert apart." I could read the admiration in his voice.

I'd never met R. G. up to that point, but I knew his work. This Alabama-born actor had broken into television and films with bit parts in the mid-1950s before director Henry Hathaway gave him a strong supporting part in the 1958 Western *From Hell to Texas*. He possessed a powerful screen presence, one that kept him working past 2000.

I needed to take a day off from the film to drive into Las Vegas to visit with Benny Binion, the Las Vegas entrepreneur, hotel owner, gambler, and (some say) mobster whose motto was "good food, good whiskey, good gambling." R. G. also knew Benny and asked if he could drive in with me, so I had a meeting with both R. G. and Benny at the Golden Nugget. (Benny's place, the Horseshoe, was across the street.) To my great surprise, the conversation with R. G. Armstrong covered many subjects far beyond the scope of filmmaking. I discovered that R. G. was a mystic. Sam must have known that. That might describe, in part, their affinity for each other, for R. G. appeared in several of Sam's films.

R. G. was just beginning to study the art of healing through massage, muscle manipulation, and a spiritual force he claimed he was able to tap into. Some years later, Pat and I were staying at the Golden Nugget when, for some reason I cannot recall, we ran into R. G. Armstrong. We had some drinks—slow drinks—and I jokingly mentioned the wild stagecoach ride I'd taken with Slim Pickens during the shooting of *Cable Hogue* in which we went up on two wheels and almost tipped over. The coach stopped, and Strother Martin, L. Q. Jones, and the other actors riding within the stagecoach got out and refused to get back in. (I guess they didn't trust Slim's driving.) Sam had to hire stunt men to replace them for the next round, but Slim and I had to do our own stunts. My one arm was under a heavy strap and I held on to Slim's belt as he took off for another take, and the force ripped my shoulder out of joint. Slim weighed at least 250 pounds. (It still hurts, years later.) R. G. said to me, "I can fix that," and he began massaging my shoulder. He worked on it and it helped considerably. As he worked on me, he told me that he had started a second career as a mystic healer and that his clients included Warren Oates, Bo Hopkins, and James Coburn—all members of the Peckinpah acting ensemble who were probably much in need of spiritual healing after a bout with ol' Sam. Coburn later swore to me that R. G. saved his life when his hands suddenly crippled up. He had tried all the standard treatments as well as Eastern mysticism, and they didn't work. But R. G. took over, and Coburn gave R. G. full credit for saving both his career and his life.

R. G. had a booming voice and a booming presence that dominated any picture he worked on. R. G. was a man of peace, but I would say it would have been very difficult for God to help anyone who tried to hurt R. G. He was a gentleman, a strange and peaceful man who didn't care how big his part was in any movie. He could appear in the worst piece of crap, and he'd give it everything he had. I noticed when I was out with him that people would recognize him and stop to visit with him. They would remember a certain scene in a certain film and then shut up about it and end up talking about anything in the world—their dog, going fishing, politics—with him. He had that rare common touch where he could adapt to any conversation.

I remember the last time I saw him. I was in Hollywood, and he was staying in a hotel nearby, shooting a picture. He invited me over for a drink. I made my way to the hotel, found his room, and noticed the door was slightly ajar. Figuring he was expecting me, I knocked on it as I opened it, and lo and behold there was R. G. in bed with two beautiful naked women. He didn't act embarrassed, so I didn't act embarrassed. He offered me a shot of whiskey, which I accepted, and one of the two ladies got out of bed—quite nude—poured me a drink, and handed it to me. We talked awhile, and then I made my way out. He did not invite me to join the party, and I'm just as glad. It would have diminished my view of him, and as it was, when I walked in and found him with these two ladies, my respect for him grew greatly.

• • •

In the late 1960s there was a screenwriter named Mark Hanna who latched on to me when I was staying at the Sands. He was sort of a has-been, though you wouldn't know it by talking to him because he talked a good game. He had written some science fiction films that are now somewhat well known, including *Attack of the Fifty Foot Woman*, and he'd written some grade-Z Westerns for Roger Corman. He had made one good movie, a low-budget 1960 drama called *Raymie* that starred Alan Ladd's son David. Hanna was a script packer. He got ahold of a script and pitched it around town to try to turn it into a movie, cutting himself in for a share. He fell in love with one of my short novels, *The One-Eyed Sky*, but he recognized he'd have a hard time turning it into a movie, being that its main protagonists are a mother cow and a hungry coyote. I met Hanna when he was down and out. His wife was working as a secretary for Danny Kaye, and he was embarrassed that she was the one making the living.

Hanna wanted the rights to *The Hi-Lo Country*. One day he said to me, "You know Stuart Whitman? I brought him a copy of *The Hi-Lo Country* and he likes it. He's gonna be up at La Taverna tonight. You wanna meet him?"

When I was broke, I was broke. Hell, 90 percent of the world is broke most of the time. At least 80 percent of making money is luck or chance or whatever you want to call it. This seemed like another chance—lucky or not—so I thought I'd take it. Chance and luck—good and bad—had driven Stuart Whitman's career, too. Whitman was not a big star, but he was well known. He'd been in the Army and boxed some, and he broke into Hollywood with small roles in movies in the 1950s. People forget that he was nominated for an Oscar for his role as a sex offender in *The Mark* (1961), and he'd made a big Western with Duke Wayne, *The Comancheros*, that same year. But he never seemed to get that big break. Everyone I knew liked him; all the writers I talked to kept hoping he'd break through and become a big star. I met him after the failure of his 1967–1968 TV series *Cimarron Strip*, which he produced and acted in. I know it was before *The Wild Bunch* came out, because Stu had never heard of Sam Peckinpah, which I found surprising. But like Fess Parker, Stu invested well in land, so he didn't have to worry about money.

We went to La Taverna, and Stu was there waiting for us. He had a reputation for being a helluva fistfighter. He really could play up the women—they loved him. Men were jealous of him, and some of them would incite him into beating the hell out of them.

He invited me out to his house in Beverly Hills, off Sunset, to talk about *The Hi-Lo Country*. I drove up there, and we sat down and started talking about the book. He was pretty honest with me. He said, "I want to make this movie, but I'm not a big enough star to get it made by myself. I need a big picture to put me back on top." But his mind wasn't on the story. I soon found out why.

He was having an affair with the actress Kim Novak. She lived on the same road as he did, and she believed he had some famous French actress up at his house, so she showed up at his place, pulled a .45 on him, and threatened to kill him. This all happened the day I got there. He told me about the incident, said he hoped it didn't get into the papers, but he didn't seem too bothered by it at first, though I could tell he was distracted. Novak quit Hollywood shortly after this incident and moved away, up to Oregon, I believe, to live a fine life without the film world.

All of a sudden, Whitman said to me, "I'm going to break all my rules and show you the most beautiful sight on the face of this earth."

He led me out to the guesthouse, and carefully and quietly opened the door. On the bed inside was a nude woman, asleep, belly up. She was tan all over. And she was indeed one of the most beautiful sights on the face of the earth.

Whitman wasn't being lewd. This was a gesture, a gift. Embarrassed he could not get me a movie deal, he gave me the next best thing: the most positive dismissal I ever had on a book deal.

Novak was right: Stu was keeping this young lady at his house while they engaged in their affair. I don't remember what I said to him, but I remember thinking she looked like a beautiful living landscape. She's still quite active in movies, and I'm too much of a gentleman to reveal her name. Anyway, your guess might—just might—be better than the truth.

Whitman and I met a few more times to talk about the book, but he never optioned it. He was about forty at the time, and I do believe he would have been great as Big Boy because he had the same attitude Big Boy had: a confidence in his physical ability to overcome any obstacle. I appreciated his honesty in acknowledging he was no longer a big enough star to pull it off.

About forty years later, a friend of mine ran into Stuart Whitman at the Cowboy Hall of Fame in Oklahoma, where they were giving him some award. He told my friend, "Say hey to Max for me and tell him I owe him a kick in the shins." I have no idea what he meant.

As for Hanna, he got pissed at me because he swore that I had given him permission to pack *My Pardner* around town as a possible film option. If I had done it, it was inadvertent, because I don't remember giving him permission. I found out he was meeting Sam and had used *My Pardner* to get to him, and he was putting me down to Sam, no doubt thinking that would get him in good with Sam. One evening, Sam and I were drinking at my corner table at the Sands. There were two steps leading up and out of the bar, and on our way out, sitting at a table by the entrance, we saw Mark Hanna and a beautiful lady. He was drinking and grinning all over. Yet he was in a precarious situation. He said, "Hello, Sam!" and reached out for a handshake. Sam reached out for Hanna's hand, but instead grabbed his necktie and began tightening it, choking that son of a bitch there and then. Sam did not say a word as he did this. He left Hanna choking, and we headed out to Sam's car. I expected Hanna to come out after us into the parking lot, but he did not. He didn't pursue me anymore; he never came to the Sands again. Sam did me a big favor that night. Nobody shopped my work around town without my authorization again—that I was aware of, anyway.

• • •

Burt Lancaster. I can't really say I liked him, but I admired him. When I visited Brian Keith on the set of *The Hallelujah Trail* in Gallup, there was a joke going around the crew about Burt hiding out on the set. He didn't socialize with either the cast or the crew on that movie. My brief association with Burt Lancaster came through an associate producer and sometimes screenwriter named Mitch Lindemann, whom I met because of my book *The Great Wedding*, which he read and admired. I took an immediate liking to Mitch, and by our second or third meeting to discuss the book I realized he was afflicted with a really small germ of genius. I wondered why he had not attained greater heights. Mitch loved fun and booze a little too much to become the big wheel he was capable of being. He was the man who saved *Cat Ballou* and told the producers to play it up as a comedy. They did, and it made a lot of money. He was the man Lee Marvin told to seek me out to write the sequel to *Cat Ballou*, *Kid Shelleen*. During the McCarthy hearings and the terrible turmoil it wrought in Hollywood in the 1950s, Mitch had stayed tough and stuck his neck out for many writers in that blacklisted group. He, too, was impacted by the blacklist and wrote some scripts under a pseudonym. I learned that in spite of his drinking, producers and directors listened to him out of loyalty and because they realized he was capable of coming up with brilliant ideas to make a successful picture.

So when he recommended *The Great Wedding* to Burt Lancaster, Burt listened. And he read it because it was something Mitch told him to read as a possible starring film for him. This was before Mitch told me—almost breaking into tears—that Burt had hit a subordinate in the gut in front of a lot of other people on the set of *The Professionals*. So once Mitch set up the meeting between Burt and me, I had some doubts, because I did not intend to take any crap from him.

Burt had his own offices and his own studio within the Goldwyn Studio lot, and that's where we were to meet. Mitch found out that I had a little Indian blood in me, although I never talked about that with anyone except Sam. And Mitch had apparently passed this information on to Burt Lancaster, though I did not know it then. So I was amazed when we sat down for the first time in a meeting room at Burt's studio and Burt treated me with enormous respect. I was sitting there, probably hungover, an ex-cowboy, miner, and painter, and this SOB is treating me like royalty! He didn't ask me about the story or a concept or anything. I sensed right away that I was going to get a deal to write an outline and earn some much-needed cash.

He said, "Come on Max, I want to show you my gymnasium."

And lo and behold, he had a gym—a circus—set up in his studio. He introduced me to his little acrobat friend there, Nick Cravat. To my amazement, there were Thomas Hart Benton paintings all over the place—millions of dollars of great original paintings hanging on the wall of this sweaty circus gym.

Burt was dressed in casual clothes, and he jumped out there on a rope hanging from the ceiling with his buddy, swung around in the air, did some acrobatic stuff, swung back up onto the platform, and went on talking about *The Great Wedding*.

Whatever he was trying to do, it worked. I was impressed. I think he was trying to show me he was much more than just an actor. It was like watching the Crimson Pirate work out.

In the film version of *The Great Wedding*, Burt wanted to play Dusty, the guy wanting to get his buddy married to a rich woman in Santa Fe so they could both stop working as cowboys. He never mentioned who he had in mind for the other part. Someone once asked me whether the story would have worked with Burt and Kirk Douglas, and that got me to remembering how Mitch, who was working with Kirk on *The Way West* (1967), told me, "Kirk Douglas has spent his entire career wanting to be Burt Lancaster." I never did figure out what that meant, because those two actors seemed to play off each other very well in films.

I left the meeting with Burt thinking, "This is pretty good. I'm working with one of the biggest stars in Hollywood."

Burt assigned Mitch Lindemann to oversee the treatment. Mitch didn't provide much to the script except laughter. It tickled him. I don't remember any specific suggestions he made, although he called a lot of meetings mostly to get drunk and have fun. Now this was a problem for me because I would never take a drink while working, so I had to sometimes hide from him until I was finished writing. I did not want to break this creative vow to myself. But then we'd meet, he'd read what I wrote, and we'd drink. He loved Nat King Cole songs, by the way. You couldn't stop him: if there was a piano nearby he'd sit down and play Nat King Cole songs, which seemed to annoy a lot of people, but not me. Maybe this was because I'd been drinking and having fun.

Burt would sometimes stop by and visit with me. He'd start talking about the Taos Indians. I said to Mitch, "I don't know why Burt pays me so much respect and talks about Indians so much." Mitch said, "He really cares about the American Indian, and I told him you were one."

Mitch approved the script, and we sent it to Burt. We had to wait a week until he read it. Mitch called me one day and said, "Burt's ready to meet us and talk about the script." Mitch was very excited—evidently Burt liked what he read. I ended up meeting Burt alone at his huge office. He got behind his desk and asked if I wanted a drink.

I said, "Hell, yes, brown whiskey."

Burt poured me a drink. He didn't take one for himself. I didn't like that; I felt he was being impolite. Then he says, "OK, Max, I want to know what drives these two men."

This disappointed me. He had been so down to earth and logical up to this point, and now he's getting psychological? I'd been there before.

I said, "It's simple, Burt. These boys want to ride into town, get in out of the wind, have a couple of drinks, and fuck something."

My response stunned him. In a very fast ten seconds, I knew I had blown the deal. And I didn't give a damn. Because I could already envision the endless discussion from then on about every move these cowboys made, and what motivated them, and I realized I didn't care how much money I'd be paid. I wasn't going through all that bullshit with Burt Lancaster.

He reared back, got friendly, had a drink with me, and we talked about nothing. We both realized we weren't going to work on the script together. It was over. And I felt relief. I remember he offered me a cigarette—a Camel. Burt couldn't think of any other gesture to make, so he offered me a Camel and flashed that big grin of his. He was a charmer when he wanted to be—a snake charmer! And I was the snake.

Later, Mitch praised me for being such a damned fool. He got me some other deals, including a script deal at Paramount. I dictated and Mitch typed. I don't remember the plot, but I recall he threw a whole town square full of hippies into the story, and I just went along with his ideas and had fun. But I made a vow to *not* take a job writing a script with Mitch Lindemann again.

I was just doing what came natural to me with Burt, but I realized years later that he was not used to a writer—or anyone else—being that honest with him. He was a gentleman to the end because at least he offered me a drink and a cigarette. Yet the thing I remember most about Burt Lancaster—besides his amazing gentility toward me—was the artistic display of one of America's great landscapists hanging so proudly in his circus gym. Looking back at it, I doubt there was ever another human being who had such a beautiful experience with Burt Lancaster.

I should note that some fifteen years later Burt worked with Sam on the latter's last, misguided film, *The Osterman Weekend* (1983). Burt, who liked to play a creative hand in just about all his film projects, understood that money was tight and that the producers—as always, it seems—were at odds with Sam's vision. Burt met privately with Sam several times, no doubt trying to figure out a way to salvage the production and make it better. But there were some challenges that even the Crimson Pirate could not overcome, and the film remains a failure.

• • •

Like Stuart Whitman, Dale Robertson achieved a helluva lot but never quite achieved top stardom. He'd done some boxing, served in the military, and landed some small parts in pictures in the late 1940s before 20th Century Fox signed him on and gave him lead roles in mostly B Westerns. He did a couple of TV series and stayed busy working for decades. I met him sometime in the 1960s. Dale had read *The One-Eyed Sky* and got in touch with me to see if the rights were available. My story concerns a rancher out hunting predators, a mama cow looking out for her newborn calf, and a hungry coyote that's fixin' to eat the calf.

Dale said, "I love this story. Let's have a meeting and see if we can get this made." I drove out to Studio City where he had optimistically built a small movie studio with a sound stage and a small raised theater stage.

There, Dale started telling me how he was gonna do it. He said, "Let me show you how to play this out!" He sent me down in that theater alone, got up on the stage, and started acting it out for an audience of one.

And . . . he was playing Clark Gable.

Years before, when he was breaking into Hollywood, someone told him he looked like a young Clark Gable, and that stuck with him. He went on acting out all the parts from my book—for what seemed to be a quarter of a century. At one point, I wanted to go out in the parking lot, cry, and just keep running. I don't know why I didn't. I'm not saying it wasn't good, because it was, but it was like watching the best of Shakespeare—forever! There was nobody else there to share a laugh or a sigh or a breath of air.

Dale did have some fantastic ideas about how to get it done. Sam had plenty of ideas on how to make it, but he could never quite figure it all out. I believe ol' Dale could have accomplished the impossible, but

Hollywood had caused me to become impatient, and impatience is a fatal affliction in Hollywood.

Later, Sam and I talked about it briefly, and Sam said, "It would have to be animated." And I had forgotten that Dale Robertson suggested that to me that very day; he had thought about that approach long before Sam Peckinpah did. I'll give Dale credit: he was ahead of everybody else— Sam Peckinpah and Pixar and DreamWorks—when it came to thinking up a way to do my story on film. But he talked himself out of it before he talked himself into it.

Years later, I went to a Western Writers of America convention in the Hotel Del Norte (now called the Camino Real) in El Paso. It's about a mile from the Mexican border. They had booked Dale Robertson as their guest star. Publisher Luther Wilson and I were standing in the back of the bar. At this convention, I first introduced Luther to the WWA, and he became a member, right there in El Paso. I also named to him the writers I thought were comers. One was Robert Conley, who was on his way to becoming an award-winning novelist and the greatest of Cherokee historians. Luther, Robert, and I had gotten into a discussion about Sam's *The Westerner* series—as well as *Ride the High Country*—and all of us liked Sam's films (to that date). Dale stopped us right there and started discussing his dream project, *The One-Eyed Sky*. He had to have known about Sam's obsession with that project, too. We listened to Dale talk about the different facets of the story. We listened, and we listened. The three of us had the Cherokee background in common, and right here we became best friends forever. Luther would publish many of Robert's histories and many of my books as well. So ol' Dale Robertson's obsession with *The One-Eyed Sky* helped a lot of other works to be read.

Dale had by then sold that studio. He kept working, but his days as a leading man ended in the 1970s. One little line can change a life. Someone said to him, "You remind me of a young Clark Gable," and that blew it for him. Later on, he got over that. He stopped talking like Clark Gable and went back to being Dale Robertson, and that's very special.

Dale passed on at the age of eighty-nine in February 2013. I am sorry we didn't get one more chance to reminisce, and maybe dream about making *The One-Eyed Sky*—just as Sam, L. Q., and countless others so often did.

10. The Green

One day we all watched as Sam's brother-in-law, the towering Walter Peter, played with all the kids at a typical Sam Peckinpah party at Broad Beach. In pulling all sorts of shenanigans to entertain the kids, Walter toppled backward out of a window and, part of a second later, appeared at the front door as if nothing had happened. To all of us, he had just disappeared.

In a way, the creation of the Nation of Green, also known as the Country Green, was magic. How else could six-foot-six Walter Peter fall backward out of a window on the side of the house and instantly reappear ducking into the front door? It was true magic created by what had to be the King of Kings, lowering his own exalted position a twig to create Green and its president in less than the blink of an eye. Obviously, it was magic.

And so it came to be that Walter was elected president of the Nation of Green. His wife, Fern Lea, was elected secretary of war. (With Sam around, you knew there would be war.) I held the position of vice president for years, but most of the time I was just the court jester. Other insiders, including Chalo González and Jim Silke—who was the roving ambassador and the Green's poet laureate—took up positions as well. Sam, of course, became a major player, but he would never work with me to unseat Walter, who I felt earned the presidency unfairly. Walter took my rebelling efforts in stride. "You will never pull it off," he said. "My wife is secretary of war."

The Green was just a satire on government. None of us were very political—the only time I heard Sam talk politics, in fact, was when he was on the phone talking to his brother, Denver, about Richard Nixon. I could tell by the way Sam spoke that he hated Nixon's guts and was happy that the Watergate hearings were being televised. It's odd, really: Sam, who despised the illegal tape recording that was aired during those hearings, would later be accused of bugging others even as he feared being bugged. In truth, Sam was the power behind the throne on which Walter Peter sat.

Our power at that time now makes all similarly named "Green" organizations look like amateurs in comparison. We didn't rely on science to prove our theories. We knew them, acted on them, and nobody got in our way. We moved forward with grand exuberance, courage, and vision. We really had no official laws, just unwritten rules. David Weddle called it "a crazy, make-believe nonsensical country. . . . like the Marx Bros. country of Fredonia in *Duck Soup*, Green was their own world and operated by their own topsy-turvy rules."

Everyone who heard about the Green got curious and wanted in. Jim Hamilton and Jeb Rosebrook both longed to be part of this organization. Ed Honeck was just as curious as anyone else. He tried to approach Sam once about joining, but I told Sam no; we had to protect our privacy and power and couldn't allow just anybody to join. Years later, when I became president upon Walter's death, I broke my own rule and let Jeb Rosebrook in. He had often called me and asked me what he could do to fulfill his membership, and subtly talked as if he were a member of the Green, even though we had only made him a "trainee." I let it go but finally, unofficially, since there was nothing official about the Green, allowed him to become a member. To my dismay, he decided a couple of years ago to allow his son Stuart into the group as a "trainee." He caught on by the tone in my voice on the phone—and my threat to stand him in front of a firing squad—that this would not be acceptable.

We held cabinet meetings, each one getting progressively wilder. Still, sometimes when one of us got a brilliant idea we found we could seldom get enough members of the Green on the phone to get any movement going. My ideas were always agreed to, with the exception of one effort: the dethroning of our king. Yes, Walter was supposed to be our president, but that son of a bitch acted like he was king. Attempts to dethrone Walter were to no avail, as he had the women under his control—Pat included. In fact, they appointed Walter to a second term as president after watching him dash out of the surf naked one afternoon during a gathering of slack-jawed guests. Only Chalo González would join me in attempting to overthrow Walter. I figured since Sam loved Mexicans so much he would help Chalo and me start a revolution—that word in itself should have appealed to Sam. But those two insisted that I define my concept of what a revolution was supposed to be about. We had a lot of fun discussing that idea, drinking, and getting nowhere with the actual revolution. In desperation I told the duo, "My platform is revolution. My ideas will make this a better world even if I have to kill every son of a bitch in it but me."

That tickled Sam. He laughed the hardest and longest that I ever heard him laugh. And he did love to laugh.

The only way the Green lost a member was through death. After about three quarters of our members had passed on, including Walter, I declared myself president and have remained so to this day. After Walter's death, Jim Hamilton called me and made himself a member. From then on, he has talked with me as if he is a member, but I have never acknowledged it until this moment.

Today, early in 2014, the Green is down to just a few members: I am president. Pat is secretary and treasurer. She allows no debts or borrowing. Fern Lea Peter is head of the War Department. Screenwriter Jeb Rosebrook is vice president. Chalo González is head of Entertainment. Jim Silke is head of Records. It's still a small nation. There is no work because Green is perfect in its rarified atmosphere. Stuart Rosebook, son of Jeb, a fine author, editor, and friend, is the only acolyte desperately wanting to be a member. This fact shows his innate intelligence.

We have fewer meetings, but we are all still loyal members. And even though Jeb Rosebrook took advantage of my weakness toward highly creative people, I am glad he is there to connect with on occasion. Who knows—there may be a whole new Nation of Green created after we're all gone. In fact, if I can find the phone numbers, I am going to try to contact the remaining members of the Green and see how they feel about letting two or three members of the next generation in.

Of course, they would probably go crude by falling back on the *digital* generation. All those smart phones, computers, apps, and iPhones are ancient, rusting, creaking, and, even worse, old-fashioned. Green knew, and knows now, *everything* without having to move a thought or a thumb. Sam Peckinpah's Broad Beach house helped create the word *everything* and most certainly the best of the best fun.

11. The Brothers Kowalski

Sometimes Sam made long-term friends. Sometimes he made long-term enemies. Sometimes he made both in one.

The late writer Jack Curtis broke into writing for television about the same time as Sam, in large part because of their growing friendship in the late 1950s. Jack wrote some *Gunsmoke* episodes, a few shows for *The Rifleman*, and some of Sam's *The Westerner* scripts. Sam had a script, *The Authentic Death of Hendry Jones*, that he was trying to turn into a movie for Marlon Brando. Part of the torment in Sam's soul came from Brando, who promised that Sam could finish the script for the film that became known as *One-Eyed Jacks*. Instead, he took the project away from Sam, whose respect for actors was shattered to hell—temporarily. This event was one of the main reasons for Sam's breakup with his first wife, Marie. Somewhere along the way, Sam had asked Jack Curtis to help him with the script for Brando.

Jack Curtis was temporarily living with Sam and Marie at the time. Jack's own house burnt down in a fire of his own making in a wood stove. Sam took him in and gave him some writing work. But tensions began to flare along the way, and as Jack told it to me in a lengthy letter, Sam began acting like a top dog, putting Jack down whenever he could. I've heard different versions of the incident that broke up both the friendship and the marriage. The way Jack once told the story, Sam got drunk and in a mood one night, called Jack a second-rater, and in an effort to strike Marie, smacked a dish she was holding in her hands, causing it to fall and break on the floor before Sam ran out to his Corvette and drove off. Jack said he realized he had to get out of the house, so he kissed Marie good-bye just as Sam barged back in. Sam saw Jack kissing his wife and let loose with a left hook at Jack's nose, drawing blood. Jack claims he didn't hit Sam back—just held him until he calmed down. Later, Sam invited

Jack to lunch to celebrate the launching of his new show, *The Westerner*, but the damage was done. Years later, when Sam was descending into dark places, he would call Jack up and say, "You son of a bitch, if you were here, I'd put my .45 in your ear and blow your brains out."

Now here is the story that Sam told to director Bernie Kowalski, brother of Frank Kowalski, who worked on most of Sam's films: Sam said he left the house one morning to take a *Gunsmoke* script to the studio. He got halfway there, realized he left the script home, and returned to the house to find Marie and Jack in bed. He told Bernie he walked over to the bed, pulled Jack out of it, and violently twisted his nose. Bernie was on Sam's side, but who will ever know the truth? They're all gone now.

Bernie was the kindest man you could ever meet. He was from Browns-ville, Texas, by way of Mexico. His father was a Polish Jew, his mother was from the border area, and they migrated to Hollywood where Bernie and Frank got into the film business. Bernie and Sam were both going into the studios for television work in the late 1950s. Bernie quickly became a really good television director on episodes of *Broken Arrow*, *The Rifleman*, and *The Westerner*, among other shows. He worked as executive producer on *The Losers* with Sam. He also directed some low-budget horror films in that period, like *Night of the Blood Beast* and *Attack of the Giant Leeches*.

Bernie's wife, Helen, was a beautiful, lovely, open window. One day, around the time Sam and Marie broke up, Sam said to Bernie, "I love Helen."

Bernie said, "Thank you."

And Sam said, "No, Bernie, you don't understand. I love her. I'm taking her for mine." He was dead serious.

When Bernie realized Sam wasn't kidding, he threw him out of his house and never spoke to him again. Sam was the only guy I ever heard Bernie talk about in a manner that made you know that he despised him. He never went out of his way to say anything bad about Sam, but if you brought Sam up, he'd say, "You cannot treat this guy as a friend."

The break with Marie probably hurt Sam so deeply that he was seeking revenge on the world by hurting the person who was helping him the most at the time—Bernie Kowalski. I feel the combination of all these personal and professional events—Brando's betrayal, the problems with

Marie, the misunderstanding between Sam and Jack Curtis, and now this business with Bernie and Helen—probably led Sam to feel a great deception was being played out against him. I feel it caused a great influence of pain for the rest of his life.

I first met Bernie at the William Morris Agency. We both had the same agent, Irv Schechter, who later formed his own company. Irv was a smart, articulate man who always kept his word. He was one of the "good guys," and surprisingly there were a lot of them in Hollywood, just as with any business. Irv suggested to Bernie that he take a look at the only shoot-'em-up story I ever wrote, "Big Shad's Bridge." Bernie was really good friends with actor James Franciscus, a wonderfully sensitive man and actor who had big success with a pair of television series called *Longstreet* and *Doc Elliott*. I remember telling Bernie, about James, "I finally met a man who is too damn good for Hollywood." Really, he should have been playing Hamlet on the London stage.

Bernie's brother, Frank, who was probably more talented than Bernie, was slaving away as court jester, second-unit director, dialogue director, and drinking buddy to Sam Peckinpah—the man who had insulted his brother Bernie and given him reason to throw him out of his house. The two brothers were alike in being loyal to whomever they chose to be loyal to. I knew Bernie better than I knew Frank, but I drove out to the Valley to visit Frank once, years after he stopped working for Sam. He had come down with a major affliction of Parkinson's disease; he was all twisted and in pain. He made me a sandwich and a salad—I was impressed and amazed that he could do that much—and told me, "All I can do is lean back on my couch and watch the soaps. I've learned to enjoy them." He talked about Sam, and, contrary to what you might expect, he spoke of him with a grand nostalgia.

Once, near the end of filming of one of Sam's movies—I think it was *Convoy*—Frank Kowalski planned to take several other people on the set to dinner on a Sunday, their only day off. Sam was driving a Porsche at the time, and Frank asked if he could borrow it to drive people to dinner. Sam said yes. They all went off and had dinner, and when they came back to the hotel bar, where Sam was drinking, Sam jumped all over Frank and accused him of getting drunk and doing all sorts of terrible things to his Porsche. It made no sense. Frank turned to Sam, Jeb, and the others and said something like, "Sam, you're going to lose so many friends that when you come to die there won't be enough people to carry your coffin. Say good-bye to one less coffin bearer." He tipped his hat and left, and he never worked for Sam again. And there went another friendship, all because of a big, bright-red piece of metal. If it had been a horse or a dog or a well-trained house cat, you might have understood. Besides Katy Haber, Frank Kowalski probably contributed more to Sam Peckinpah's film career than anyone else. For all he had given, he got very little in return.

Bernie never got to experience Sam's success. He did not have Sam's brilliance. He was just too damn kind. He made one of the first mafia films, *Stiletto* (1969), with an actor who hadn't been able to "make it," Alex Cord. And it bombed. I thought for a pioneering effort that both the film and Cord were a lot better than credited. Bernie's one big hit as a director was *Krakatoa, East of Java* (1969), and they got the direction wrong—Krakatoa is west of Java. He made one Western after that, *Macho Callahan*, and he blew it, and he told me so before that film was released. But he still had the weight and reputation to make one more film.

He chose to do a horror film with Strother Martin that was pretty good, but it had a stupid title: *Sssssss!* (1973). We went to the screening, and afterward we went to Bernie's for a drink, and I went into the kitchen for a beer or something and in comes Strother Martin, a quiet, unheralded genius. He sat down and we started visiting. He picked apart all the holes in the film just as if he were a master editor or film critic. He said the biggest mistake of all was that damn title. It turned people off. If you saw the film and wanted to tell people about it, you couldn't pronounce the title! Strother also worked for Sam, and those two played games. Strother pretended to be deathly afraid of Sam, and Sam would pretend to yell at him. Strother was the only actor that Sam would constantly yell at, and I think it was just a big game between the two masters.

I felt bad for Bernie. Something told me this was his last shot at directing a theatrical film. Maybe he could have become a cult director, but he never made another theatrical movie after that. But he came close.

I was having a drink in a bar on Hollywood Boulevard one day when in came Bernie and James Franciscus. They said, "We were just talking about 'Big Shad's Bridge,' and we want to option it." I told them I didn't want to do the screenplay, but I'd write the treatment. They paid me, and it damn near worked in a big, big way.

Bernie was friends with Michael Wayne, who ran Batjac Productions for his dad, John Wayne. I became friendly with both men and later wrote a script—*The Ace and the Deuce*—that was intended for John Wayne before he died. It was a lighthearted thing; they didn't want to give him another downer Western like *The Shootist*. But by that time, Wayne was already having medical problems related to the cancer that would take his life in 1979, so the movie never got made.

I wrote the treatment for "Big Shad's Bridge"—a vengeance tale about a falsely imprisoned man seeking revenge on the town that hurt him— and Michael Wayne took it to his father. Duke Wayne read it and liked it and agreed to commit to it, which was a big deal for Bernie.

Somewhere along the way, Franciscus dropped out of the project. In the meantime, Bernie got a regular TV series—*Baretta*—starring Robert Blake, in 1975. Bernie introduced me to Blake. I got along really well with him. He was always testing everybody, but he never tested me. I told Bernie I got along with Blake, and Bernie said to me, "Yeah, because he knows you would hit him back."

We had a meeting, and Blake was stunned when we told him that we had a commitment from Duke Wayne to play the older sheriff, and we wanted him to play the younger man, the guy plotting a big robbery in the mining town, in the movie. He plans this robbery while in prison and kidnaps the first woman he's with after he gets out of prison—a whore.

The project suddenly became exciting. *Baretta* was a big hit, and Blake was always making the news saying something people didn't want to hear or getting into trouble with somebody. Blake was really talented. I don't know what torments he had. I didn't care to analyze him. Blake was the biggest TV star in the world at that time, and John Wayne was still the biggest movie star in the world. Wayne wasn't big on Bernie Kowalski, but Michael Wayne sold him on Bernie. Everything became dependent on getting a good script together.

Then Blake went on *The Johnny Carson Show* and made some cracks about Duke's kids. Duke heard it, called up Carson, and said he wanted to tear Blake's head off. Duke was very protective of his children. He was in such a rage against Blake that he cancelled the film. Bernie took it all in great stride, but there he was, stuck with Robert Blake every day of his life, for several years, with a hit series. You have to wonder whether his career may have taken a different direction had he made the film with Duke and Blake. Regardless, Bernie did continue working in TV— directing shows like *Magnum, P.I.* and *Jake and the Fatman*—into the 1990s. He also directed at least one-third of the *Columbo* shows starring Peter Falk. They were the most consistently fine shows of his career and made one wish that this was the period when he helmed feature films.

Bernie and Sam had one thing in common: they both put their money in Mexican banks. Sam once said to me, "I'm getting 21 percent down there. Give me all your money and I'll fix you up." I said, "What money?" It didn't matter what kind of interest he was getting, for Sam died close to broke.

There was a big difference between the two men. Bernie didn't express regrets on a personal or professional level, while Sam would brood about something going wrong forever. Most of the time failure will give you a gift somewhere down the line, but Sam didn't have the ability to see it that way. He had made some real enemies along the way, but near the end, he began seeing ghost enemies. They weren't really there; he just imagined they were. Bernie was still working in TV regularly, with no bitterness to slow him down, while Sam struggled to land a job, any kind of job, by returning to his roots, directing television episodes. Near the end, Sam begged his agent to get him a job directing an episode of a contemporary Western series that Jeb Rosebrook was producing and writing, *The Yellow Rose*, with Sam Elliott, in the early 1980s. The studio producers wouldn't take a chance on Sam. That spoke to the great slide he was experiencing.

How do you measure the value of a man? Frank was a part of every single thing Sam Peckinpah created during his finest period; the only person who gave more to Sam was Katy Haber. Frank, Bernie, and even Sam, with all his faults, were exemplary human beings. When you think about what they gave instead of what they took, how do you figure out who gives the most? Bernie was very helpful to me—he set up appointments for me with studio executives, and if I wanted the phone number of any-body in the entertainment business, he had it. Bernie gave to everyone, Frank gave to Sam, and Sam, well, he gave to the future, and he's the only one of those three men who remains known today. Sam lasted. Who the hell would have figured that thirty or forty years ago? Bernie died about five years back. I don't know who still remembers him. I know I do, with great admiration and fondness.

12. Charles Champlin, Sam, and *The Wild Bunch*

I tried to get Charles Champlin and Sam Peckinpah together for years. A meeting between the two finally happened, but I wasn't there. My friendship with Champlin had roots in Denver, Colorado, where I had a close friend, Bob Palms, whom I had met in Taos while he and his wife, Maggie, were there visiting clients. He was an attorney who represented the Couse Family estate of the famous Taos artist, E. I. Couse. Palms and Champlin had graduated from Ivy League colleges at the same time: Champlin from Harvard, where he majored in literature, and Palms from Yale, where he studied law. They ended up working in separate departments at *Time* magazine, where they became conversational and drinking friends. Red Fenwick, once the most highly regarded columnist in the entire West (for the *Denver Post*), read *The Rounders* and drove down to Taos to meet the guy who had written it. We became close friends, and I would then drive up to Denver to visit with him. I introduced Bob to Red, and Red sometimes mentioned Bob Palms in his columns, and Bob would get some business from the mention. Palms got a contract to work for Travelers Insurance, which led him to travel around the country to deliver big insurance checks.

I was staying in a small hotel off Wilshire Boulevard in Los Angeles, working on some project, when Palms came out to Beverly Hills to deliver a settlement check to somebody. He booked a room at the hotel I was staying at and said, "You introduced me to Red Fenwick and Rex Allen (the last of the B-Western cowboy actor-singers), so I owe you one. I've got it all set up for you to meet somebody special."

We went down to this little bar in this little hotel, and there was Charles Champlin. At the time, he was the principal film critic for the *Los Angeles Times*, and he was about to start his lengthy tenure as entertainment editor of the *Times*. I had read and admired his columns and film reviews over the years. He had read *The Rounders*, *The Hi-Lo Country*, and *The One-Eyed Sky* by the time we first met (about 1965), and we had a mutual admiration for our written words. I had learned long ago that the greatest relationships were usually built upon this sort of mutual respect.

At some point, Palms said (very unlawerly), "I have to go over to this place a few blocks away and deliver this settlement check." He pulled the check out of the inside pocket of his jacket and showed it to both of us: it was for $10 million! Champlin and I both showed the proper respect for this piece of paper, assuming it would not bounce at the bank, of course. I wish to God I could remember who it was made out to. I'd try to sell them a book.

Champlin and I finished our drinks and our talk, and we would meet after that both in Los Angeles and back in Denver, where Palms lived until his death. I remember at Red Fenwick's retirement party they had, as honored guests, myself, Pat, Rex Allen, and Dean Krakel (then head of the Cowboy Hall of Fame in Oklahoma City). Krakel sat next to me, and we all had to make a speech about Red. Slim Pickens was there, as well as Champlin. The room had a capacity of about eight hundred, but more than a thousand people showed up for the celebration! It was a great send-off for a truly great writer of the West who was almost universally adored by readers. Red only lived a few years after that celebration, dying in 1982. The night after this party, some of us had a party in Champlin's suite, where he was entertained by the humorous tales that Slim Pickens could spin so masterfully. Many were Madera County stories—the county that both Slim and Sam Peckinpah called home. So Sam Peckinpah was in our midst. Champlin admired Slim's film work because he recognized the authenticity behind those roles, and his reviews, including his review of Sam's *Pat Garrett and Billy the Kid* (1973), often mentioned Slim in praise. Champlin's mention of Slim's one great scene in *The Honkers* (1972) gave Slim's career a boost, too.

In Hollywood, Champlin and I would often meet in the bar at the Sands Motel. He was recognized and honored in the most elite places in Los Angeles, and yet here we would have a rip-roaring time in the little common Sands. Around this time, my book *My Pardner* was published by Houghton Mifflin. I had no idea at that time how to promote a book or hold a signing or participate in autograph parties. The City of

Los Angeles notified me that I would receive some sort of city commendation for the book. The Los Angeles Public Library set up a display of my work, with photos from my childhood, and I remember Mayor Sam Yorty presenting me with an award at the press room in the city's court house. This whole event came as such a surprise that I didn't think to invite anyone but Charles Champlin—he was the only attendee. After the presentation, he and I went over to some small restaurant nearby and had lunch. I realized that he was amazed by my amazement. He caught on as to how terribly naïve I was in matters of publicity. He told me he actually liked that. I would have used the word "stupid," but he had a warm laugh about it.

Both of us geared our meetings toward a discussion of films, directors, screenwriters, and actors. We had another thing in common: we had both been combat dogfaces in World War II, although we didn't know this for a long time and talked about it for perhaps a total of one minute. Of course we both looked forward to my inevitable suggestion that we arrange a lunch—which would segue from day to night with much drinking and laughing—with Sam Peckinpah. I knew those two had a mutual respect for each other, and I knew we could probably meet in the little Sands bar where these two famous men could relax and not worry about being unduly approached by anyone. We talked about this idea for years, but it never quite worked. Sam would be off making a picture, or I'd be back in New Mexico writing a book, or Champlin would be out of town on assignment—there was always some reason it just didn't happen. Finally, Champlin said to me, "I think Sam is avoiding this meeting because he's mad at me."

I couldn't imagine why. For years I had only heard Sam speak in admiration of Champlin's writing. But then Champlin told me that word had come to him that Sam resented his movie review of *The Wild Bunch*. While this came as a surprise to me, Walter Peter later told me that Sam was pissed at Champlin for placing so much emphasis on the bloody parts of the film and not spending enough print on the transitional elements of the story that Sam so loved. In his 1997 book titled *Hollywood's Revolutionary Decade: Charles Champlin Reviews the Movies of the 1970s*, Champlin picked reviews of about sixty films that had impressed him from that decade—not a "best of" list but films that had stuck with him over the years. I reread his review of *The Wild Bunch* (which was actually released in the summer of 1969) and feel that this one little paragraph near the end describes the totality of the review, and I can see, in retrospect, why Sam would react to such a viewpoint when he felt that he was under attack from the press: "The squeamish, the weakhearted or the simply tenderhearted are quite seriously warned away. Those who go will see a wondrously made, thought-provoking movie."

Champlin also called the film "the most graphically violent Western ever made, and one of the most violent movies of any kind . . . not so much a movie as a bloodbath."

The luncheon between the two finally occurred, quite by chance, according to Champlin. They both mentioned how much they enjoyed the experience. There was no animosity expressed anywhere, anytime, and from what I heard from both sides, they had an open discussion of their favorite films and directors. Damn, it was my idea to hook them up and be there when it finally happened, and I missed it.

In December 1982, while Sam was shooting his last film, *The Osterman Weekend*, Champlin paid a visit to the set (which, on that particular day, was the old Robert Taylor estate) to interview Sam. In that piece, Champlin called Sam "one of the relatively few genuinely original, if controversial, voices in the directing community" and noted that Sam was still trying to get two of my works, *My Pardner* and *The One-Eyed Sky*, made into films. He quotes a tired Sam as saying, "No creative control, but they've let me have a damned good cast and a damned good crew and that means a lot. . . . Whether it'll be a Sam Peckinpah picture when it gets to the screen, I've no idea." (Most critics agree it's about Sam's worst film.)

Toward the end of his career, and before his eyesight became a huge drawback to his work, Champlin hosted a television show on the Bravo cable channel called *Champlin on Film*. He interviewed a lot of famous film artists. I'm not sure if he ever interviewed Sam on that show. But over time, Champlin's eyesight began to dim, and he had to give up the program, which was part of his life's blood. He retired from the *Los Angeles Times* in the early 1990s, though he kept writing articles and books. In 2001 he published *My Friend, You Are Legally Blind: A Writer's Struggle with Macular Degeneration*.

I cannot express my admiration for his wife, Peg, enough. She realized what was happening to this great man, and when he could no longer read on his own, not even with enlarged-print books, she read to him. As of this writing, I believe she still does. I understand the wonder and value of this gift, because Pat has done the same thing for me during a period when I was unable to read. The world makes very few Sam Peckinpahs and is just as stingy turning out the equal of Charles (Chuck) Champlin.

13. An Interlude with Katy Haber

Katy Haber kept Sam Peckinpah alive. With the possible exception of Frank Kowalski, I don't think anyone gave so much to Sam and got so little back. Her family was from Prague, and they were all in the arts. When Hitler started putting people in camps, where he could destroy them with ease, the Nazis sent a lot of her family to a special camp for artists. Some of them had already gotten visas to get out, but one of the boys in the family got a real bad case of the flu, and they didn't want to move him right away, so they waited a week for him to improve. At this point, it was too late. They were ready to escape when the Germans sent them to Auschwitz. All of Katy's relatives were wiped out—except her parents, who somehow got out in time and immigrated to London. A few years later, in 1944, she was born there. Her father was working as a doctor, but for some reason he was only allowed to practice medicine in the army, as a civilian doctor. Because of his service to the government, after the war he was allowed to set up his own practice. Katy's mother was thin, tired, and run down. Her father loved her so much, but he didn't have faith that she was going to live, and he became depressed— depressed about his own life and about the inhumanity of man. Part of his depression was brought on some years later, in the early 1960s, when he read of a resurgence of the Nazi party. Some twenty years after the war, he traveled to Scotland where he was given an award for his service. He returned to England, where, in the early 1960s, he killed himself.

Katy's mom survived for quite a while, outliving her husband. Katy went to college, got into the film business, and met Sam Peckinpah when he was shooting *Straw Dogs* (1971) in England. (He later paid off the mortgage on Katy's mother's house.) Katy never expressed this directly, but I always thought she felt guilty because she left her mother for Sam. I think that's why she's done nothing but good for the impoverished since

Sam's death in 1984. She never married. She never had children. Katy currently serves as manager of the Compton Cricket Club in California, which, among other missions, teaches impoverished and homeless children how to play cricket as a way to improve their self-esteem and teach them team-building skills. Not quite five years after Sam's death, I interviewed Katy about him in my room at the Mikado Motel. This is the unedited transcript of that interview, conducted in July of 1989.

MAX: How did you get into the picture business?

KATY: Originally, I was going to be a doctor.

MAX: An MD?

KATY: An MD. Then, when I was eighteen years old, my father committed suicide because he felt my mother was dying. She wasn't, but he did. So I took a secretarial course and decided I wanted to go into the film business. I started working for a company called the Rank Organization, a big film company. Then I worked for a film producer in London for about five years, worked on about three different films and did some theater and stuff and some development. And the producer went back to the states.

Some guy called Jimmy Swan rang me up and said, "There's this guy, Sam Peckinpah, in town. He's going to make a movie called *Straw Dogs*. Would you be interested in working with him?" I said, "I don't know who he is, but sure." He said, "Well, he's going to call you next week and set up an appointment." At the time that he was going to call, it was Wimbledon. I was a great tennis fan at the time, and I was going to Wimbledon every day. I was there at two o'clock and I stayed till the bitter end. He said, "Call me around five o'clock on Friday." I called him from Wimbledon, which is about an hour out of town. I said, "Mr. Peckinpah, this is Katy Haber." He said, "Can you be at my place in twenty minutes?" I said, "Well, I'm about an hour away from where you are; it'll take me an hour to get there." He said, "That's too late. Call me back next week on Monday." Same time next week, same place, I was again at the tennis [match]. I rang him and he said, "Can you be here in ten minutes?" I said, "I can be there in about an hour because I'm an hour away from you." He said, "Fuck you!" and hung up. That was the end of that.

Two weeks later, I sat down and had a meeting with the same guy,

Jimmy Swan, again. He said, "Katy, what are you doing?" I said, "I'm still not working." He said, "Remember that guy Sam Peckinpah?" I said, "Yeah." He said, "Well, he's had about ten people work for him in the last two weeks and he still doesn't have anybody. Why don't you come over to the office, it's just around the corner, and he's there. Why don't you meet him?" I walked into his office, and there was ol' Sam sitting at his desk. He looked at me, and I looked at him, and I said, "I suppose you want me to give you another chance, huh?" He said, "Sit down and start typing!" I sat down and there was this script that looked like a spider had walked across it with ink on its paws. It was covered with little scratches. About an hour later, I had typed the rape scene from *Straw Dogs*. He said, "You're the only one who can read my writing, so you may as well work for me, huh?"

MAX: Which of Sam's movies did you work on?

KATY: *Straw Dogs*, *Junior Bonner*, *The Getaway*, *Pat Garrett and Billy the Kid*, *Bring Me the Head of Alfredo Garcia*, *Cross of Iron*, and *Convoy*.

MAX: Seven pictures, yeah. That's the same he did with Gordy Dawson. Just the other day, Gordy told me he won a Value Award last year; we won one at the same time. We went to San Diego to accept them, and I ran into him. He told me something that really shocked me that I didn't know about. He told me that approximately six days before they wrapped up *Bring Me the Head of Alfredo Garcia*, Sam came up to him and said, "I gotta leave, Gordy. Take it over." Did you know about that?

KATY: Uh-uh.

MAX: He said it was the most shocking day of his entire life.

KATY: Where did he go?

MAX: He just left. That's what Gordy said. I don't know where he went.

KATY: Well, he certainly came back because he finished the picture.

MAX: Gordy said he had to finish it, and he didn't know what the hell to do—he had no idea what to do.

KATY: Did I go with him? (*laughs*)

MAX: I don't know. That's why I'm asking ya. You don't remember? Well, I'll just drop that.

KATY: I drew a blank on that one.

MAX: What do you want to tell me about ol' Sam?

KATY: The good bits or the bad bits?

MAX: What I want is tragicomedy. Anything that's both tragic and funny about the man.

KATY: God.

MAX: There's just so much, I know, to try to recall it all.

KATY: I've got stories that could go on forever. When we first started working together, he went to Ireland to look for locations. I went out to dinner, and I came home and my mother was sitting there looking like she'd seen a ghost. I said, "What happened?" She said, "Sam's been calling for the past four hours." I said, "Well, I've been out to dinner." She said, "Well, he thinks you've run off with his passport and his money and his traveler's checks and all his papers and he's calling the police and the police are going to be here." I said, "Why?" She said, "Because he can't get ahold of you; he wants you to be at the phone at all times." Finally, he called around one o'clock, and he said, "Where the fuck have you been?" And I said, "I've been out to dinner." He said, "You're not allowed to go out to dinner! Where the fuck is my passport?" I said, "Where you left it; I've got it."

When we were in Scotland looking for locations, he would kill deer out of season, and I once had to keep a doe in the back of my car for three days while we were driving around Scotland so the guys wouldn't catch us for shooting a doe out of season. We kept the heart and the lungs and the liver in a pot in the top of the closet in the hotel.

Or the time that we had this big meeting and Danny Melnick came up to Scotland, and I said, "Gentlemen, I have to go because I have to go to work." I said, "Good night, Danny, good night Jimmy, good night Sam." About two hours later, he came in and destroyed the room, beat the shit out of me, ranting and raving, and said, "Get out of here; I never want to see you again." I said, "What did I do?" He said, "You said good night to Dan Melnick first."

MAX: Oh, God almighty. He had to be first on the list for good-nights!

KATY: He was so fuckin' jealous and so fuckin' possessive of me. The night he married Joie (Gould), he rang up from his honeymoon suite at the Camino Real in Juarez to make sure I was in my room on my own. When we went on *Junior Bonner*—I'm going backward and forward, but Sam and I lived together for ages—Joie kept popping up, and he said to me, "When we're working, we have to keep our distance; we can't get that close. Otherwise, Joie . . ." I said, "OK, fine, OK." We were over in Arizona on *Junior Bonner,* and I thought Joie Gould was out of my life, and here she pops up in the middle of Phoenix. They had this big row and she went back to England. A week before, we were due to finish shooting *Junior Bonner,* and he said, "I want you to go back to L.A. and I want you to take everything from storage and put it into this apartment that Kip Dillinger has just rented for me."

I showed up in Los Angeles at this two-bedroom condo in Studio City with boxes of stuff from his five-bedroom house in Malibu that I had to make into a living place. The place had been packed by his kids; they had taken boxes and just put the box on the table and swept everything on the table into the box. So when I opened boxes, there was shit in there like books, there were ashtrays, there were cigarettes—all piled into one box. That's how they packed it. It took me six days to unpack these boxes and make this place like a living place. I got a phone call from Sam, who asked, "Have you finished yet with the apartment?" I said, "Yes, it's ready." He said, "Well, Joie and I have been at the Century Hotel in Malibu the last three days waiting for you to finish the apartment. Can we move in?" I don't know whether you would call that tragic or comedy, but I packed my bags and moved back to England.

MAX: How in the hell did you handle his—well, I know how you did it. I watched some of it. I didn't know how you could handle Sam when we all know he spent a great part of his life prone. He was in bed most of his life. I never understood how you could handle him and ever get him to eat when he'd get on that vodka-and-pills-together thing.

KATY: He used to wake up every morning and throw up. I used to force him to eat. The problem with me was, he used to stay up all night and then at five o'clock in the morning he would finally fall asleep. I had to get up at 8 a.m., and he was in bed all day. And I had to work. I slept about two hours every night for about seven years. I was living and working with the man. When these women came into his life, at first I was insanely jealous and upset, and then it was such a relief because I thought, "Oh, I can sleep. He's got someone else to spend the night with." The relief of being able to go to my own hotel room to sleep was wonderful. Of course I was jealous and the whole thing. . . . But there was a "thank God."

MAX: His women finally became your lifesavers, actually.

KATY: I look back at my life with him, and I wonder who that person was because that was not the person I am today. Now that I'm older and wiser, I don't think I would have taken as much mental and physical abuse now. How all you guys had any respect for me, I'll never know, because I don't respect that person very much.

MAX: Yeah, but we all did because you were the only one who could handle the guy.

KATY: And I was the only one who was there. You guys could run away. I remember the wardrobe people used to turn their phones off at night when they finished working; everybody turned their phones off at night when they got to the hotel because they knew that in the middle of night Sam would say, "Oh, I want to talk to Kenny," and I'd say, "Sam, it's three o'clock in the morning." And he'd say, "Fuck 'em, I want them in my room." Everybody took their phones off the hook. Everybody knew that I was the only person who was there for Sam. Everybody was gone at six o'clock. He couldn't find anybody. I suppose that's why everybody respected me; they knew I was the only one who could stick with him.

MAX: I imagine that all those who were close to Sam had this tremendously mixed emotion about him.

KATY: I know. He was like an infection; he was like a disease. Once you caught the Peckinpah disease, you couldn't get rid of it.

MAX: The whole damn family is pretty strong. One of the things that got me the other day when Laurence Olivier died (July 1989) was that so many commentators of both sexes were commenting on what a hole is left in the theater world. In my lifetime, there have only been two people who did that. I had the same feeling when Sam died as I did when Olivier died the other day. The hole was just as great with all the people who were close to Sam and loved him in spite of all the terrible things he did to people. To this day, if anybody has been around Sam, really around him as much as a month out of their life, they can sit down and talk all afternoon telling Peckinpah stories.

KATY: I remember one July the 4th we had a big party at his trailer, and there was this woman hiding in the closet—a journalist whose name I won't mention because she's still around. She came to interview Sam. I went to work in the other room, and when I came back they were lying

140

in bed together, this very prim journalist and him. There was another girl who used to work at Warner Bros. who was so crazy about him that she would stand outside the fence at Fox—when he had that office at Fox that he lived in—all night and just wait. An educated, intelligent, and bright woman. Once touched by the man, it was like they had a disease.

MAX: I think the admiration . . .

KATY: I think it's being involved with the devil. I'm not sure.

MAX: It may be a little bit of that. But you're the only one who held it together. He destroyed all the other women except Marie and Begoña—they had to leave.

KATY: Um-hmmm.

MAX: But all of the other women, they were forever destroyed. Their minds were gone. Of course you weren't—you stayed through all of them, outlasted all of them, outlasted Sam, outlasted the whole damn bloody bunch. You're the only one who did it.

KATY: But he sure as hell tried.

MAX: He damn sure did. I wonder if the truth of it is that he had grown to admire you so goddamn much that. . . . The last time I was with you guys is when you told me, "He's gonna die," and you went to the store and got all those vegetables and made that wonderful big pot of soup and just sat there and spoon-fed him. It'd been three days since he ate, and he threw up all day. I went in and talked with him twice, and he wouldn't listen. I guess you spent hours and hours, but I just went off. I thought, "What is she gonna do with him? He's gonna die right there." I know you must have gone through that over and over and over, year after year.

KATY: I sometimes slept on the floor outside the door with him because he was so drunk he'd get to the door and say, "I think I'm just gonna lie down here." And he would lie down outside the door, and I just had to fall asleep next to him outside the door until morning. I woke up one morning when we slept outside the door thinkin', "What the fuck am I doing here outside this door?" We slept on cots in the studio. When he moved into a studio, he immediately wanted me to move in. I've lived at studios in rooms that people have used as cutting rooms. I've lived in the weirdest places with that man. In a trailer in the middle of Goldwyn Studios in the middle of winter—we lived there. We lived in a little office on the MGM lot. We lived in an office on the Fox lot behind the greenery, behind the plants. We lived in an apartment in Hollywood Studios. We had apartments everywhere, and he ruined every single one of them. Every time we moved out, I had to buy a new wall and new doors because of the knives he was throwing. The house in Mexico City—he obliterated the wall in the bedroom; he used it for firing practice. I had to explain myself out of more situations with him than anyone else. I don't know what it is—maybe I was possessed by the devil—but I kept bouncing back.

I'll never forget this one fight we had. It was in Albuquerque—no, not Albuquerque, it was Phoenix . . . Prescott, Arizona! I don't know how much you want to write about this . . .

MAX: Just go ahead and tell it.

KATY: I suppose every man has this fantasy of being with two women. And Sam had a thing for this woman in a bar in Prescott and decided that the three of us should get together. And I really didn't want to. He ended up just giving me a left hook. I was black and blue. I didn't want that; it's not my bag. I'm sorry. I grew up as a nice Jewish girl of middle-class European parents in London, and a ménage à trois was not something I was very good at.

The next morning, I had this huge black [bruise] on my chin. McQueen came up to me and said, "Jesus Christ, what happened?" I said, "Well, Steve, I was running upstairs and I fell over," and he said, "Well, I suppose if you run upstairs hard enough and someone pushes you hard enough you end up falling over." I made more excuses. Sometimes I told people that I walked into a glass door. I never told anybody the truth and everybody knew.

MAX: Oh God.

KATY: It's like fucking a rubber ball. You bounce back all the time.

MAX: I understand about sleeping on the floor with him. We got drunk out there—I don't know where you were, you were gone somewhere, but out at the trailer house. Sam and I got drunk on red wine and got down on the damn floor and couldn't get up. He was crawling on his hands and knees, and he kept running into the wall. He was only a few inches from the doorway, but he couldn't find it. So I just rolled over; he slept right up against the wall all night. When I woke up, I had evidently crawled over and tried to get up in the bunk but hadn't made it. He was still on the floor. I was on the floor. He had this ol' shaggy white rug—I think you got it for him, didn't you?

KATY: Um-hmmm.

MAX: I'm sure you're the one who cleaned it up. There were red wine tracks all over the damn thing. I don't know where you went.

KATY: I probably saw that you two were going to have a night out and went back over to the Fielding [Hotel] to sleep in a proper bed. I thought, "Fuck it, Max can look after him for tonight. He can have him."

MAX (*laughing*): Oh, Lord. What do you think of his best work now? After all these years now, and you look back—I know you look back at his pictures . . .

KATY: I love *Cable Hogue* with a passion. I love *The Wild Bunch.* I think for a commercial film, *The Getaway* did very well. I love *Junior Bonner*—I think it's a really great piece. I hate *The Killer Elite.* Hate it. I thought it was a mess; I thought he was influenced by too many different people. He had about ten or twelve different karate experts all trying to do their shtick. *The Killer Elite* was when he first got introduced to cocaine by a lot of those people who were on that picture, and I'll never forgive them for that. That was the turning point for him, because that's when he met all those people who were on that stuff, and that's when it all started. That's why *The Killer Elite* was not a good movie.

MAX: Wasn't he on coke on *Alfredo Garcia*?

KATY: No.

MAX: He was on pills, wasn't he?

KATY: He was boozing on *Alfredo Garcia.*

MAX: Just straight booze.

KATY: He was always on booze, and he was always taking sleeping pills and valium. One of the funniest stories of all time was when Ken James and I were driving Sam's Porsche to San Antonio from another city in Texas when we were making *The Getaway.* I was driving Sam's Porsche, and he had all his luggage in the back, and of course all his luggage was all the shit he was taking—everything that was illegal in Texas was in the back of that car. I went through a red light right in front of a cop, and Ken sat there and said, "Oh shit, what are we going to do?" Before I even stopped the car, I jumped out of the car and said [to the cop], "Am I glad to see you. We're making a movie, I'm lost, and I have no idea how to get to San Antonio. I am so glad I found you because we have been driving around for hours." Long story short, this guy convoyed me all the way to San Antonio with a flashing red light. He got me all the way into town. I knew exactly where we were going. He never checked the car, and he never even asked me why I shot the red light. Ken said, "I am always going to travel with you for the rest of my life." Had that car been checked, you know . . . all Sam's shit was in the back.

Convoy was not my favorite movie, because everybody wanted to be a genius on that picture. Everybody had an idea of how to elevate *Convoy* from just a commercial picture to some sort of movie with meaning. Kris [Kristofferson] wanted to play Christ. Ali [MacGraw] wanted to intellectualize it. Burt Young had his ideas about it. Everybody was bringing pages; everybody was rewriting their own part to make it not just a trucking movie. Had it been done as just a trucking movie, the way Sam wanted to do it—a simple, straightforward Western in trucks—it would have been great. But he hired actors who all wanted to intellectualize it so they could justify the fact that they were in a commercial movie.

MAX: Why do you think he allowed this to happen when back in the early pictures he didn't let anybody contribute to anything?

KATY: He was not in control anymore.

MAX: He had already lost it because of the chemicals?

KATY: And that's really when I realized that I could no longer help him. That there was no recourse, I'd run out of lies, I'd run out of excuses to save his ass, you know?

MAX: Um-hmmm.

KATY: I just thought, "He's gonna go under, and I'm going to go under with him, and maybe the best thing in the world for me to do is get away so he can realize that he's got to do it alone." I'd been saving him for so long that my saving him became detrimental because he was relying on me so much that he knew he could do whatever the fuck he wanted to because I would always be there to make the excuses and keep the producers and the distributors and these people away from him. And I thought maybe that was bad instead of good, and he had to stand up and realize what he was doing. I realize after the fact that he made one more movie before he died. And I don't want to sound like maybe it was me, but I probably kept him alive for the seven years I was with him and kept him working because after that, he made one more movie and that was it.

MAX: I got a letter from that girl who worked for him for just a little while—Barbara Engel or something like that—on *Osterman Weekend* and he fired her. She wasn't mad at him; she heard I was writing this book, and she sent me the damndest stack of papers she'd kept from the production, and they really ripped Sam off on that movie.

KATY: Really?

MAX: I'm not gonna write about it. This is not what I'm doing; I don't want to go too much into people stealing money.

KATY: You know what you should do someday? There's a guy called Jessie Graham who is a real Peckinpah fanatic. He's a good friend of mine, and he's a good friend of Matthew's. All of Sam's files are at the Academy [of Motion Picture Arts and Sciences], and you can go in there and look at his files. There's one file of mine called "Memorable Memos," and it's about *this* thick, and it's got all the really hysterically funny memos that Sam wrote on every picture that I compiled and put together, and that in itself should be published. It's a priceless piece of work. Some of them were eaten by Felice the mule and the goats on *Pat Garrett and Billy the Kid*, because they were all over his desk and we had a mule, two goats, two sheep, and a pig that we kept in the garden in the house in Mexico. And I came in one morning, and they were all in the office eating those memos. A lot of them were eaten up; a lot of them are missing. But there is a file at the Academy that someone should go in and look at. They won't let you remove it, but they will let you open it up and have a look at it.

MAX: These are memos on all the productions?

KATY: All the memorable ones, like "Fuck you!" . . . all the really funny ones.

MAX: Let me give you my opinion—what I've already written down, which I'm gonna rewrite. After all the years go—and I've studied and studied and studied—as far as the West I can't conceive of anybody doing what Sam did when he was at his best: *Ride the High Country, The Wild Bunch* . . .

KATY: *Major Dundee.*

MAX: *Junior Bonner, Ballad of Cable Hogue,* I can't see anyone . . .

KATY: . . . who did it better.

MAX: That touched it. John Ford certainly did, and he only had two pictures you could compare, and I always thought Sam was spoofing people when he bragged about Ford because the only person I ever remember influencing him in the picture or literary world was Robert Ardrey.

KATY: Yes, Robert Ardrey, of course.

MAX: In fact, I read Ardrey about the time he did and I can see his influence, and I knew damn well and I kept my mouth shut when Sam was touting to everybody—the Germans and everybody—about John Ford. I knew he was putting them on. Didn't you?

KATY: Yes. Absolutely. Robert Ardrey was his mentor who really sort of guided his beliefs. *Straw Dogs* is everything Robert Ardrey ever . . .

MAX: Of course.

KATY: Territory is imperative, what's mine is mine.

MAX: And the strong exist. But anyway, I wonder if you agree with me on that as far as the West is concerned . . .

KATY: Of course.

MAX: In *The Wild Bunch*, called one of the most violent pictures of quality ever made, I don't understand why people go on about that. There are moments of such wonderful tenderness . . .

KATY (*overlapping*): Since then, violence has taken leaps . . . the violence that is in movies now makes *The Wild Bunch* look like a fairy tale. But he was the first person to really show that death was not just falling over. That is what Sam showed for the first time. Usually, in Westerns, in cowboys and Indians, you went "bang bang" and people just fell over.

MAX: And it didn't hurt.

KATY: And it didn't hurt. And you knew they were actors, and you knew that they got up. But Sam showed that when you hit someone with a bullet, it fuckin' hurt, and it would fuckin' kill you. I asked him, "Why in slow motion?" He said, "Have you ever been in a car accident?" I said, "No." He said, "When you are in a car accident, all of a sudden everything slows down, and that car coming toward you starts to come real slowly and you see everything. Everything is in slow motion. That's how death is, that's how pain is, and that's how I see it. Everything goes very slowly at the end."

MAX: Did he ever tell you about that metaphysical experience we had? We had three. Actually, we had four, but for some reason my mind just lost one of them. The time we ran through the car?

KATY: Yes, he did tell me that.

MAX: I'm gonna put it in a book. Not this book, another book, a metaphysical book. The car phone rang—and there was no phone—and then this car honked and drove right through us. It wasn't a car, it was two dimensional. We rode right through it, on the freeway. Cold sober going to the studio to work.

KATY: Yeah.

MAX: The car came at us, and Sam spun around to get away from it; there was sort of a guard rail between us and the other place, and all of a sudden I heard the goddamned phone ring. We stopped and I said, "Sam . . ."

KATY: Did he ever tell you about the dream he had that he was out hunting deer, and he shot the deer and went and looked closely and the deer turned into a woman, and then he never wanted to shoot deer again?

MAX: Yeah.

KATY: Did he tell you about the time we were driving to the location on *Pat Garrett* and we were just about to have a head-on collision? Chalo González was driving, Walter was in the front, and Sam slipped down in the back seat because he thought he was going to die. And my reaction was to hold his head; I was sitting there holding his head as we missed the other car by inches.

MAX: With Chalo driving?

KATY: No, it wasn't Chalo; it was just one of the Mexican drivers. Anyway, we got very close to a head-on collision. I said, "Sam, did you notice what happened? You went under the seat to save your head and my reaction was to hold your head so you wouldn't get hurt." And he said, "You were just tryin' to get my fuckin' drink."

MAX (*laughing*): Goddamned dirty bastard!

KATY: I really must have loved this guy. My reaction was to save his ass, and I just sat there holding his head watching this head-on collision. He told everybody, "She was just trying to get my fuckin' drink out of my hand."

MAX: He had me go to a meeting. He said, "Meet me down here . . ." at one of the hundred places we met—I can never remember all those joints. He'd have his lawyer, his agent, and he'd have me there as a foil, nothing in the world but as a damn foil right in the middle of the goddamn thing. I didn't even know what the game was, nothing. But because of this phone ringing when we had this metaphysical experience, I finally caught on when he said, "Max, did you hear the phone?"—I'd have to make an excuse for us to get the hell out of there. He expected me to think of it. I'm sure he did the same thing to you over and over and over. I felt sometimes that his mind was so great that he was just out there everywhere and you could just read it all the time because he. . . . So much was unspoken and yet he expected you to know.

KATY: Um-hmmm.

MAX: It was very difficult. I used to watch him when he was younger, directing, and he'd be marvelous with newcomers or stars, but old, experienced character actors—he expected them to do the job without saying a damn word. I said to him one time, "You are overlooking those people; you expect too much of them." He said, "Oh, hell, if they don't know by now, they can read the script." I said, "Sam, they like to be directed; they really do care to be directed." I don't know if it had any effect.

KATY: Certainly got good performances out of them though—ol' Dub Taylor and Jack Elam . . .

MAX: And Strother Martin. He'd just terrorize that poor guy.

KATY: Oh, Strother would be terrified of him.

MAX: But I think what they miss on *The Wild Bunch* even now, the critics. . . . There's moments of real tenderness in it.

KATY: Are you kidding me? The scene with the bird, and the whore, and the love between those two. . . . I can see that movie a thousand times and be moved by it every single time, because there's so much of Sam in it. The words are coming out of the actors' mouths, but I can hear Sam's lingo.

MAX: They've been running *The Wild Bunch* on television for months now, more than any of his other films. It may not have the largest audience of any film, but I believe it has the most loyal audience of any Western film. *Cable Hogue* is finally getting the attention it deserved in the beginning. He was ripped off on that terribly, and I know that had to be part of his destruction. That was the third film that he really got shot in the guts on. I've had that happen in minor ways with books and things, so I partially understand how he would feel. I know it was a terrible tragic influence on his life and everybody around him. Part of the madness. . . . I went out there when you guys were fixin' to screen *Pat Garrett and Billy the Kid*, and I took him this machete, and I had some poem written out for it. He was so paranoid, he said, "Let's turn on the radio; everything's bugged." From then on he had that [paranoia].

KATY: He was constantly taking apart the earpiece to the phone and checking to see if there were bugs in the phone.

MAX: How many years was he paranoid about this?

KATY: He was always paranoid, but it got worse and worse.

MAX: I mean, about this idea that people were spying on him and he was being bugged.

KATY: Always. He finally bugged me in the end. He bought this little bug in Japan. That was the beginning of the end when I said I finally had it. I opened the drawer to the desk next to my bed, and there was this little bug in the drawer. I was paying the bill for a Mr. Robinson in the room next to mine. I thought, "Who the fuck is Mr. Robinson?" It was Bob Grey, Sam's friend, in the room next door with a receiver listening in to everything that was going on in my room. What he thought was going on in my room I have no idea, because all I did was work in there.

The day after I found it, we were driving in the car on the way to location and he said, "Katy, we have to go back to your room and get some files"—I had all the files in my room. I said, "We have to be on the set in half an hour; we'll never make it." He said, "We have to go back to your room." I took the bug out of my purse and said, "Is this what you were looking for, Sam?" He said, "Goddamn it—you found it! I wanted to go back and leave a funny note about it." He realized what he'd done and figured "I've got to get it out of there before she finds it." When I found it, he was mortified. He made some excuse like he wanted to write a note, saying, "Ha-ha . . . it's a joke."

MAX: I've wanted to ask you this for a long time. I never could give Sam a present. If he accepted it, he said nothing and went and hid it. I went to an awful lot of trouble one time getting him a bucking horse. . . . There was a bucking-horse carver in Santa Fe who was getting famous, and I took about every penny I had in the world and bought Sam a carving of a big cowboy bucking on a horse. It was very difficult to get there. He didn't even say thank you or anything. I went through hell to get him that bucking horse. I thought it was funny. He never put it out.

KATY: He liked to give more than receive. Gifts always embarrassed him. If you said to Sam, "That's a really nice jacket you're wearing," he'd just take it off and give it to you, and if you didn't accept it he'd be mortified.

MAX: Slim Pickens told me once that he heard Sam needed money. So he said, "Max, let's go down there and see him. I've got quite a bit of money and I could help Sam out." I said, "Well, I don't have any damn money." Slim said, "No, just go with me." For some reason, he took his wife, Maggie, along. I don't remember who all was there, but Sam was back in bed, obviously. I think even Marie and the kids stopped by and visited. Maggie and I were visiting, and Slim went back there for about two hours, I guess. I thought, "Boy, he's staying a long time to give him some money." When we were driving away, Slim said to me, "I'll never work in another picture for Sam. It offended him deeply that I wanted to loan him money. He's madder than hell. He'll never hire me again." And he never did. He never hired Slim again.

KATY: That must have been after *Pat Garrett*?

MAX: Right after that, right after that. He was so proud that Sam had given him that role that expanded his whole life and his whole career for his family, and he thought the least thing he could do was make sure Sam had some money. He just heard Sam needed money. I didn't know if he needed money or not. I never could tell. He always would tell me he was broke. That was Slim's reaction.

KATY: I think Sam had money. He used to stash it all over the place. I'm sure there were bank accounts that nobody knew about that were stashed away somewhere, you know? Sam was so paranoid about his files that when we went down to Mexico City to shoot *Bring Me the Head of Alfredo Garcia*, I had to ship all his files. Eight full filing cabinets. Can you imagine going on location and taking eight four-drawer filing cabinets and putting them in the basement of this house? I mean, there was shit in there—production notes from *Major Dundee* and *Ride the High Country*—but who gives a shit? He was so paranoid that people might get into his files that we had to ship eight filing cabinets.

MAX: I think five of those Westerns will survive longer than anyone else. I don't think there's anybody around who can make another great Western. I don't believe there's anybody who can make 'em. How do you top *The Wild Bunch*?

KATY: You can't. And every time they do make a Western, they make comparisons to Peckinpah—*Young Guns*. They just did *Billy the Kid* for television for Turner, did you see that? Gore Vidal wrote it—that's ironic.

MAX: I didn't see that.

KATY: I have it on tape.

MAX: Is it good?

KATY: It's not *Pat Garrett and Billy the Kid*.

MAX: There's another Western that Jeb Rosebrook did a rewrite on called *Montana* based on a book by Larry McMurtry. Ted Turner bought it, and HBO is going to release it. They hired Jeb to rewrite it. He's not going to get any credit, but he said it's a possibility for another good one. I haven't seen anyone make a good one for so long. It's understandable why the Western died. No one has been trained in the form. There are probably a dozen people in the whole world who can even write one. So who would you get to produce and direct it? I don't know anyone who can do that.

KATY: No. They're still trying to make *The Cowboy and the Cossack*, Clair Huffaker's book. Robert Redford wants to make it.

MAX: I actually think that would make a great film. Well, is there anything that you would like to say about ol' Sam that you would like me to write down?

KATY: There are so many moments. I could sit and talk forever. I could talk about our life in Yugoslavia. I could talk about the night we were driving around looking for a hospital because he believed he was having a heart attack. I actually believe he was having a heart attack. And we were sitting in this little remote place in the middle of nowhere with Yugoslavian doctors trying to save Sam's life. That was the first time he had a heart attack, and it was the first time he realized he was killing himself.

MAX: That was on *Cross of Iron*, right?

KATY: It was just him and me in this distant little place. I have this image of the two of us just sitting there, and I thought, "My God he might die on me right here. We're so far away from home and it's just the two of us."

MAX: Explain to me why the two of you were alone and away from the production.

KATY: It was in the middle of the night, and he was having a heart attack. He had chest pains and I thought . . .

MAX: On location?

KATY: Yeah.

MAX: What was the name of that little place?

KATY: Portorož—a tiny little village in Yugoslavia. I didn't want to call anybody. I just got him in the car and drove to the nearest hospital I could find.

MAX: How far did you have to drive?

KATY: I can't remember. It was a local hospital; it wasn't far, but it was very quiet and very dark, and it was just him and me. That was it. I figured I'd better get him somewhere.

MAX: God.

KATY: They gave him nitroglycerin—put it under his tongue. I think that was his first heart attack. It was the first time I realized something serious was going on. There were many times when I would just wake up in the morning and hold his head in the bucket. And I knew it was blood; I knew it wasn't just vomit. I tried to save him. I tried to save him for seven years.

MAX: Well, you did. You got him through some fine work that we wouldn't have if it hadn't been for you. That's the truth. I told Pat, I'm gonna write it down someday; somebody here is not getting the credit.

KATY: Bob Grey just told me recently that when I was in England, Sam denied that he had anything to do with the fact that I was back in England.

MAX: But he was responsible?

KATY: He was totally responsible for it. He gave Bob Grey a ticket, and Bob Grey sat outside my house for two weeks like in surveillance and watched me. He told me recently.

MAX: Who was Bob Grey? He worked for Sam?

KATY: He was a close friend of Sam's. Sam said, "You have to check out what that cunt is doing over there."

MAX: Well, how come I never knew Bob Grey?

KATY: You know Bob Grey, the chiropractor, his friend . . .

MAX: Oh, that bastard. Of course I know him. I deliberately forgot that son of a bitch.

KATY: Bob Grey was the one who was in the next-door room on *Convoy* listening in to my bug. He loved Sam; he did everything Sam asked him to do.

MAX: I think he was very bad for Sam.

KATY: You do?

MAX: You're damn right I do. I watched him that night up there at Camille's after that memorial, and I didn't like that guy and I didn't trust him and I thought, "Here's a man who really helped put that . . . "—he was undoing a lot you were patching up, I think.

KATY: If it hadn't been for Bob Grey, Sam would have died earlier. It was Bob he called when he had his heart attack in Livingston, Montana, when he was living in the hotel. And Bob went and got him to the hospital.

MAX: I didn't know that. . . . But I do want to use the surveillance incident you just told me about.

KATY: In London . . . he described my house to me. I didn't talk to Bob Grey for many years because I knew he was responsible for having me thrown out of the country. Sam maneuvered it. One day, he rang me up and said, "We have to sit and talk. There's so much I want to talk about, there's so much I want to apologize for. Because Sam was very close to me—I was trying to protect you as much as I could. I don't want you to think I was all bad." He told me about the fact that Sam paid for his ticket and that he was sitting outside my house (in England), and I said, "Why didn't you come in?"

MAX: Go in and visit—have a little spot of tea, for Christ's sake.

KATY: Sam had this idea that I had run off with the script, that nobody could finish the picture. I should have known that Sam was planning something when he said, "I want you to go back to L.A. and I want you to get all my papers over to Kit Dillinger and all my papers over to Norma Fink and make sure all my personal stuff is taken care of." And the night I was about to fly back, he called and said, "Why don't you Federal Express all the papers? I don't want you to take the stuff with you on the plane." I said, "Why?" He said, "Well, the plane might crash." I said, "What about me? You're more concerned about the fuckin' papers than me?" He said, "Just Federal Express the stuff." I should have realized then that . . .

MAX: Yeah. Well, that's funnier than hell. I like that. Fern Lea gave me a picture of Sam when he was a kid in the Marine Corps with his mother. Did you ever see that picture?

KATY: Yeah it's amazing. We used that when Sam had his fiftieth birthday, the party that I gave him for his fiftieth birthday, when everybody in the world was there because I invited everyone, and I had blown-up pictures of him all over the house, blown-up pictures of him as a child. He didn't speak to me for a week; he was in such a state of shock. That's one of the wonderful stories. We had turned all the lights off, and the kids were standing at the window. You know the story of his fiftieth birthday. . . . Two days before, one of the guests, Steve McQueen, told Sam, "I hear you're having a surprise birthday party." Sam called me into his office and said, "What the fuck are you doing?" And I had to call thirty people within five minutes and say, "Be at the Formosa at lunch Friday, and let's pretend this is the surprise party." And we had a great party at lunchtime. Frank Kowalski came over, McQueen came over, and Sam thought this was his surprise party. I said, "On your way home, why don't you and Denver come over to Camille's (Camille Fielding, wife of composer Jerry Fielding) because I forgot to bring you your present." There were 350 people in Camille's house. All the lights were off. The kids had said, "The car's just driven up in the driveway. Denver and Sam just got out of the car. They're peeing in the bushes!" Denver and Sam peed in the bushes outside with everybody peering out the window. They had no idea! Sam said, "Gotta take a piss, come on Denny, gotta take a piss." Denver, who knew what was going on in the house, couldn't say, "Why don't we wait until we get inside, Sam?" because he always pissed outside with Sam. So he had to pee in front of 350 people and then walk through the door and everybody went, "Surprise!" and there was everybody who had worked for him. He was in shock. He went to bed for a week. He couldn't speak. He didn't have one drink that night. He was stunned. And everyone who could not come sent telegrams—Joel McCrea and Randolph Scott sent telegrams. Dustin Hoffman sent a telegram. Ringo Starr was there, Keith Moon was there. People were there who he had not seen in years, including crew people from *Deadly Companions* and *Ride the High Country*. I went through his production files and invited everyone he had worked with. Keenan Wynn was there. Sam came up to me and said, "I'll never forgive you for this for the rest of my life." But he loved it, of course.

MAX: But you had that picture blown up of him in the Marines with his mother?

KATY: Yeah. I don't know where it is now. I think the feelings he had for his mother he took out on all the women in his life.

Postscript

Katy broke away from Sam in 1977 at the end of *Convoy*. She joined Michael Deeley at EMI Films as a post-production supervisor on Michael Cimino's *The Deer Hunter*. In 1981 she was the executive in charge of production with Deeley on Ridley Scott's cult sci-fi film *Blade Runner*, starring Harrison Ford. She served in a similar capacity for Paul Bartel's *Not for Publication* and Michael Cimino's *The Sicilian* and was the production coordinator on *At Close Range* starring Sean Penn and Christopher Walken. In the early 1990s she began raising funds and volunteering for a homeless shelter in Los Angeles, which, in Katy's words, "turned into thirteen years of running a homeless shelter"—namely as executive director of Justiceville/Homeless USA's Dome Village transitional housing community. She founded the Los Angeles Krickets, a cricket team made up of homeless youth, and, through them, started the Compton Cricket Club, which, she said, "started with me recruiting all these gangbangers from Compton to play cricket." The team is also known as the Compton Homies and the Popz, and it toured England in 1995, 1997, 1999, and 2001, even playing games at Windsor Castle under the auspices of Prince Edward.

Katy has been an active board member of the British Academy of Film and Television Arts in Los Angeles for over twenty-two years, and she also serves on the board for the Association for the Recovery of Children, a nonprofit dedicated to rescuing missing and exploited children around the world. She has coproduced documentaries on Sam Peckinpah, including *Sam Peckinpah: Man of Iron* in 1993 (with Paul Joyce) as well as Mike Siegel's *Passion and Poetry: The Ballad of Sam Peckinpah* (2005). She continues to develop various film projects as of this writing. In 2011 she cofounded the Inner City Shakespeare Ensemble, coproducing three Shakespeare plays with inner-city students from George Washington Preparatory High School.

In 2010 Katy was awarded the Martin Luther King Keeper of the Dream Award for her work with disengaged youth in Los Angeles. In 2011 she became an honorary doctor of arts at the University of Bedfordshire in recognition of her career in the film industry as well as for her contributions countering homelessness and crime and advocating for transformational education. In the spring of 2012 she was awarded an MBE (Member of the Most Excellent Order of the British Empire) in the Queen's Honours List for her services to the community in Los Angeles. She was also presented the honor at Buckingham Palace by Her Royal Highness Princess Anne and also earned certificates of recognition from the City and County of Los Angeles for her community service.

Katy is working on a book called *The Puppet Box*. Though her parents escaped the Nazi-fueled Holocaust, the rest of her family perished in concentration camps. "My parents spent their entire time in England trying to find out what happened to my family," she said. "They had escaped from Prague in 1939—two weeks after Hitler's troops entered the city." In 2009 Katy and Ali MacGraw were invited to present a Sam Peckinpah retrospective at the Karlovy Vary Festival in the Czech Republic. During that time, they were invited to spend a few days in Prague. She recalled:

> I'd never been to my parents' homeland, and I spent a week there
> visiting the Jewish Quarter, where I found the names of all my family
> members inscribed on the walls of a synagogue and information
> on where they were born, where they died, and what concentration
> camp they were sent to. Ali and I then went to the Theresienstadt
> concentration camp memorial museum and found a tribute there
> in a museum exhibition to my uncle, Franta Zelenka, who was a set
> designer and director of a children's opera called *Brundibar*, which
> was performed over fifty times in the concentration camp. I also

identified a photograph of two unknown victims of the Holocaust—
my aunt and cousin, Franta Zelenka's wife and his child, Martin.

Sometime later, I got an e-mail from this guy who said he had
lived next door to my family in Prague. He said my aunt had given
his mother all of her family possessions, including twenty marionette
puppets. "We were going to give them to a museum, but I wonder
if you would like to have them," he said. So he sent them to me. My
book *The Puppet Box* is my family history through this journey of
discovery.

Katy, who now lives in a West Hollywood apartment with a cat, is also
working on a book about her cricket team, called *Straight Bat out of
Compton*. When asked how she looks back at her years with Sam, she
said, "That was a strong and powerful segment of my life. My only regret
is that it was during my prime childbearing years, so I never thought of
having kids, which, I suppose, is the result of me working so closely with
Sam on eight pictures over seven years. I think I dedicate my life now to
other people's children because I didn't have any of my own."

14. A Pirate Guarding His Gold
L. Q. Jones

L. Q. Jones is a strange son of a bitch. He has held on the longest and stolen more movies than any character actor I know. L. Q. came to Hollywood at the same time as two of my other friends, Morgan Woodward and Fess Parker. Ol' Fess—what he had the most of was charm, and that charm made him rich. Morgan was smart with money. When he was not working in Hollywood, he'd buy old houses, get a couple of carpenters to fix them up, and sell them. L. Q. probably knew Sam better than anyone else, film-wise. L. Q. is an actor, writer, director, and producer, so when he decides to observe something or someone, I'm going to listen to him. He will bullshit you about anything—except film. L. Q. appeared in five of Sam's Westerns and several of his television shows. L. Q. took no crap from Sam, and Sam gave no crap to L. Q. because L. Q. knew his lines, did his job, and acted like a total professional. He would never hang around with the rest of us in the bar. He would get up every morning before the shoot and go for a long run.

L. Q. and Morgan are still neighbors in the Hollywood Hills area, with Morgan in the hills and L. Q. down below in the flats. Whenever I ask Morgan, "How's ol' L. Q. doing? Is he still sitting in his window with a shotgun across his lap?" Morgan always says, "Oh yeah. He's guarding all his money that he buried out there in the yard. He's buried every dime he made somewhere out there." And it's the truth. It's a running joke, but it's the truth. L. Q. knew every penny counted when he was making low-budget films of his own. He squeezed all the copper out of a penny and then remade it into a dime.

L. Q. was born Justice Ellis McQueen in Texas in 1927. He took his screen name from a character he played in his first movie, *Battle Cry* (1955). I first became acquainted with L. Q. because of a successful Don Siegel film called *Hound Dog Man* (1959). L. Q. really wanted to be in that film; he had a feeling that it was going to turn out well. Somehow he still thinks to this day that I got him that part. I can't shake him of the idea that I had a hand in that. I don't know where he got that idea—I may have made a slight suggestion or recommendation about him to somebody, but I can't recall. L. Q. thought that it was his best role, a real step up the ladder for him.

In 1961 he played one of the villainous Hammond brothers in Sam Peckinpah's *Ride the High Country*. He would be linked to Sam's career forever. Even in this early stage of his film career, he had that old hound dog sense of smell. He knew Sam was unique, so he observed him and noted every move he made and every mood he displayed during the shooting of that film. Sam's sacrifice to get that movie made left a deep and lasting impression on L. Q. After observing Sam's manner of getting performances out of actors, setting up shots, and instigating creative madness on the set, L. Q. decided that Sam was a genius when it came to mood, action, and camera setups. This led to L. Q. making films of his own, displaying this same finesse. This is what L. Q. told me about Sam: "Sam Peckinpah was a genius. He saw things no one else observed. He involved all the characters in every scene." L. Q. emphasized, "Everyone is engaged. Sam never failed. But he never fully succeeded either."

Sam's first acquisition of my *Hi-Lo Country* caught the attention and respect of L. Q. and a lot of other Western-film character actors. They all craved to be part of this Sam Peckinpah film. It would be more than thirty-five years and countless scripts and concepts later before Walon Green solved the problem and wrote the script that would be filmed by Stephen Frears. L. Q. never got a shot at making *The Hi-Lo Country*, but he fell in love with another of Sam's obsessions, my 1963 novella *The Great Wedding*. Sam was between options on this one when L. Q. and I teamed up on it and made a long, hard run at trying to get the damn thing made.

L. Q. decided to make some low-budget films of his own. The average budget for these pictures was somewhere in the neighborhood of $17,000. That figure is as unbelievable as a sudden earthquake and just as true as an ocean tide. He showed a small profit on every one of them. Our friend Morgan Woodward only acted in one of them—he liked to get paid. Still, L. Q. filmed with professional actors, edited the films and scores himself, worked on the scripts, hired the cameraman and tiny crew, and completed them. Many Hollywood insiders felt that L. Q. was as crazy as Sam. Before launching these films, L. Q. would show the scripts to all the friends he respected and ask them to make any suggestions they liked. Then he'd throw away any of those suggestions he didn't like and keep—for free—any of your ideas he thought would help the film. I was among the chosen. L. Q. would come to me and say I was the only one who could help him with a particular script. It was the same line of bullshit he'd give to every friend. And yet it wasn't bullshit, because it worked. His directorial debut was on the now-forgotten exploitation film *The Devil's Bedroom* (1964). One scene called for lead actress Valerie Allen to be trapped deep in a dark, cold, spider-infested well. She didn't want to do it, and L. Q. kept cajoling her until he said, "Baby, Barbara Stanwyck would do it." To which Allen replied, "Then get Barbara Stanwyck." And yet, in the end, pro that she was, Allen climbed down into the well and did the shot.

L. Q. made *The Brotherhood of Satan* (1971) in Hillsboro, New Mexico, my own favorite village in the world, with a vast desert to the east and a great mountain range and Gila wilderness to the west. It starred Strother Martin and himself, as well as other professional actors, including Alvy Moore, and in the end L. Q. made a pretty good horror film. He knew he had a fairly good film, so he approached people who distributed low-budget horror films. I think he wrote a paperback novel to go along with the movie. He took that entire package to these distributors and was turned down quite a few times before he found one who wanted it. The head of this company tried to force L. Q. to tell him what the budget was, but L. Q. wouldn't do it. They met several times and this distributor kept asking what the budget was. Finally, the man laughingly told L. Q., "We're going to make you an offer. It'll be a good profit. But we want to know the budget. Write it down here." And it was a good profit, because L. Q. told them he made it for $67,000. No matter what you hear about the economy of low-budget films, that was impossible. But L. Q. was capable of pulling off the impossible.

L. Q. read a fine short story by Harlan Ellison called "A Boy and His Dog." L. Q. had good taste in writing. I know that because he liked everything I wrote! I think L. Q. bought the rights to Ellison's story outright. He started out by getting the script written in his own inimitable way, and then set about raising the money. He had a lot of help from Alvy Moore, who would become his producing partner on several films. Moore had recently been a costar on the successful television series *Green Acres*, with Eddie Albert and Eva Gabor. L. Q. talked Jason Robards Jr. into starring in *A Boy and His Dog*, and he cast Don Johnson, who had not yet become world famous with the television series *Miami Vice*. He also cast himself, Moore, and Strother Martin. Tolstoy once said that everything is connected, and connections in Hollywood are as close as threads in a fishing net. Sam's *Cable Hogue* certainly contributed to *A Boy and His Dog* in terms of casting. L. Q. talked everyone, including the lead girl, Susanne Benton, into working at bargain rates. And of course he had the dog and his trainer on hand. Miraculously, L. Q. made this movie for about $400,000.

A Boy and His Dog, released in 1975, is one of the first quality post-apocalyptic stories written and sold as a movie. I've looked at countless fine pictures from around the world made for under or around $1 million, but what L. Q. managed to do for less than half that amount was a monumental achievement. He conned everyone he could, any way he could, to direct a pioneering science fiction film—a little classic. He and Alvy Moore set out to sell it at a profit; they knew it could be a sleeper. They were made a few small offers, and Alvy wanted to take 'em. L. Q. had the guts to turn 'em down. You might call that foolishness, but he had faith in his judgment and kept on fighting to get a decent deal and a release for what was to him, at this time, his life's work.

I was invited to one of the screenings he was constantly holding to try to sell the movie to distributors. I instantly fell in love with the film and complimented all concerned. I knew what L. Q. was going through—I'd been through the same thing many times in other worlds. Later, I returned to New Mexico to finish a story and when I returned to Hollywood sometime later, L. Q. told me he still had no luck with his baby. He asked me if I could get Charles Champlin, then entertainment editor and principal film critic for the *Los Angeles Times*, to look at the film and tell L. Q. what he thought of it. I had become close friends with Champlin, so I called him—at a really busy time for Champlin, as it turns out. It was a sacrifice for him to find time to look at the film, but he said yes. He insisted that no one be in the screening room except him and me. He didn't want to have to duck and dodge anyone.

L. Q. set up a screening at Warner Bros. That's where Champlin and I saw the film. We got out at about eight o'clock at night. There was a bar near the studio that a lot of people in the movie industry frequented. We went in, and Champlin told me he had time for just one drink before he ran off to another film to review around nine o'clock.

I began to feel some pressure to say something, but I kept my mouth shut. Champlin raised a toast to me, and this was the only time I ever heard Champlin use an off-cue word: "That is one fine fucking film."

I called L. Q. and told him that Champlin liked the film. L. Q. was already thinking about how to use this. He asked me to ask Champlin about what L. Q. could do to get the movie released. A few days later, Champlin called me and asked, "Do you think L. Q. would be interested in selling the film in France?" Champlin had a friend who bought films for French distribution, and he said his friend wanted to see the film. I got L. Q. and Charles Champlin in touch with each other to sort this out, and I stepped out of it. Well, the guy saw it and liked it and bought the French rights for about $20,000—more than the budget of L. Q.'s early movies. L. Q. called me again and asked if I had any other ideas for distribution. I had a friend in San Diego, a newsman named John Sinor. He had a wondrous talent for wrapping up a full column with one sentence. I asked L. Q. if he would be open to showing him the film. He was. Sinor, who was writing a worldwide-syndicated column for the *San Diego Tribune* then, invited the film critics for the *San Diego Union* to see it, too. They loved it. I asked how all this could help, and Sinor told me, "We know a guy who runs an art house in San Diego; L. Q. can open it there."

So L. Q. took part of the $20,000 and opened the film in San Diego. The critics gave it a rave review. Sinor gave it two columns of ink in advance. It was a smash hit at this theater, and distribution people started calling L. Q. about it. He knew then he had something. He called me once to say, "I still don't have a deal, but we're going to open in two or three more cities."

Variety had noted the full and enthusiastic run in San Diego. I knew Lou Avolio, who ran the Commonwealth Theaters in Albuquerque, and he said he'd open it. Tulsa, Oklahoma, was also on the itinerary, and four other cities were lined up. It was a hit at every cinema.

L. Q's bluff—well, it wasn't a bluff, but faith—paid off. The trade papers gave him ink. United Artists' distribution arm made a deal with L. Q. The film started grossing millions. I would imagine that film's success has supported him to this day. He never gave up the rights, and I don't believe he ever sold the television rights. But it did come out on VHS and DVD.

L. Q. had the help of people who love film and who did something about it. He never called to thank me, but he would pay me back much later.

Now L. Q. was in good with United Artists. We met several times about *The Great Wedding* and decided we should make it even though it would piss off Sam Peckinpah. L. Q. set up a meeting with United Artists executives in San Francisco. Robert Naify and his kin owned at least six hundred UA theaters around the country. Bill Kelly, who I discovered to be a true gentleman, ran the UA theaters for the Naifys. We went up to meet him sometime around nine o'clock one morning in San Francisco. Bill was glad to meet me; he was interested in *The Great Wedding* because it had all the same characters from *The Rounders*—though I wouldn't call *The Great Wedding* a sequel. It's more of a continuation of the same story. It is about one cowboy who tries to marry off his friend to a rich woman in Santa Fe so they can both retire and live a life of ease. Kelly told me that *The Rounders* saved a number of big pictures the studio released around the same time because they could double-bill the other films with *The Rounders*. He told me, "I guarantee you more people saw *The Rounders* than *Mary Poppins*."

We started talking about *The Great Wedding*. The deal was, I would write the first draft, and L. Q. would produce and direct. I don't know what we told Bill about the actual screenplay; I think we just made it up as we went along.

And then I almost blew it. I was staying in a modest hotel—L. Q. wasn't footing that bill—and I didn't have enough money to pay the rent. I started thinking, "I don't know if I can get out of this hotel." There was a law in San Francisco at that time that stated that you could be arrested if you didn't pay your hotel bill. I panicked and suddenly blurted out, "We all know what we can all do. I guess *The Rounders* saved you, but I never saw a penny of it. As of today, I want what would be considered a pittance—a certified check for $20,000 and a handshake."

That was the first time I ever saw L. Q. Jones sweat. The two men sat there, stunned. Bill said, "You have to wait until we sign a contract."

L. Q. grabbed me and pulled me out into the hallway to try to salvage the deal. I had seen a cashier's sign down the hallway, and that's what put the idea into my head. L. Q. was a master talker, but it was to no avail on this deal. I didn't tell him I was on credit at the hotel. I can't remember how much I owed, but it may as well have been the national debt. I told L. Q., "Somebody has to show faith here beyond a handshake."

L. Q. stopped contesting me. He went in and quietly told Bill, "Max won't make a deal unless he gets a check."

Bill stood up, shook his head, walked down the hall, got a check for $20,000, and came back. It worked out—a true miracle.

I made a deal with L. Q. He would pay me $3 out of every $4 of that $20,000 for writing the script. L. Q. got $5,000 for overseeing it. I believe I was breaking all Writers Guild rules by accepting that deal. But I'd learned a simple truth a long time ago: if you don't figure out how to survive, you're gone. Adios.

L. Q. was both helpful and hellish with the script. He would come up with wonderful ideas, but they were usually jokes. I don't write jokes. My humor comes out of the nature of the characters. We never really fought. We just disagreed. And he did have some very good suggestions that I incorporated into the script.

Meanwhile, United Artists started coming down on Bill. No matter how successful this film might be, the company was in the business of distribution, not production. If this got made under these terms, they would be inundated with producers, directors, agents, actors, and so on—and they were right.

I had previously dealt with L. Q. on a filmscript based on my 1974 novel *Bobby Jack Smith, You Dirty Coward*, which was about a cowboy who uses the strategies of Napoleon to advance himself. I made a deal with Nash Publishing, who released it. They asked me to get a portrait of myself made, and they blew it up to a life-size cardboard likeness for promotional purposes. Nash wanted me to do a cross-country promotional tour, but I couldn't. I still had tremendous problems and pain with my blown-out inner ear due to my infantry experiences. Maybe I could have made four or five states, by driving, but to this day it's difficult for me to fly without it causing me intolerable discomfort and pain. But Nash was putting together ads to run in *Publisher's Weekly*, the *New York Times*—everywhere. It didn't matter. Nash's offices were at the top of a big business building at the end of Sunset Strip. They had a long hallway of offices up there, and I went up there to talk to the publicity department, which was right next to the exit or entryway. I was up there when I heard this noise coming from down the hallway, a voice, a buzz of voices. Guess what was happening? The New York office was closing, and the manager's assistant was walking down the hallway telling everyone. This young pioneering company was slowly failing. They published my book anyway, and it got some good reviews.

I took it to Sam Peckinpah. It was a raunchy comedy and I thought he would like it. He saw it as a satire of the Old West. It's actually the only project I ever took to Sam; he usually came to me. He said he couldn't get it made—this was after *The Killer Elite* (1975) and before *Cross of Iron* (1977), when he was stumbling a bit—but he knew a director who could: Tommy Gries, who had made the marvelous *Will Penny* (1968) with Charlton Heston. Tommy had just made a successful Western with Charles Bronson—*Breakheart Pass*—and he was about to make a film under contract about Muhammad Ali called *The Greatest*. Sam gave the book to Gries, who called me. We hit it off, had a few drinks, and talked about the book. He told me he didn't want to make *The Greatest*, but by contract, he had no choice.

I remember Tommy took me up to meet the production head of one of the studios—MGM, I think. This guy resented me for some reason. I didn't have much respect for him, and he seemed jealous of me. I don't know why; I was clad in worn-out Levis, a denim jacket, and cowboy boots, so I couldn't have impressed him or anybody else. He invited me to play in a poker game held in a certain room of a certain hotel on a certain night of the week. I knew these film executives would be playing for some mighty big money, so I turned him down jokingly with an "I'm not gonna let you guys take advantage of a little ol' cowboy like me." Sometime later, I found out that he had a camera and microphone built into the ceiling light fixture of that room so he could see what all the other poker hands were. I wouldn't have lasted one shuffle in that game.

Tommy Gries and I talked about *Bobby Jack Smith*, but he was constantly committed to *The Greatest*. He said as soon as he wrapped that film, we could start talking a deal on *Bobby Jack Smith*. I remember sweating the last few days of the production of his film; I knew Tommy would call me a few days after it wrapped. Well, he finished the picture, and a few days later, in January 1977, he dropped dead while playing tennis. He was about fifty-five years old.

I then met with L. Q. about all this, and we put together a damn good first act and outline for the rest of the film. We worked on it without a contract. L. Q. knew I would keep my word on any handshake. When it came to him keeping his word, all I had to say was, "Remember, I'm a dead shot."

L. Q. thought he could get it produced out here in New Mexico. He made several trips here to scout locations and found a place where we could build a set about fifteen miles west of I-40, off I-25, near where Route 66 Casino stands now. Everything seemed set, except the money. L. Q. wasn't going to put up money. I had to return to writing books, novellas, short stories, and magazine articles. So the momentum began to slow down.

Around this time—1977 or so—*San Diego Tribune* columnist John Sinor had written a book, *The Ghost of Cabrillo Lighthouse*, based on a historic lighthouse in San Diego that supposedly had a ghost in it. He felt it could make a fine film. I thought so, too. We wrote a screenplay for it. We decided to raise the money in San Diego. We set a budget of about $400,000 and started looking into casting the children's roles. John's wife was the stage actress Diane Sullivan. She agreed to be in it. Well, L. Q. read the book and wanted to be in on it, too. He would act in it, produce it, and maybe even direct it. Gene Gregston, once editor of two San Diego papers—who had written a book about the golfer Ben Hogan—got into it, too. He had connections, and he got four powerful, rich men to consider financing it. He set up a meeting.

L. Q. did everything right in that meeting. He was charming, smart, and confident. This was just a few years after *A Boy and His Dog*, and his name still carried weight. We left with warm handshakes exchanged all around. The men said, "We like it; we're going to check this out."

A week later, John called me. He said one of those money men wanted to talk to us. I knew in my gut that if he wanted to talk to us alone, something had gone haywire. We met with him, and he didn't waste words.

"Everything was a go until we discovered, with all due respect, that Mr. Jones does not know how to divide up the money," he said.

We were stunned. But it was true that these were friends of John's and highly successful businessmen. What could a couple of dumb writers say but "Thanks for your time"? And that was the end of that. We didn't have the heart to start over on our own. It wouldn't have done any good. You can't put an exploded shell back together.

I told L. Q. what happened. He threw a small fit. "Businessmen, what do they know?" he said.

After the failure of Sam's last movie, *The Osterman Weekend* (1983), L. Q. and Sam teamed up to make a film version out of James Gould Cozzens's novel *The Castaway*. Sam's friend Jim Silke would cowrite the script, and L. Q. would star and help put together the money. It never happened. L. Q. and his business manager raised some money and set it up in a trust fund. Somebody involved stole all the money. L. Q. told Sam this, and Sam told L. Q. he was filing suit because L. Q. hadn't kept his part of the deal! It didn't go anywhere, of course, and Sam was dead before the end of 1984, anyway.

L. Q. really did pay me back tenfold for my assistance in getting *A Boy and His Dog* released. He was the one who suggested Martin Scorsese read *The Hi-Lo Country* at the end of shooting Scorsese's *Casino*.

L. Q. said, "Marty, why haven't you ever made a Western?"

Scorsese said, "I've never found a good Western story with characters I like."

L. Q. told him, "Well, Sam Peckinpah spent his entire life trying to get this book made."

Marty had a great respect for Peckinpah's work. He said, "You think the rights are available?"

L. Q. said, "I think so," and he gave Marty my address and phone number. And Marty would eventually produce the film version of *The Hi-Lo Country*, directed by Stephen Frears.

Now I know damn well L. Q. had an ulterior motive. He wanted to play Jim Ed Love in the movie. However, he did not play it because of his own choosing. But we will get to that later.

About ten years ago, a German filmmaker named Mike Siegel made a documentary about Sam called *Passion and Poetry: The Ballad of Sam Peckinpah* (2005). The Germans like Westerns, and they love Peckinpah. Siegel knew L. Q. would be the key to the success of that film. He called L. Q. to arrange an on-camera interview, but L. Q. wouldn't answer the phone. So Siegel and his crew decided to go out to Los Angeles with a cameraman and confront L. Q. at his home. They caught L. Q. putting out his trash! L. Q. told them, "The reason I didn't return your call is because you didn't offer me any money." Siegel understood. They got together some money and paid L. Q. for his contribution. A real thin dime is a big fat dollar bill to L. Q. Jones.

Incidentally, L. Q. kept $1,330 back from my wages on that script job—money he still owes me. I have joked with him for nearly forty years about getting that money back, with compound interest. He won't pay. And he's still out there in Los Angeles, a shotgun across his lap, guarding his pirate treasure. Somewhere in his unholy attic is the only copy of the script for *The Great Wedding*. Somehow, some forty years later, he just can't find it.

15. *Junior Bonner*

Junior Bonner (1972) is the best rodeo film that's ever been made. It was the best script Sam ever got his hands on. Sam called me and asked me to work on the script in Arizona. He offered me $1,000 a day plus all the whiskey I could drink. I don't know why he wanted me out there; writer Jeb Rosebrook had done a wonderful job with the story. Imagine if I had gone: between Sam and me and Casey Tibbs, who worked on the film, somebody would have lit the fuse, and it would have become another botched Peckinpah movie.

Here's how I first met Jeb: I got a phone call from Sam, who said he was working on a script at Warner Bros.—he had an office there, but he didn't have a picture. He said a young lady brought a script to him and asked him to read it. I don't know whether he read it or not. He told her that he did. I guess he offered to buy it from her, and they haggled over the price of writing or rewriting. She told him, "You buy it, because you can fix it." The truth is, he wanted to screw her—and he did, right there in the office! Then he told her to get the hell out of his office. I don't know what the script was, so I didn't ask.

She went to the Writers Guild and filed a complaint regarding the price of the script. Sam called me and said there was going to be a hearing there, and he needed some writers to back him up. He had Jeb Rosebrook there as well as a once-famous writer named John Gay, who had written some scripts for Burt Lancaster's company, and another guy whose name I can't remember. Sam told me, "We'll have all the big guns there." I said, "What big guns? We're all BB guns except John Gay."

The woman told her side of the story, and Sam told his side, and I told the truth, which was that Sam always paid me what he said he'd pay me, and right on time, and he never abused me about it. All of the writers told the truth, including John Gay, who was the last to testify. He said,

"I think Mr. Peckinpah's work speaks for itself." The members voted, and Sam won. On the way out, in front of the Writers Guild building, Sam invited us all to lunch. Only Jeb went. He later told me that Sam got drunk and started playing football with the butter. So that's when I met Jeb. He had read my short story "Xavier's Folly" and told me, "I know a guy back in Virginia, Fielder Cook, who I'd like to send this story to." I wasn't familiar with the man's name, even though he had directed a lot of the best Hallmark Hall of Fame films, such as *Patterns* and *A Big Hand for the Little Lady*. He got such charm out of the stars of that latter picture (Joanne Woodward and Henry Fonda). You forgot that the script gets a little too silly for good humor.

I told Jeb to send my story out to Fielder, who read it and said, "I love it. We need a screenplay. Jeb, can you write it?" Jeb was thrilled to get the job because he had gone into debt before *Junior Bonner*. I remember his wife, Dorothy, saying to him, "Now we can replace the four slick tires on the station wagon." I understood that scenario well.

Fielder—who directed the 1966 TV version of *Brigadoon*, starring Robert Goulet—went to producer Barry Corbin, who was Goulet's business partner. Goulet and Corbin had a production company, Rogo Productions. Rogo optioned "Xavier's Folly" for the screen. Goulet loved the story. He was then engaged at the Frontier Hotel in Las Vegas for big money—mob money—and he was married to singer Carol Lawrence at the time. Goulet was not going to act in it, just finance it, with his partner and agent as producer. Goulet treated me like a king. He invited me to Las Vegas and put me up in a big suite with a private swimming pool, and I don't swim. I told Goulet, "If you want to do something nice for me, I like to drink Crown Royal." In less than an hour, a metal cart of about thirty bottles of Crown Royal arrived at my suite. I could have stayed there drinking for a year. Goulet wasn't drinking during this time, though it was known that he liked alcohol. He seemed to get along with everybody, but I heard wild things about him. I remember once he invited me to meet Carol Lawrence at his home. She wasn't there, but he walked me around the house and showed me where the walls were patched up because he had gotten mad at his wife and punched the walls in anger. He started sharing weird stories with me. I remember he told me he had read my story "Candles in the Bottom of the Pool."

"That's a spooky story," he said, and that was that.

The film version of "Xavier's Folly" never got made. Barry Corbin got divorced and his life went down the tubes. Goulet's life also went down the tubes, and then things turned around. Fielder Cook went crazy. He called me and told me that he had a way of getting it made. He asked me to fly out to where he was living in the Sportsman Lodge on my own dime to talk about it. He said, "I know how to get this made. I have to run off to Europe for a few days. Stay here until I get back." I waited three weeks. He never called. He never showed up. I called Corbin, who tracked Cook down somewhere in Europe. Cook called me. I said, "Fielder, you better stay over there. Don't come back here, because if you do I'm going to teach you a lesson about keeping appointments that you will never forget. I'm going back to New Mexico, and I don't ever want to see you again." He really pissed me off. I never saw him again. Too bad—he was a true talent.

Then Corbin called me and asked me to come meet him at some small hotel off Wilshire in Los Angeles. I went out, hoping he had the funding. I told him, "This has been a wonderful ride, except none of us is getting anywhere." I told him if he wanted the deal, we'd have to make it over breakfast the next day.

The next day, Corbin told me that Goulet was pulling out of the deal. I said, "OK, if you want this property, I'll write the damn screenplay myself."

"What's it going to cost?"

"$90,000, but I want the check now."

He pulled out a check and wrote it out to me for $90,000. It was from a bank in New York City. I went back to New Mexico and showed the check to my wife before taking it down to the bank. I asked them to call the bank in New York to make sure it was good, and they said it was. I deposited it, and what do you know—the check bounced! So much for bank confidence.

Corbin married a woman he was dating and moved back to New York to make a comeback. He kept changing his phone number, but I got ahold of it once and called him. His wife answered, and I said, "I know you must hear this all the time, but this deal with him cost me about $6,000. Tell him I want him to wire me $5,000 [how much I was willing to settle for] tomorrow by Western Union."

It didn't happen. I called and got him on the phone. He said, "I'm having a hard time."

I said, "You don't know what 'hard time' means. If that money is not here by noon tomorrow, I'll be on your doorstep in New York the day after."

The money arrived the next day.

A year or so later, I got a special delivery of the book *The Stockholm Syndrome* and a note from Barry Corbin asking me to read it and write a film treatment. I read it, called him, and said, "I'll do it if you can get it together—but bring cash."

Two weeks later, he called me. "I need to borrow a plane ticket from you. I found a guy in L.A. who can make this happen if I can get out there to meet him." I wired him the money. A few weeks later, the phone rang in my house. The guy on the other end of the line was hysterical.

"Are you Max Evans?"

"I'm the remains of Max Evans," I said.

"Our friend Barry Corbin blew his brains out last night in my guest bedroom. I found a note from him saying, 'Please call the following people to inform them.' You were third on the list. I dug ol' Barry, but he didn't have to do this to me: his brains are all over my damn walls!"

Thus the first phase of the Hollywood adventures of "Xavier's Folly," the movie, ended.

But Corbin had recommended that story to some theater people in England, the Carringtons. They called me from London and said they wanted to take an option on it to make it into a stage musical. I was with William Morris at the time, and my agent said they were genuine producers. It was a solid five-year option for a modest amount. The plan was to open it in London and then take it to Broadway and then make it into a movie. They hired Don Black to compose the music, and he was doing such a good job that Andrew Lloyd Weber hired him before he could finish it. He ended up writing four or five great musicals for Andrew Lloyd Weber, and none for me! Meanwhile, they hired a teacher at Long Beach State who had written a few television episodes to write the script. I got ahold of him and asked him to send me the script. I'm not saying it was a bad script, but it had nothing to do with my original story. He had turned it into a rock 'n' roll musical! Still, to my amazement, in came the checks for five years.

When I stayed at the Sands in the 1960s, I would see thousands of hippies walking by the motel. I watched them pack the streets so tight that the cops couldn't get by in their squad cars. I couldn't make sense of them. Sometimes, I tried to go out and speak with some of them. Late at night, they would disappear, and I always wondered where to. I saw in them a generation of chaos. I didn't resent them; I was just puzzled. I started thinking of my own filmscript, a movie that could be set in a medium-sized city dump in New Mexico featuring a young man, a young woman, and a little boy who were lost but made beautiful crafts and jewelry out of the items in the dump. I wanted to say that anyone who wanted to pull themselves up by their bootstraps could do it. I got obsessed with it, and I was pissed off that nobody was thinking about those thousands of hippie kids walking the streets.

So around 1970 I wrote a script for *The Wheel*, and I took it to Sam, who didn't understand it and turned it down. I then took it to Robert Altman, who was almost offended that I even asked him. I decided to direct it myself. I raised $229,000, which left me with no room to hire any professional actors, although I did hire Slim Pickens's daughter, Daryle Ann, as the female lead. I thought she had more acting experience than she did. The lead actor had done some acting, so those two were really the only so-called professionals on the set. The rest were amateurs. Several directors I knew, including Sam, sometimes hired amateurs. But they had all the money they wanted and could do all the takes they needed. I only had one take. I hadn't realized before that big directors could get good performances out of amateurs because they had a lot of time, and takes, to craft the work. Half of the film was rank amateur stuff. The other half of the film was really, really something: pretty damn good.

I needed at least another $40,000 to finish the film the way I wanted. Sam knew I needed money. He was working on the *Junior Bonner* script in Prescott, Arizona, and he kept calling me, offering to hire me to re-work Jeb Rosebrook's script. I said, "I can't leave my film. You know damn well that if I come out there, you, Casey, and I will drink so much that we'll ruin both films." Sam even offered me cash under the table. I said, "Quit callin'. I ain't comin'."

I later told Jeb, "You're lucky I didn't take Sam's offer." Jeb was lucky in another way, and so was Sam: on one of his phone calls, I told him how I was using a bulldozer in my production. He inserted the idea off the cuff in *Junior Bonner*, and it was a perfect fit. So, something good comes from my disaster after all, and at least a couple of good friends benefited from *The Wheel*.

We held several screenings of *The Wheel*, and I knew I needed more money to give it polish. I paid everyone, but I didn't know enough to get good performances out of the actors. Three or four of my investors began riding my ass, so I made a deal with Shapiro Entertainment to handle the foreign distribution rights. Another company that used "Universal" in the title, but wasn't Universal, put it out, and it got some limited screenings and some good reviews and some bad reviews. A woman who worked for Shapiro double-crossed the company, and she and her boyfriend stole my negative. They just vanished, and there I was without a negative. I wonder now, if it had played on TV, whether it wouldn't come off so much better than most of the stuff you see in reruns.

Anyway, I had made a big mistake. I thought young people would want to see the film. They didn't. At one of the previews, a hippie kid told me he didn't know what the film meant. A few older people told me they loved the film. I'd gone after the wrong audience. For years afterward, people would ask me, "Whatever happened to that film?" It's gone, that's what happened.

Back in Arizona, Martin Baum and Joe Wizan were producing *Junior Bonner*. They were good producers who worked well with Sam. There would be the usual madness that erupted on all of Sam's pictures, but the producers decided to surround him with top-notch people. They flew Susan Hayward in from Florida to play Junior's mother. Sam, star Steve McQueen, the producers, and Jeb all met with her, but they didn't know what to say to her, so they didn't talk about the movie. She figured they didn't want her, so she got up, got on a plane, and took off! She thought they weren't treating her right. Ida Lupino replaced her. Sam had directed her in a forgotten television series she did with her husband, Howard Duff, called *Mr. Adams and Eve*, in the late 1950s. She was a wonderfully talented woman, and she recommended Robert Preston for Junior's dad; they had made a film together some years before. Sam insisted on Ben Johnson. Sam told Steve, "I just saw *The Last Picture*

Show. Ben's going to win an Oscar!" Sometime later, on the set, Steve said to everyone, "I just saw *The Last Picture Show*. Ben's going to win an Oscar."

Sam wanted Jeb on the set for rewrites, but he got mad at him; that's why he would call me sometimes. He was trying to hire me behind their backs to finish the script. He told Jeb that if he didn't get the script down the way Sam wanted it, he'd tie a can to his tail and run him out of town.

Sam disappeared for a week during the shooting. He blamed it all on Jeb. He took the script, rented a cabin up in the mountains somewhere, and rewrote the whole thing. He put his name on it and gave it to the producers. They tore the script up and told Sam to let Jeb rewrite it.

Sam started riding some members of the crew. He was good with actors—he had respect for actors, but he was renowned for firing crew members on sets. He even started riding Casey Tibbs. Carroll Ballard, no relation to Lucien, was the first to go—he was the second unit director. Sam fired him and another four unit directors, one after the other. Imagine how Jeb was feeling: here's his chance to get a big film with the biggest movie star in the world, and here's this madman Peckinpah putting people on the bus.

Over time, Sam began to accept Jeb. They would have some drinks at the Palace Bar, where much of the film was shot, and play pool. They got to joking about being the worst pool players in the world. They'd wager drinks on who was the best or the worst, and pretty soon pool balls were ricocheting off the walls. Jeb later had a pool cue made for Sam, in a case, on which he engraved, "For Sam Peckinpah, the world's worst pool player." It vanished. Jeb never saw it again. You couldn't give Sam a gift; he was very uncomfortable accepting gifts.

Sam would invite Jeb to see some of the dailies. One day, they watched the scene where Robert Preston and Ida Lupino are out talking on the back steps of the bar/brothel. Sam had worked some dialogue into that scene. Jeb looked over and saw tears coming down Sam's face. It was the only time he saw Sam cry. That scene must have brought back memories of his grandfather and grandmother. Sam and Jeb had a drink the night before they were going to shoot the final scene between Junior and his dad at the railroad station. Sam said, "When I was a kid and I did something my father didn't approve of, he'd just cuff my hat." And by God, that's what they shot the next day in the scene between Preston and McQueen. In all the madness, Sam could think of one little scene or line, drag it out of his actors, and run with it. And it would be a moment that would last forever—much like stealing the bulldozer scene from me and being justifiably proud of it.

Sam was running two women on the film, Katy Haber—his mistress and Girl Friday, by her own admission—and Joie Gould, whom he would later marry. The first night in town they all stayed in the same hotel. Sam and Katy got drunk, and Sam started calling everyone late at night, which he would often do. She told him he'd get in trouble and get fired if he kept bothering people. For some reason, he hauled off and hit her. I never saw Sam hit a woman in his life, but she later told me about it (for details, see chapter 13). Sam had this nasty trick of pretending he was walking away from you, and then he'd whirl around with a left hook and whack you.

That's what he did to Katy. He hit her on the chin, and it turned black, and when she went downstairs to get some ice for it the next morning, she ran into McQueen, who asked her what happened. She said, "I was running upstairs and fell and hit my chin." He said, "I guess if you were running, and somebody pushed you, you would bang up your chin."

Joie would sometimes visit the set, and Katy would disappear into the scenery. One morning, Sam told Jeb, "I hit Joie last night." McQueen must have heard about it. And he let Sam know that he did not like the idea of a man hitting a woman.

It was the first and only day that McQueen messed up. He was drinking tea between takes, and he kept goofing up his lines. Sam said, "Why don't we go on to another scene?" McQueen took the cup of tea and threw it over his shoulder at Sam as he walked away. That was his way of letting Sam know that he didn't like what Sam was doing with his women.

Jeb Rosebrook probably didn't like what Sam was trying to do with his woman either. Jeb's wife, Dorothy, visited the set of *Junior Bonner* for a week. She described herself as a naïve thirty-year-old, and she set out to prove her naïvety on that set. The film's principals usually had lunch on Sunday—their day off—at one of the local restaurants. When Jeb and

Dorothy attended one, she noticed that Casey Tibbs and the script girl were missing from the group. Dorothy blurted out, "They must be on a date." Uproarious laughter from the assembly followed because everyone else knew that Casey and this girl were shacked up in a motel nearby. They *were* on a date.

Sam invited the Rosebrooks and three or four other couples out to dinner at a restaurant one night. Under pressure to rewrite the script, Jeb told Sam that he and Dorothy had to get back to their hotel so he could work. They left the restaurant, and Dorothy said to Jeb, "We didn't even thank Sam for dinner. Let me run in and thank him." She ran in, and Jeb noticed that she was gone quite a while. When she came back, she told Jeb, "My God, Sam gave me a French kiss in front of all those other people." Jeb shrugged and said, "I told you not to mess with him."

At some point Sam had Mexican actress Elsa Cardenas, whom he was sometimes having an affair with, fly up to Prescott for a weekend during the shoot. Sam invited the Rosebrooks to go to the racetrack with him and Elsa. They had a great time, even though Sam lost every race. He was always losing at the track. On the way out, Sam pointed to Dorothy and said to them, "Tomorrow Jeb is going to Hawaii with Elsa and I'm staying here with you." Dorothy thought Sam was joking. Jeb knew he wasn't. Jeb later said that if his wife had said, "OK," Sam would have hired a bunch of stunt men to put Jeb on a plane to Hawaii.

Sam was the ultimate paradox. He tried to steal Jeb's movie and put his name on it, and then he goes and gives this film a few little scenes that make all the difference, and it has Jeb's name on it. And he probably would have stolen Jeb's wife if he could have gotten away with it. That action certified that Jeb was now a "close" friend.

They got the movie made, and everyone felt pretty good about it. McQueen wanted to release *Junior Bonner* like an art-house movie, slowly, city by city, giving people time to appreciate it. Sam agreed, the producers agreed, but the studio didn't agree. It opened at all the big theaters all at once, with no advance word of mouth. It wasn't a failure, but it only did mild-to-moderate box-office business. It got good reviews, and over time people have come to appreciate it more and more. The producers had told Sam that they didn't want it to be just another rodeo picture.

The rodeo goes on for three hours, but the backstory of the family goes on for days and weeks and months and years before and after that rodeo. *Junior Bonner* is truer to the human element behind the sport than any other rodeo film. It's Sam's one Western film where the protagonists survive the transition—at least for another day. The wreck might still be coming for Junior Bonner another mile or so down the road. That was the story of Sam, too.

Ol' Max staring out the back of the Broad Beach house at the great Pacific Ocean. (Photo by Pat Evans, courtesy Max Evans)

My twins, Charlotte and Sheryl, ready to frolic in the ocean at Broad Beach. (Photo by Pat Evans, courtesy Max Evans)

(*opposite*) Behind the Broad Beach house of pleasure, Sam's daughter Melissa and two of his nieces frolic in the Pacific. (Photo by Pat Evans, courtesy Max Evans)

Matthew Peckinpah, Sam's only son, in his birthday suit with Max Evans. Matthew loved Max, according to Sam, because he urinated on Max's boots—a sure sign. (Photo by Pat Evans, courtesy Max Evans)

Two unsung players in the world of Max Evans and Sam Peckinpah: business-man Ed Honeck (left) and Peckinpah's brother-in-law, Walter Peter (right). No one seems to know who provided the comic captions. (Courtesy Max Evans)

Sam in a pensive mood on the set of *Junior Bonner* with his son in the background. (Courtesy Max Evans)

(*opposite*) Sam talks with Steve McQueen on the set of *Junior Bonner* (1972), long before both men went crazy. (Courtesy Max Evans)

Sam's fiftieth birthday party was orchestrated by long-time friend, lover, and aide Katy Haber. That's Sam's nephew, David, sitting on his lap, with Stella Stevens and a blow-up doll among the other guests. (Courtesy Katy Haber's private collection)

(*opposite*) Barbara Leigh, Steve McQueen, and Sam crossing the rodeo grounds on the set of *Junior Bonner*. Max always felt he would have messed the film up had he accepted Sam's offer to cowrite the screenplay. (Courtesy Jeb and Dorothy Rosebrook)

Though Sam came to hate his mother, there was a time when he appreciated her. Here Sam (second from right) and three service pals pose with Sam's mom, circa 1945. (Courtesy Max Evans)

(*opposite*) Katy Haber put up with a lot of nonsense from Sam. Here she wheels him in a cart doubling as a wheelchair through the Belgrade airport following the completion of the troubled production of *Cross of Iron* (1977). (Courtesy Katy Haber's private collection)

Brian Keith was *The Westerner* (1960). He also appeared with Maureen O'Hara in Sam's first feature film, *The Deadly Companions* (1961). (Courtesy Max Evans)

Bernie Kowalski (left) never made it to the big time, but he was a genuine friend to Max Evans and, for a while, to Sam Peckinpah. That's Bernie visiting with producers David Brown, Dick Zanuck, and David Striepeke on the set of the horror film *Sssssssss!* (1973). No one knew how to pronounce the title, which is probably why the film flopped. (Courtesy Max Evans)

Lee Marvin (left) was perfectly cast as Kid Shelleen in *Cat Ballou* (1965). He was a drunk playing a drunk, according to Max. That's Jane Fonda, Michael Callan, and Dwayne Hickman on the right. (Courtesy Max Evans)

Sam always wanted to adapt Max's novel *The Hi-Lo Country* into a film, but it was British author Stephen Frears who did that some fifteen years after Sam's death. Billy Crudup (left) and Woody Harrelson (right) were perfectly cast as two postwar cowboys fighting a losing battle against progress. (Courtesy Max Evans)

Sam at his Broad Beach house. He was probably never happier. (Photo by Pat Evans, courtesy Max Evans)

Sam gives Max the boot from the Broad Beach house. The picture is fuzzy because both men were drunk. (Photo by Pat Evans, courtesy Max Evans)

Though Sam had a wild sense of humor, he never quite understood what Max was doing with all those dead skunks on an isolated New Mexico road. (Courtesy Max Evans)

(*opposite*) Hugh Cabot III ran through money and women as fast as Sam Peckinpah, but he remained the "black but happy sheep" of his illustrious family all the same. One wonders what happened to the brunette in Hugh's arms. (Courtesy Max Evans)

Max took this photo of a pensive Sam Peckinpah standing in the Nevada desert during the *Cable Hogue* shoot. "It says something," Max succinctly said of the image. (Courtesy Max Evans)

16. Pat Garrett, James Coburn, and the Taos Talking Pictures Festival

I believe that Sam Peckinpah made at least five great films: *Ride the High Country*, *The Wild Bunch*, *The Ballad of Cable Hogue*, *Junior Bonner*, and *Pat Garrett and Billy the Kid*. I call the latter, released in 1973, a flawed masterpiece, but all great works have faults in them. It's part of nature: there will be things that will be neglected in the reach for brilliance. Is there any possible coincidence in the fact that these five films are all Westerns that deal with transition?

James Coburn was magnetic as Pat Garrett in *Pat Garrett and Billy the Kid*. I would not call him so much a friend as much as a working acquaintance, but he was very loyal to Sam and, as noted in Robert Nott's introduction, he and I were two of the very few friends from Hollywood who stuck with Sam up to the end, for by the late 1970s, many of Sam's friends and working colleagues had left him, refusing to work with him again after his erratic behavior and violent outbursts of temper. Coburn has been associated with the Western since his early days in Hollywood when he first appeared in one of Randolph Scott's best pictures, *Ride Lonesome* (1959), scripted by Burt Kennedy and directed by Budd Boetticher. Coburn also played Britt in in John Sturges's 1960 Western, *The Magnificent Seven*, and he played a supporting role in Sam's botched production of *Major Dundee* a few years later. He also appeared in a Sergio Leone Western, *Duck, You Sucker*, in the early 1970s—so, with the exception of John Ford, you could say Coburn worked with just about all of the best-known directors of the Western genre. Though I've suggested that it was Coburn, and not James Caan, who got Sam hooked on cocaine in the early 1970s, it should also be said that Coburn helped Sam get through both *Cross of Iron* and *Convoy* in the late 1970s, when Sam most needed support.

You could argue that most of Sam's films were troubled productions, but in truth he got through some of them with more creative control and less conflict with producers than others—*Ride the High Country* and *The Wild Bunch* immediately come to mind. The weather stymied Sam on *The Ballad of Cable Hogue*, but it's still very much his picture, and a fine one at that. There may have been headaches and bumps during the making of *Junior Bonner* and *The Getaway* in 1972, but he got them done without too much angst. And with a major force like Steve McQueen serving as an anchor, Sam wasn't going to go too far off.

Pat Garrett and Billy the Kid really was the first big cinematic mess Sam got involved in since *Major Dundee*. He wanted to shoot it in New Mexico, but at that time MGM, who produced the film, deemed it cheaper to shoot in Mexico. Rudolph Wurlitzer, who had written the cult film *Two-Lane Backdrop* (a financial flop in its time), wrote the original script for *Pat Garrett*, and Gordon Carroll, who had produced *Cool Hand Luke*, served as producer. With Coburn and some familiar, loyal friends on board—Slim Pickens, L. Q. Jones, Jason Robards Jr., Chill Wills, R. G Armstrong, and Emilio Fernández, to name a few—Sam must have felt pretty confident going into the film.

All that changed over time, as many Peckinpah historians (including David Weddle) have already documented. James Aubrey, the head of MGM, was known as "the smiling cobra" for his disdain for creative artists and his penchant for backbiting. "Aubrey was a challenge to Sam, and Aubrey saw Sam as a challenge, too," Coburn told Weddle years later.

Sam was rarely good when working with limited budgets and deadlines, so when MGM cut both back on him and refused to give him the technical support he needed to ensure the 40mm Panavision camera and lens were operating properly, he reacted in typical rebel style—defying Aubrey's orders, taking his time and going over schedule, and, of course, pushing up beyond the initial budget of $3 million. The climate and influenza also took a toll on the cast and crew. Sam was drinking, and, if Walter Peter is correct, starting with cocaine thanks to Coburn. But Sam got the picture done early in 1973, bringing back a rough cut of about three and a half hours that Aubrey would cut in half by the time the picture was released later that year. I remember when Katy Haber called to invite me and Slim Pickens to the first screening of the finished product at Metro. I heard that Sam had his troubles trying to keep it all together in Mexico, and, wanting to show him support, I spent time searching for a special gift for him. I found a machete in a store on Melrose and had it engraved (it cost me a small fortune). I had it wrapped up and—imagine this—walked onto the lot at Metro carrying a machete for Sam Peckinpah. Slim and I went into the office behind the screening room at Metro. Fern Lea, Walter Peter, and a few other people were there. I had written a poem and enclosed it in this long, slim package, suggesting that if MGM had cut his film unfairly, he could take this machete out and cut off the producers' heads. Sam opened the gift, the slightest smile passing over his lips, and almost immediately passed it on to a nearby assistant. He did not say thank you; that wasn't his way. Then he pulled me into a side room, turned up a transistor radio he had in there, and said, "They're bugging me—they've got all my rooms bugged." This was the first time I realized he was actually infected with this paranoid belief. He told me, "They've cut my film, though I don't think they cut Slim's part. He has a great part." He was right—Slim's role as an aging sheriff who wants to avoid gunplay and retire on the river was marvelous.

But that small victory for Sam didn't help him or the picture. MGM cut seventeen minutes that were particularly special to Sam before they released the movie. I couldn't believe this was happening to Sam again, though I don't think the film was destroyed by those cuts in the way that *Major Dundee* was. Some of the critics did notice the abrupt jumps and commented in their reviews that this was a byproduct of the conflict between Sam and Aubrey. *Pat Garrett* received mixed reviews and, according to Weddle's biography of Sam, may have made a very slight profit at the box office. The only good news to come out of this is that Slim Pickens's asking price did go up after the beautiful scene where his wife in the film, played by Katy Jurado, cries as she watches him die from a gunshot wound. And it was L. Q. Jones who shot him.

Sam had taken a great gamble in casting Kris Kristofferson as Billy the Kid and an even greater gamble in casting Bob Dylan as a reporter who turns outlaw. Sam thought Dylan was a great symbol of a press that was making up phony accounts of the Old West; he basically cast him to stand around and observe. You'd have to see the entire film with all the original footage restored to understand how well that casting works.

Sam was dead by the time the first screening of a restored version of the film took place in Los Angeles in 1986. In the early 1990s, Ted Turner, who by then owned the MGM film library, agreed to finance a complete restoration of the film. The restored version was screened in the spring of April 1995 during the first Taos Talking Pictures Festival in northern New Mexico, founded by Josh Bryant and Melinda Mullins. James Coburn was invited to the festival to receive its first Maverick Award. (Over the years, that festival would also honor Elizabeth Taylor, Edward James Olmos, and Susan Sarandon.) Josh Bryant called me in Albuquerque and asked if I would drive up to present the award to Coburn. I had misspent my youth in Taos just as hard as I could misspend it, so of course I wanted to go back. I decided that, in my presentation, I would not make a speech. I was almost speechless by the fact that one of Sam's films had been saved. I remember saying, "Jim Coburn and I are amazingly strong survivors of the Sam Peckinpah clan. We maintained our friendship with Sam throughout his life." Coburn laughed, and that's when I asked him how we had survived Sam Peckinpah. It was during a post-screening party that he replied, "Maybe we should ask how Sam survived us." I had not seen Coburn in some time, and this is when I first noticed that his hands were crippled with arthritis. He reiterated that he would not have been able to maintain his career if it hadn't been for the healing hands of R. G. Armstrong. Later, when we were alone, Coburn said to me, "Max, Sam *was* crazy, but we were crazier than he was." I shut up.

There were a lot of film lovers in that crowd in Taos, and you could feel the ripple of excitement as the film began. That's when I saw the film for what it is: a wonderful, leisure-paced saga of transition, friendship, and betrayal, and I love it to this day. *Pat Garrett and Billy the Kid* had come back after having its limbs cut off more than twenty years before.

Josh Bryant had already enjoyed an impressive career as an actor in film, television, and on stage. He starred or guest starred on a ton of television shows, including a recurring role as Sergeant Scully on *M*A*S*H** and a role as Mary Tyler Moore's boyfriend on her series, *The Mary Tyler Moore Show*. His partner, actress and fine painter Melinda (known as Em), is a Julliard graduate who appeared in the long-running AMC cable series *Remember WENN* and played Lady MacBeth opposite Raúl

Juliá on the stage. The goal of the Taos Talking Pictures Festival was to set a comfortable, relaxed atmosphere where film artists and audience members could visit and have fun around film. The festival also became renowned for hosting seminars that looked at the role of media in culture. It lasted nine years, gathering debt (much like Sam Peckinpah!) before it closed its doors in November 2003—a year after James Coburn died. Josh and Em bought a piece of land out in the Taos desert northwest of the Rio Grande gorge, and Josh built a great house with a big porch up there that looked out over the magnificent views. They bought some mustangs and had dogs, and they took care of those animals better than any person ever cared for a child. I remember taking them out once to a place about seven or eight miles north of their home, where I had established a perlite mine in the 1950s. They knew about it, and they drove me over. The Yucca was already growing up all around it; it looked like a miniature version of White Sands in southern New Mexico. I remember saying to them, "You've got your own beach here. No water, but a beach." Em agreed and said, "We'll get us an umbrella and have a beach party." Years later, some filmmakers got in touch with me to discuss making a documentary about me, so we had reason to go back to that site. The offroaders had found it by then and had driven over all that beautiful white sand, turning it grey. It broke my heart. I'm happy to say that my creative friends, Josh and Em, had already moved from Taos to France—taking their mustangs with them—so they did not witness this man-made destruction of the earth. They are now happy, creating in the beautiful south of France. (The documentary about me never got made due to a complicated case of mistaken politics.)

I never ran into Coburn again after the festival, but I was pleased when he won an Oscar for his supporting role in Paul Schrader's 1997 drama *Affliction*. There's a great story I heard about Schrader interviewing Jim for the part, and urging him to really get into the character, to which Jim said, "You want me to act? I can do that. I haven't been asked to do it very often, but I can do it." And he did. When he accepted his Oscar at the awards ceremony in 1998, he said, "Some of them [movies] you do for money, some of them you do for love. This is a love child." I'd like to believe that he felt the same about the films he made for Sam, as flawed as they may be.

17. Why Bob Boles Never Became a Movie Star

Director and writer Burt Kennedy, who was a helluva nice guy, came out to New Mexico sometime in 1964 to scout locations for the film version of my novel *The Rounders*. The film didn't end up getting shot here, but Burt became one of my best friends from my Hollywood days. We were meeting at Maria's Mexican Kitchen in Santa Fe, the place to be for working cowboys, politicians, mining promoters, and all kinds of go-getters. I remember introducing Burt to Don Hammond (yes, *that* Don Hammond), who eventually bought Maria's and ran it for many years.

We were in the back room, Burt and me, sitting in a little booth by the bar, and I happened to look into the dining room, and there was Bobby Boles. He had been raised near Truth or Consequences, New Mexico, and he was a cowboy, an athlete, and a charmer. He was about thirty and already had pure white hair. Women fell madly in love with him. So did his wife.

Burt asked me, "Who is that guy?"

I said, "A cowboy, a hustler, a con man."

Burt said, "You know, if he's got a good voice, I can make him as popular as John Wayne."

As Burt and I were eating, Bob walked out with two or three other people and got away from us. I didn't realize at that time how Bob Boles would impact my life or Sam Peckinpah's life.

Later that night, we stopped in at La Fonda Hotel, where Burt was staying, for a nightcap. A message came in that Glenn Ford had called. He wanted to know what kind of chaps to wear for his role in *The Rounders*. That's how sincere Ford was about this part. He wanted everything to be authentic.

Bob Boles came into La Fonda with a briefcase in his hand. He nodded to me, ushering me into the lobby there. I followed him, and he slipped a small revolver into my pocket.

"I need you to do me a favor," he said.

Now Burt was worried about Bob Boles's voice, but it must have been pretty good because he convinced me to deliver this briefcase to Tiny at Tiny's restaurant. (Tiny's restaurant is still in Santa Fe, but at a different location, as of this writing.)

"What's the pistol for?" I asked.

"Just to ensure that there's no trouble delivering the briefcase. Don't give it to him until you get into his office."

Crazy as it sounds, my sense of loyalty led me to say, "OK." I started walking to Tiny's. It began to snow. I got to Tiny's, and the bartender sent me into Tiny's office. I said, "Bob Boles told me to bring you this brief-case." Tiny took it, put it in a desk drawer, and never said a word about it. He offered to buy me a drink, which became two or three drinks.

Then who walks in but Bob Boles with a beautiful blonde woman who was married to a prominent Santa Fe golf pro. Somebody in the bar said, "Hi, blondie," and Bob hit the guy in the mouth. In less than a second, a pack of people grabbed Bob and had him stretched out. I think they were going to hang him. And that's when I made one of many great mistakes in my life: I pulled the revolver out of my pocket and told them to drop him or I'd blow them away. They believed me and dropped him, somebody called the cops, and Bob and I got out of there just in time. He disappeared into the snowy dark, and I wandered around for a while before feeling safe enough to walk back to La Fonda.

I got to the front door of La Fonda, and lo and behold, there sitting in a parked car by the front door was Bob Boles lovin' on that blonde woman. I had to fight the instinct to go over there and shoot him with his own gun. I thought to myself, "I don't think I'll introduce him to Burt."

The next day, Burt, Richard Lyons, and I, as well as some film-location people, jumped in a company van to drive to Pecos to scout locales for *The Rounders*. It was still snowing. There was about ten to eighteen inches on the ground, and when the vehicle got bogged down around Rowe, I had a sinking feeling that we weren't going to film *The Rounders* in New Mexico—and I was right. A snowplow truck showed up, helped pull us out of the white stuff, and began clearing the road to Santa Fe.

We followed the plow back. The film's producer, Richard Lyons—who had also produced Sam's *Ride the High Country*—told me that the studio couldn't afford to waste even a day of shooting on uncertain weather conditions. The film was modestly budgeted with a limited schedule, despite having two big stars—Glenn Ford and Henry Fonda. He told Burt and me, "We've already checked out Arizona. It's clear there. We're going to film it there." And that's what happened with that dream.

Well, the next morning, I was having breakfast with Burt at La Fonda and in came Bob Boles just bouncing around. I was pissed. I realized I still had the revolver in my pocket, so as he walked by I took it out, slammed it down on the table, and said, "There's your damned gun. Now get out of here!" Bobby just smiled and said, "Thank you," and left. Burt never brought him up again, and there went Bobby's shot at movie fame—though he never knew it.

Some years later, I ran into Bob Boles again at the bar in the Albuquerque Hilton. By then, he had a good-looking redheaded wife who knew what he was and stayed in love with him for the rest of her life. They told me they wanted me to introduce them to Sam. They knew Sam was working in Mexico—I think this was while he was shooting *The Wild Bunch* down there—and they wanted to solicit his help in smuggling mercury out of that country in film cans. Mercury was a popular black-market product in those days.

Bobby was working with a local dairyman in Albuquerque on this deal (and probably on a lot of other deals, too). They figured nobody would inspect the film cans Sam was sending back to the studio. People did that kind of thing in those days. In fact, they still do, only now they're smuggling dope and guns. Smuggling was considered an honorable American profession then. Now, well . . . I told Sam about these two guys, and he got excited. He got to thinking about how the hell he could take part in this smuggling operation with the film cans.

Bobby couldn't help himself when it came to smuggling. He and this dairy guy got caught with some $50,000 bank certificates from Texas that they weren't supposed to have on them. They were sent off to jail, bailed out, and were set to go to trial. Bobby vanished; he didn't show up for the trial. The dairy guy was trying to hold it together, but he didn't know where Bobby had gone. Now around this time, Sam's daughter

Kristen decided she wanted a pony. Sam asked me if I could help, and I told him, "I'll get her a pony." I started to think of this dairy guy, who had some ponies, and I told him I wanted one. He owed me a favor—I can't remember why, but he did—and I gave him a deadline for the birthday gift. He was under the gun, being sued, worried about going to court, and he told me, "I can't do it. I need everything I've got." I said, "You will deliver, because if that pony does not arrive that little girl will lose faith in humanity. And if you don't deliver the pony by tomorrow, all your troubles will be over because I'm going to kill you."

I was bluffing, but he believed me. He came through and ran that pony out to her in California in a pickup and trailer.

The dairy guy disappeared shortly thereafter.

Now it turns out that Bobby had moved to Mexico with his wife, and he was flying dope in a biplane. Besides being a good calf roper, Bobby was a licensed pilot. At first, the Mexican government turned a blind eye, but then one day they set a trap for him. What happened was he started fooling around with some higher-up's wife. You don't do that in Mexico—not even now. But you can't blame poor ol' Bobby Boles be-cause all these beautiful women just fell down in front of him. He was a kindhearted ol' boy, and he couldn't help being of help. He'd just pick those women up and comfort them, being the tenderhearted soul that he was. So off he went to jail. Both Sam and Emilio Fernández, who knew a lot of the higher-ups in Mexico, confirmed this story for me.

They sentenced him to ten years, and to the best of my knowledge he served every day of it. His wife stood by him. He had spoken Spanish since childhood, so communication wasn't a problem. While in prison, he made rugs (or more likely had them made), and she sold them on the outside to make a living. Bobby would sometimes write me, and I would sometimes send him twenty dollars. Sam went to visit him in prison, and Bobby told Sam that I was a chickenshit for not sending him more money!

Bobby Boles began writing his life story while he was in prison. Sam liked the idea and gave him $2,000 in cash for the manuscript, and he never read a page of it! So Bobby was one rich lawbreaker in prison.

Around this time, Sam was looping *Bring Me the Head of Alfredo Gar-cia* (1974) at the old Goldwyn Studios in Hollywood. He invited a bunch of us to lunch at Formosa, a popular but plain place, to meet some people, including Kris Kristofferson, who had been in Sam's film *Pat Garrett and Billy the Kid*. The rumors suggested that *Alfredo Garcia* had been a troubled production.

Kris and Bobby Fritz, his guitarist, were at Formosa. So was Emilio Fernández, who sat on my left, and on the other side of him was actor Gig Young, which surprised me, because he didn't fit Sam at all. Gig had a part in *Alfredo Garcia* a few years before he killed himself. Gig was drunk and kept interrupting everyone at the table, including Emilio Fernández—and if you knew anything about Emilio, you knew not to show any rudeness at all. But somehow Gig got away with it.

Sam was staying in the Marilyn Monroe Suite at 20th Century Fox at the time. I think he was talking with them about a picture. He invited me to stay with him there. The Marilyn Monroe suite was on the far southwest corner of the lot. I walked in, and it was filled with boxes of Sam's papers and scripts and production notes that Katy Haber had moved there for him. It was a two-bedroom suite with a kitchen and a living room; it was often quiet.

I remember at night I'd be sleeping on a cot there with my head by the wall that faced Century Boulevard, and I could hear the traffic passing by all night long—so close that at times I felt a car would take my head off.

After lunch one day, Sam, Kris, and I went to a really fancy clothing store in Beverly Hills that was closed for the day. The owners opened the place for Sam, but I could tell they were pissed. Sam needed a tuxedo, and we were clearly drunk. It turns out that Sam needed the tux to attend the AFI Life Achievement Award banquet for James Cagney at the Century Plaza Hotel the next night. Cagney was only the second person to receive that award at that time. The AFI had given it to John Ford the year before.

So the owners let us in, locked the door behind us, and tended to Sam. Kris had gone out to rustle up a bottle of whiskey at a nearby liquor store, and when he returned, we got bored, so I said to him, "We ought to get something out of this." So we stole socks from the store. We filled our pockets with them. I have no idea what we did with them. Sam got his tux fitted and we drove back to the Fox lot and the Marilyn Monroe

Suite. The three of us got drunk, and then even more drunk. Sam played Kris Kristofferson records on his record player. I could tell Kris did not want to hear his own music, but Sam would do that with a musical artist he liked—whether it was Kris or Bob Dylan or Roger Miller or the Beatles, he'd play the same damn records over and over again until you wanted to break his phonograph, no matter how much you might admire the musician.

I got more than socks out of the deal that night. On one of the walls in Sam's bungalow was a framed photo that photojournalist John Bryson took of Ernest Hemingway kicking a can. I believe it was one of only thirty copies made. The photo was signed "To Sam." I met Bryson, and he had promised me a copy of this photo, but he never delivered, so I took it off the wall and told Sam, "You can always get another one. I can't. I'm taking this." Sam never said a thing. That photo is still hanging on our kitchen wall. Coincidentally, Bryson also shot some famous photos of Marilyn Monroe and did a bang-up job acting in Sam's film *The Getaway*.

Kris got very drunk that night and said he had to get back to his wife, Rita Coolidge, who was pregnant with their daughter, Casey. We got a cab for him and sent him off. We later heard he got home, stumbled over some furniture there, and passed out on the floor. She found him the next morning in that condition, and I don't know whether this is true or not, but I have heard that it was one of the last straws for her and helped convince her that she wanted a divorce.

The next day, Sam, still drunk, caught a cab to pick up Isela Vega, the Mexican star of *Alfredo Garcia*. He had quite a day. He was waiting in the bar at her hotel for her to come downstairs, and he got into a fistfight there with some guy. This was caught on camera by a photographer for one of the Los Angeles papers. For some reason, they didn't put him in jail. Vega showed up, and she and Sam went off to the AFI event for Cagney.

Jack Lemmon was scheduled to introduce Cagney and say something nice about him. Well, he said a lot. I met Lemmon once. He was playing piano in a bar when a mutual friend introduced him to me, and Lemmon never shut up that night—he was drunk. He may have been drunk the night he introduced Cagney, because he went on and on and on. And Sam, who was sitting there in his tux with a red bandana tied around his head, had had enough. He jumped up and yelled out as loudly as he could, "Jack, we didn't come here to hear you talk about yourself. Shut up and get off the stage!"

Well, everyone in Hollywood was at that event, and they all turned around and looked at Sam Peckinpah—another nail in the coffin. How he got out of there alive, we'll never know. He managed to alienate everyone at the AFI in less time than it takes to run one hundred meters.

When Sam came back to the suite with Vega, I knew something was wrong. I don't know if he had tried to make a pass at her or what, but she suddenly turned on him and let loose a bunch of curse words in Spanish. Then, in English, she simply said, "Call me a cab now." And he did.

The fun during that time kept going. Sam had three or four knives— one was so big that the blade couldn't stick into anything solid. When producers came to visit him there at the bungalow, he could spot them by the way they knocked on the door—or so he claimed. He'd greet them by throwing the knife at the door. You can imagine their surprise standing on the other side, being welcomed by a blade coming through the door. Why any producer would come to visit him is beyond me. I don't believe he ever got a deal with Fox to make a picture, and you can see why.

Sam screened a rough cut of *Alfredo Garcia* and managed to insult the intelligence of his friends and relatives by inviting us. I sat next to Frank Kowalski, Sam's dialogue director, friend, and court jester, who had come up with the concept for the film. I didn't like the picture, and I felt a terrible sinking feeling in my stomach as I watched it. Up until this time, like him or not, Sam had made some great works, nothing less than solid—*The Getaway* and *Junior Bonner* in 1972 and *Pat Garrett and Billy the Kid* in 1973—but this one just wasn't well done. When the screening was over, Frank turned to me and said, "I'll sell you my interest in the film for one hundred dollars." That was proof enough of the great slide into the abyss. Sam had started on this slide of gravel and glass, and there would be no turning back.

Sam asked me my opinion of the film. I said, "Well, you still kill people with the same ol' beauty." That was the best I could do. He knew what I thought because of what I didn't say.

Everybody's life includes big changes. I do believe *Alfredo Garcia* represented a big change for Sam. His glory days were over. Yet I owe him—and the film's screenwriter, Gordon Dawson—an apology. Pat and I watched *Alfredo Garcia* again recently and I enjoyed it, especially Warren Oates's performance. I forgot what Sam often did in the editing of a rough and misunderstood cut of a film. The film is now unforgettable to me.

Isela Vega should have become a bigger star. I remember after Sam's memorial service early in 1985, several of us went to her house to visit. David Weddle drove us. I sat with her for several hours and found her to be an enormously talented person, a great lady, and an individualist. I finally figured out why she didn't make it in Hollywood. She was too honest and blunt. Nobody could buy her. There was no way she could fit in there and become the star she should have been. I don't know what's happened to her since. At least Warren got to star in a cult film playing his hero—Sam Peckinpah.

During all this madness, Bobby Boles was with us—in manuscript form. It was while we were in the Marilyn Monroe Suite that Sam asked me to read Bobby's life story. It was about two thousand pages long. I could barely pick it up. It started when Bobby was just a kid near Truth or Consequences, New Mexico; there was some damn authentic stuff in there. Somehow I finished it, and it annoyed me that I had to take the time to read it because I had sold a film option to one of my short stories and I needed that time to get back to my own work. I approached Sam one day when he was sober and said, "There's about a fourth of this that's really good. You need to cut about 1,500 pages out of it. You need to hire a good editor to cut, paste, and fix it." I told him I didn't want the job. He said, "If you're not going to do it, it'll never get done." He didn't get mad about it, but I think he somehow took perverse enjoyment in knowing that I was reading another author's work and not writing myself.

Sam liked Bobby. He was attracted to these types of con men and thugs. How else can you explain his love for Emilio Fernández, the meanest son of a bitch on earth? Emilio carried a gun with him at all times and once shot a bus driver on the set of *The Wild Bunch* for no reason. Sam told me the Mexican government approached Emilio and politely asked him to stop shooting people. When I had met Emilio at the Formosa, gregarious and grinning as he was, he scared me. I was a dead shot, so I think Emilio would have gotten to like me for that one reason alone. I remember he liked the hat I wore at that time. Somebody stole it. It was probably Emilio.

Sam could get into dark moods. Around the time I finished reading Bobby's book, Sam fell into a black hole. Things were just not working out. The door was full of knives he'd thrown at producers. He was drinking, and there was nobody there for him. Katy was having one of her "stay away" times. One weakness Sam had was he could not handle being alone. And I was the only one around. He and I would walk around the big lot; the studio security guards wouldn't bother us. One night, around midnight, while we were walking out there, he turned to me and said, "I've hired a hit man. I've paid him $5,000 to blow your head off after I'm gone."

I said, "You're too late. I've already paid a hit man $10,000 to kill you right now."

He never said another word to me about it. But why would this son of a bitch do something like that to a friend like me? I covered for him. I wrote for him. I read that damn Bobby Boles book for him. I thought that's what friends did—not kill one another! (Although there have been times when that thought has made me smile.)

I tried to cheer Sam up during these dark times. Early in 1974, he received some letters, care of the Motion Picture Association, from animal-rights activists who expressed outrage that live chickens were used for target practice in *Pat Garrett and Billy the Kid*. (One of these letters, which I still have, ends with the writer signing off with, "By the way, I hope your picture is a flop.") I helped Sam draft a satirical letter in response, in long hand. (No one could read Sam's handwriting, with the exception of Katy Haber.) I had been reading articles about people talking to their plants around that time, so I wrote that the guy running this animal-rights organization was probably verbally abusing his plants, and that when he walked on his lawn, the grass was screaming, and when he ate cold cereal the wheat stems in it were wailing in anguish. The studio secretary typed it up for us and mailed it off. I don't believe we ever got a response. Sam got a kick out of that, but it wasn't enough to deflect the blows hitting him from all directions.

Bobby Boles never became a star. His book never got published. Sometime in the late 1990s, I got a call from a guy who said he was a friend of Bobby Boles, and that Bobby was out of prison, had found an aluminum mine in Belize, and wanted me to help him develop it. Bobby probably had found a mine—somebody else's. I was told sometime later that Bobby died of a heart attack and is in Belize for eternity. I don't know what happened to his wife, or the dairyman. Maybe they're all together somewhere celebrating a score.

Whether Sam helped Bobby smuggle mercury out of Mexico in film canisters, I cannot say. I don't want to know. And if I did know, I'd plead the fifth.

18. Beverly Hills Max

The place: the Polo Lounge of the Beverly Hills Hotel. The time: the late 1970s. They got to where they liked me in there; the help could sense who was genuine and who was not. There was a certain gentleman from West Texas whose father had run a huge chain of theaters, which this gentleman inherited. This gent and I were born about a mile apart on the same day, and he thought that made us kin. He stayed in the Beverly Hills Hotel, where he ran $1,000-a-day whores. He'd make out like they were his girlfriends and go out on the town with them. There was a phone in the bar, and a bunch of guys always hung out around that phone. They were running the operation with those $1,000 whores out of the bar. These call girls were beautiful women, and most of them were very well educated. They had a guy named Andresson who was the head pimp. Andresson took a liking to me. The theater guy who was born the same day as I was wanted to be a producer, and he fell in love with my 1965 book *The Mountain of Gold*. He knew the Mexican film director Roberto Gavaldon, who was a very gracious man, and he arranged a meeting between us. He actually flew him in from his palatial home in Mexico. We met over the course of two days in the Polo Lounge to discuss what a filmscript of that story would look like. I liked and respected Roberto. He had class. But I didn't quite have faith in my would-be producer pal. He said he would option the rights to the book, hire Roberto to direct, and Roberto would hire a screenwriter from Mexico to write the script. We talked about casting Ricardo Montalban, whom I had met at Burt Kennedy's party after he wrapped *The Money Trap* (1966), as the lead actor for the film. Montalban was a first-class multitalented gentleman, and he loved the whole idea.

This little book had quite a history. Several major publishers wanted me to increase the length before they would publish it. I refused. After Houghton Mifflin turned it down for the same reason, one of their editors, a noted Southern bookman named Norman Berg of Atlanta, called me. He said he wanted to launch his own private publishing firm and publish my book. Berg had carried Margaret Mitchell's huge manuscript of *Gone with the Wind* in a suitcase to an Atlanta hotel to show it to Macmillan's editor-in-chief, Harold Latham. Latham was numbed by its length but agreed to start reading it on his trip back to New York. Upon reading it, he agreed to publish it if Berg would take on the huge task of editing. After this world history–altering event, Berg published over one hundred books at his Sellanraa Press, which included thirteen out-of-print Pulitzer Prize winners and two Nobel Prize winners. This is what we were dealing with in the company of mob pimps, a drunken wannabe producer, and a scrambling writer.

Anyway, my friend took me up to his hotel room to discuss the deal. "How much do you want for an option on this book?"

"$10,000 for six months, payable right this minute," I said, as I was short of cash.

He wrote me out a check there and then. Then he called down to the lounge and hired a hooker to celebrate. He was going to pay, of course. Everybody paid because the mob was sitting right there by the phone. They knew me, and they liked me, but they didn't like this producer, I could tell. To them he was a rich, cheap, big-mouthed son of a bitch. They knew we were upstairs talking business. When I came down to the lounge, they were like a little bunch of blackbirds sitting on a fence: "How'd it go?" I showed them the check for $10,000 and said, "That's pretty good for two days' work, and you guys get $1,000." (Because the producer called down for a girl, mind you.) I never had to pay for a drink during this period; I was accepted as one of them.

Andresson had a good-looking daughter who wanted to work in the movies. He once saw me meeting with Burt Kennedy there in the lounge, and he asked if I would introduce him to Burt. I did, and Burt said he'd give the girl a bit part in his next picture. I don't remember if he did or not. Sam didn't go into the lounge a lot, but sometimes you'd see him in there, having a few drinks. I was just as glad he didn't hang out there—I was a little afraid that the gang would break his neck, particularly after he messed up a deal involving one of the ladies from the hotel.

One day, Sam called me and said he was lonely. "Tell that pimp I want the best he's got for a night," he said. That was Sam—all charm. I set it up for him. The deal was that we would all meet around 2:30 in the afternoon at the old Holiday House. The price was $1,200. I was on time, and Sam was almost on time. From the bar in that hotel you could see out the window into the garden by the parking lot. All of a sudden, here comes this woman walking down the rock stairway and through the desert shrubs toward the bar. She had class, looks, and intelligence.

"Is that her?" Sam asked.

"Yeah."

He leaned over and gave me a complimentary pat.

I thought my job was done. Sam asked me to have one more drink as she arrived. He went to the bathroom, and I was sitting there with her, and we started talking books.

"Who are you reading now?" she asked.

"Joyce Cary, an unknown Irish writer."

"I love his work!" she said, to my astonishment.

So we began talking about Joyce Cary.

Sam came in, saw us together talking, and threw his car keys on the bar. "A man can't even take a piss without you trying to steal his girl!" he screamed.

He wasn't joking. He was really, really mad. Sam could be very generous, but he was extremely jealous when it came to hookers, of all things. Sam began saying very rude things to this woman. I told him not to talk that way to a lady. Sam grabbed his keys and stormed off, leaving me with both the bar tab and a $1,200 bill for the lady.

She looked at me and could tell right away that I didn't have that kind of money.

"I can't pay you the $1,200," I said. I wasn't sure I could even pay the bar bill.

"Don't worry," she said. "Andresson already explained to me that Sam Peckinpah might be a mad man."

As it turns out, I had fifty dollars in my wallet, but after paying for our drinks, I only had about thirty dollars. I walked her to her car and gave her the thirty. It was like giving an elephant one peanut out of the bag. She didn't want to take it, but she did just to make me feel better. Sam had really goofed a dandy deal.

The next time I visited the Polo Lounge, one of the mob guys told me not to worry about it, that it was OK, but that if Sam ever came around again they would fix his ass. I was relieved Sam didn't get that woman. If he had abused her in any way, I would have had to do something to him—something painful, before someone else really hurt him.

To show me that everything was OK, Andresson invited me to an orgy upstairs. I declined. Those guys were good to me; they offered me a freebie with a particular woman I liked there anytime I wanted it. But I knew better than to accept anything more than drinks from them. You don't want to "owe" these types of guys anything.

The Mountain of Gold went nowhere. Something happened between my producer pal and Roberto Gavaldon. I don't think the producer was serious about it. I think he paid me the $10,000 so he could look like somebody big in the film world for a little while.

I left Hollywood for a while, and sometime later, when I went back on business, I visited the hotel. The bartender was there, but none of the old crew was. I said, "What happened to the crew?"

"Didn't you hear?" the bartender said. "They got busted. It was in all the Beverly Hills newspapers."

I tried to find out what happened to Andresson, but I never did. Maybe they sent him to the pen. The last I heard of him, he had come through Taos looking for me. Luckily we were out of town but we heard about a short notice in the *Taos News* that said Mr. So-and-So Andresson was in town to visit his friend and associate Max Evans.

As for the changes at the old Polo Lounge, well, I was devastated, of course—that place was a helluva deal for an old country kid like me.

19. Two Guys, Two Girls, and Me in the Middle

The Sands Motel and connecting restaurant/bar were responsible for my friendship with Ed Honeck. He was working as a PR man for rock bands with an office on Sunset Boulevard. He liked me and the Sands bartender, Cliff, and would go there to escape what he had to believe was a wonderful form of madness: the rock world. Ed was then in his early forties, and he never felt like he fit in with that world. When I speak of the bar at the Sands as a second home, you have to understand that the waitresses there were between forty and fifty years old, married with kids, and solid. They took care of you. Although celebrities came in there to eat for business meetings, including Duke Wayne, they did so because it *wasn't* a celebrity place.

Ed found out from Cliff that I was a writer. So was he, albeit in public relations. We hit it off right away. Ed was then negotiating a deal with the owner of the international manufacturing firm Tapmatic, headquartered in Riverside and owned and operated by Al Johnson, to take care of their PR. It was a different kind of PR—they ran no commercials or ads in television, radio, or newspaper outlets. Tapmatic manufactured machine-tool accessories, mainly tapping heads and precision metal-working instruments. Ed's job was to draw up catalogues for their customers worldwide. He got to travel with Al Johnson to just about every country in the world. Ed loved to travel, so it was an ideal spot for him to be.

Al Johnson and Ed Honeck became close friends because of actress Sally Fraser several years before Al hired Ed. Sally had been in some movies including *It's a Dog's Life* at MGM with Edmund Gwenn, Dean Jagger, and Richard Anderson. She also appeared in the 1950s cult horror films *War of the Colossal Beast* and *Giant from the Unknown*, as well as *Dangerous Charter*—the first film shot in Panavision. Robert Gottschalk was the producer of that film and the inventor of the Panavision photographic process.

Ed told Al about Sally while doing a play with her in Laguna Beach and invited Al to the cast party. Al arrived to find Sally sitting in Ed's lap. Al decided he needed to get to know this guy better because they both appreciated the same woman so much. Al married Sally and they have remained together ever since.

The couple built a ranch compound for entertaining friends and business associates in Wildwood, Idaho. It has a main house, a large guesthouse, and a great western bar with a full kitchen and movie screen. One of the motion pictures they would run for these invited guests was *The Rounders*, which Sam wanted to make before Fess Parker got ahold of it.

Ed was about 6'3", real slim, and he wore glasses. He loved everything to do with literature and music. Histories and biographies of World War II were his favorite books. His house was full of artifacts from around the world. He was an avid California Angels fan. He would invite me over to his place, which was wonderfully isolated. Whenever I'd get completely caught up in the entertainment business, or when I'd go broke, Ed's house became a haven for me.

Ed married young, and he and his wife divorced. We never talked about it. He had girlfriends. On his mantle in one of his rooms was a photograph of the Mexican actress Elsa Cardenas, who had appeared in Sam's *The Wild Bunch*. Ed and I never discussed Elsa in great depth, but when he did speak of her, it was with great reverence and regret. He felt that he had somehow messed it up when he dated her.

Little did I know that Sam was having an affair with Elsa. He never hit on or had affairs with his leading ladies, but supporting players were another thing altogether. Ed would later fall in love with a singer, Marti Perkins, who would live with him for about six years. There's nothing unusual about that, but she had also dated and worked for Sam Peckinpah. She had a beautiful singing voice, but it wasn't strong enough to carry her into the big time. She played clubs and recorded some demos. One, called "Rivers in the Sky," I wrote myself. She did get some wonderful benefits out of the relationship with Ed—she got to go on some of the European trips with Ed and Al. She probably imagined that one day she and Ed would marry and live somewhat happily ever after. But he was tormented about whether to marry her or not.

And he waited too damn long. One day, he came home from work, and he didn't find Marti. He found a note. It read, "Ed, remember Scott and Zelda. Love, Marti." He showed the letter to me. It was a terrible shock. She had moved back east, and that was that.

I damn sure never told either Sam or Ed about either woman. Here were my two friends, both vastly different in so many ways yet also quite alike. Both were perfectionists. Sometimes Ed would suggest that he'd like to meet Sam. Well, everybody wanted to meet Sam until they met him. It was tough to work this out. I didn't want Sam to feel like I was shoving somebody on him, and I didn't want Ed to feel uncomfortable. Since Sam had dated Elsa—when it was convenient for him—and sometimes dated Marti, I was a little apprehensive about introducing Ed to Sam. But it finally happened.

In the late 1970s I was staying at a different hotel off of Sunset, the Solana Inn on Church Lane. I had a deal to write a screenplay about mules called *Hey, Mule!*, and this place was close to the producer and director Bud Cardos's house. I had an admiration for mules, and I wasn't the only one. People come from around the world to celebrate Mule Days in Bishop, California, to this day, to pay tribute to the creature. My story would be a revelation of the connection between the human beast and this beast of burden—and full of honest fun. Cardos was a good cowboy, and he had made some low-budget horror and Western films, including some for the renowned Al Adamson. One movie that was successful was called *Kingdom of the Spiders*. Actor Robert Dix, a tall, handsome guy who was the son of the late, now mostly forgotten, movie star Richard Dix, had worked with Bud on some of those films. Now he was involved with our mule story.

At one point, Pat and I were visiting Bishop Mule Days when Monte Montana came over to do some tricks for the film. Dix pulled out $5,000 or $6,000 in cash, gave it to Monte, and told him to go ride around and do tricks. Then Dix, surprisingly, asked me if I needed any money. I stupidly said no. I was working on the script for scale and a half plus expenses. I was having such a good time that I didn't care about getting paid. Bud did some preliminary movie shots there—he shot me riding a mule and shot Monte riding a mule. It didn't matter. Little did we know that Dix would be too generous with the production money. Well, he didn't give all of it away—he just spent it! The project came to a halt. You might think that I would have gotten upset, enraged, gone mad, gone drunk, or ended up in jail when this big handsome guy dissipated all of our money. But it was just part of the game called Hollywood, and we had enjoyed another adventure with all concerned—including Dix.

Anyway, I was working on the first draft of this script back at the hotel when the Filipino guy working at the front desk called me in my room and said, "Sam Peckinpah is here. He keeps asking for you. I told him you were working, and he said he wouldn't bother you." To this day, I don't know how Sam knew I was working there. I didn't call him for two days. I was afraid he'd mess up my head and consequently screw up my script. Eventually, I ran into him. He was with this redheaded gal at the hotel. Sam was staying on the second floor in the far corner for a few days, and we made arrangements to meet later that afternoon. Then it dawned on me that I had already invited Ed Honeck to have a drink with me in the early evening.

Come seven or snake eyes, however the dice fell, it was time to play. So I invited Ed early and we called on Sam in his room. The woman was gone. Ed and Sam hit it off right away, but I could tell Sam was on co-caine. At one point, guys who are on coke feel like they are doing great—before they start going mad. I hinted to Sam that Ed, like me, didn't do dope. He got it. It was a memorable moment in Ed's life because he admired *The Wild Bunch* so much; he knew every scene. Ed had a way of laughing and getting stuff out of a guy, so he got Sam talking about *The Wild Bunch*. They were talking, so I told them I was going back to my room to call Bud Cardos about the script. I left them in a jovial mood.

As I headed down the staircase, I noticed a car that hadn't been there when we went up to Sam's room. I recognized two plainclothes detectives on stakeout. I went into my room, called Bud, and talked for a while. When I came out, the two cops were still sitting there. I thought, "What if they are staking out ol' Sam?" I went back to Sam's room. As always, he was holding court in bed. I said, "Sam, there's some cops down there." He jumped up, grabbed two plastic vials of coke, ran over to the window, and jumped up and stuck the vials on top of the curtain rod.

I started thinking, "Jesus Christ, they're gonna bust all of us and that idiot thinks he's hiding the evidence!" He didn't even bother to flush 'em down the toilet.

The atmosphere began to change. I started to get real uncomfortable about something else: I was afraid one of my pals would say something about their mutual women. I was watching the end of two worlds right there—and what could have been the end of mine! I opened the curtain and looked down at the parking lot. I could see the cops were still there. I said to Sam and Ed, "I'm going to the restaurant to sit for a while, and I'll see if they're still waiting."

I went over to the café and had a glass of tea and waited about thirty or forty minutes before heading back to the room. Now it was nightfall and the cops were gone. I went to Sam's room and told him and Ed that the cops had left. Sam had a bottle of Scotch out and was drinking. But the good times didn't return.

Ed finally said he had to get back home. We all shook hands and Ed left. He was barely gone when Sam went to the phone to call someone. About thirty minutes later, somebody knocked at the door. Sam asked me to answer it. I did, and there was this young man standing there. I was surprised when he said to me, "You must be Max." He was a dealer who came to bring Sam dope. He was an American-raised German with a wife and a kid, and we sat down to visit like we were going to have a domino game. Sam gave him cash, the guy gave Sam dope, and Sam walked into the bathroom to snort. He came back in, crawled into bed, and I bid him good night.

When I woke up the next morning, I found out that Sam had left. I don't know how Sam found out I was staying there in the first place, but now Ed Honeck could say he spent an afternoon visiting Sam Peckinpah.

One consolation of this meeting of two very special friends of mine—Sam and Ed—is that they both lived life to the fullest and beyond. And unbeknownst to everyone else in the world, I was content in knowing that they had both loved the same two creative women.

At this time, Ed was sort of on the rebound. He began dating a solid lady named Janice who had no desire to be an entertainer. She had inherited some money and owned her own home and was just as independent as Ed.

I was there visiting Ed one time, and I suffered a terrible inner-ear attack—the same ol' byproduct of my combat experiences as an infantryman in World War II—and I started getting sick and throwing up. Nevertheless, I had to get back to the Sands for an important meeting. Janice volunteered to drive me back, which took a lot of courage since I told her, "I might throw up all over your car." She gave me some Dramamine and got me some crushed ice, which slows the process down. As she drove me back to the Sands, she talked to me just the right way to keep my mind occupied. I knew then that she was a really good human being, and I was very happy when Ed married her.

Our friendship lasted for many memory-filled years. Then Ed got cancer of the stomach. They got half of it out, and it looked like he might survive. Janice nursed him and got him back to doing his job. Then it showed up in his brain. They gave him chemo and radiation treatments. The tumor was painless. The treatment wasn't. They operated on him three times. It didn't help. He succumbed. He was about fifty-five.

Some years later, I invited Janice to the premiere of the film version of *The Hi-Lo Country* in Hollywood. She came, and we visited. She was doing quite well. Three or four months later, Al called me to tell me Janice had come down with Lou Gehrig's disease and died.

Pat and I had often traveled to Al and Sally's Wildwood Ranch to visit with them and Ed and Janice. Ed's dream was to build a cabin on a select acre of land that Al had given him and write. That didn't happen.

Instead, Al built a monument of stone with a plaque to Ed on that acre. Al still invites us up to pay tribute to our friends. I keep letting Al think that someday I'll be able to come. We all know better, but it's still a lovely thing to plan.

And so this fairy tale for Sam and Ed had a bit of a happy ending, just a little moment of the universe that will remain in my memory forever, like a warm breeze on a cool mountain.

20. Crossing the Iron

Back in my Taos days, about 1957, just after I'd gone broke in the mining business and frequented the liquor joints of the city, I ran into three beatniks at the Taos Inn Bar. One of them was Impressionist painter Len Kanneson, and the other two were the writers Jim Hamilton and Calvin Kentfield (who had written for the *New Yorker*). Calvin tried to ride me a little too hard. To maintain the friendship, I once took him by the arm, led him out to the lobby of the Taos Inn, and explained to him not to do that to me again or it would instigate violence. We became friends.

All of them were from San Francisco. Jim had served in the infantry during the Korean War and was working on a novel. They had a little bit of hell-raising in their souls, and they were all crazy. I liked all three of them. Why wouldn't I like them?

One night, when the Taos Plaza was empty, we staged a one-car Indy 500 race. I was the flag man. Len drove Jim's car and Jim sat on the hood while they roared around the plaza. I took my shirt off and flagged the car three or four times before the cops came. I had hired a lot of relatives of cops to work for me in the mining business, so I just had a little talk with the cops and everybody sort of drifted on home. Taos was just an art colony back then—a great fun colony.

Calvin went back to San Francisco after about a month. Len received a grant from the Wurlitzer Foundation of New Mexico that allowed him to stay in Taos and paint. And Jim, well, how was I to know that this young ex-sergeant would write one of the first major books on combat in Korea (which was never published) and later become a key part in Sam Peckinpah's life and help salvage one of his last major films?

Georgie Gutekunst owned and operated Ondine's restaurant in San Francisco, a high-end eatery that opened in the late 1950s and is still running. Jim felt that Georgie was his patron saint. Georgie came out to

Santa Fe twice, and I missed meeting him, but the third time he called Jim, who was just finishing his novel about the Korean War. I was expected to read it the next day. We all met at Jim's house, where Georgie cooked for us and we had many drinks.

The book was real. You felt the battle. But it was also ponderous—way too long. And I had to tell Jim the truth.

Jim's wife, Georgana, was pregnant at this time. We met at the Taos Inn to discuss the book. Jim and I had a beer and she had a cup of coffee. I had no idea how to start this discussion about his book. It just came out.

I said, "Jimbo, you got the feel, you tell the truth, but the book is as ponderous as an elephant's walk."

His wife, who was always honest with Jim, immediately said, "That paraphrases what I told him."

Jim accepted the critique in good grace. He would go on to write essays, stories, and other works, and of course he helped to save one of Sam Peckinpah's later movies, *Cross of Iron*.

Meanwhile, Len—who was nicknamed Bear—returned to San Francisco and sold very few paintings there. I don't know how this happened, but he developed a following in Pittsburgh, of all places, where he had an annual show. Calvin Kentfield kept writing, lost his marriage along the way, and then went and jumped off a cliff. But Jim Hamilton and his wife stayed close to us. Georgana had the baby. Jim kept on working on his novel. We would meet and have fun and talk literature whenever we could. I was writing *The Rounders* around this time, so my drinking time was nonexistent. I ran into Jim at the post office one day, where I showed him the acceptance letter from Macmillan to publish *The Rounders*. I couldn't believe it. He couldn't believe it. He was happy for me.

Jim was out doing some "rounding" of his own, as it turns out. He was a real charmer, and good-looking, too. People thought he looked like Gregory Peck. Women liked him, and he liked women. He was having an affair with a married man's mistress when word came to me that some local people were pissed off at Jim for his womanizing of their women, and these people were planning to waylay him and seriously work him over.

Jim lived south of Taos in upper Talpa. He didn't have a telephone. I went out to the Sagebrush Inn to talk to a guy I knew who fancied himself to be a local sheriff, an FBI man, and a CIA operative all in one. I said, "You've got to do me a favor. Run out to Jim's house, pull him away from his wife, and tell him to leave town with his wife and baby now. Tell him I said for him to do this, and to do it now!"

The guy drove out to Jim's house, passed on the message, and Jim and his family took off. Then he moved back to San Francisco and kept writing. It was about ten years later, while in Hollywood, that I found out that Jim thought it was me threatening to work him over if he didn't get out of town! I was just trying to save his life.

Now Georgie Gutekunst was a wonderful Marxist who didn't put anyone down if they were something else, politically speaking. He had served in the merchant marine during World War II and was on a boat that was sunk by a U-boat as it tried to deliver supplies to Russia. He became friends with Ernest Hemingway's son, Jack. While reading Ernest Hemingway's *Selected Letters*, Georgie came across a letter Hemingway had written to his editor, Maxwell Perkins, about Beryl Markham, who, Hemingway wrote, "can write rings around all of us who consider ourselves as writers." She was a female aviator and had flown solo from east to west across the Atlantic, and she had written *West with the Night*, which detailed her life in Africa. Georgie went to Africa to find her and the manuscript. He caught planes, boats, cars, and wagons to find her. She was about eighty then and making a living training race horses. She and Georgie got along fine: they both liked gin. He got her book to a friend, who in turn got the book to William Turnbull, publisher of North Point Press in San Francisco, who in turn published the book again. It became a number-one best seller. Markham suddenly got all this money from royalties and didn't change a damn thing about the way she lived. Sometime later, Georgie got a wire from a friend saying Markham had tripped over an old dog she loved and fallen and broken her neck.

Georgie had this wonderfully strange trait: he would take a writer under his wing for a year and help him or her out, showing up to talk writing, literature, and the classics. He adopted me for a year. He could drink and drive without stopping from San Francisco to Albuquerque. He never took care of himself, though; he'd eat and drink whatever he wanted, and most of the time he could handle it. He helped Jim by getting him work as a longshoreman on the Bay. They had an understanding: Jim would work so many weeks and then return home to write.

All of their worlds began to change when Sam Peckinpah arrived in San Francisco to make *The Killer Elite*. Georgie was married to a Mexican national named Berta, and Sam loved her just as he loved all Mexicans, so he became acquainted with Georgie. Georgie employed Georgana as his hostess at the restaurant, and Sam went to the restaurant, and that's how they all met. Sam didn't pay a helluva lot of attention to Jim at the time.

Jim rented a small apartment in Los Angeles so he could travel there to work and try to make deals. It was about five minutes away from the stock brokerage firm where Walter Peter worked, so in no time at all they ended up meeting in a bar and becoming friends. Jim was trying to write screenplays, but he was a very slow writer. He'd kill himself writing just one line, but that detailed mind would later pay off for both him and Sam Peckinpah.

Jim called me when I was living in Albuquerque and said he wanted to write a profile piece on Denver Peckinpah. "Denver won't return my calls," he said. I knew Denver would return my call for one reason: I had faith in Denver's only son, David.

Sam had no faith in David. David was a better writer than Sam, but he never proved to have the same directing talent as his uncle. Sam hired David to write a first draft of a screenplay based on my book *My Pardner*. It was a damn good draft, but Sam said, "This is a piece of shit." I called Denver, and lucky for me he had just finished the right amount of bourbon. If I had called him two drinks later, it would not have worked. I told Denver that I knew Jim, that he wasn't the kind of writer to double-cross anyone, and so Denver finally called Jim back. Jim wrote a good article about Denver but didn't know where to get it published. *New York Times Magazine* had just written that the best literary magazine in America was being published in—of all places—South Dakota. John R. Milton was the editor of the *South Dakota Review*, and he had published a lot of my work, including *My Pardner*. He took Frank Waters, who had fallen out of print, and published essays on Frank until the next thing you know, Frank was back in print. He's dead, but his work remains in print. I read Jim's piece on Denver and called John. He agreed to publish it, and Denver loved it. So did Sam, though he wouldn't comment on it too much. Denver took Jim up to Peckinpah Mountain and introduced him to the family. Still, with all these "ins" to Sam, Jim Hamilton still was not "in" with Sam.

Sam was having trouble putting together a script for *Cross of Iron*, which was slated to start shooting in Yugoslavia. Because I had served in the infantry in World War II, Sam called me and asked me to help him work on this war script. I said, "I'm not your man. I don't want to write about the war." (Although I later would: some ninety pages in the eight-hundred-page novel *Bluefeather Fellini*.) I said, "We both know someone who can do this—Jim Hamilton, who is one of the best friends of your brother-in-law."

That got Sam's attention. He called Jim, and Jim agreed to help. He wasn't the only writer on the movie. Sam first got Julius Epstein, one of the famous Epstein Brothers (they wrote *Casablanca*, among other great Warner Bros. films) to write a script, and Peckinpah actor and second-unit director Walter Kelley also worked on the script. It's not that Jim contributed that much to the script, but he contributed just enough, giving it the feeling of truth, to launch the production. It saved Sam—temporarily—and probably remained the highlight of Jim Hamilton's life. I believe that Jim would have never been able to jump into *Cross of Iron* without the experience of working on his own war novel.

Orson Welles saw *Cross of Iron* and wired Sam to say it was the best war movie ever made. (Welles and John Huston were Sam's idols as American film directors.) *Cross of Iron* didn't come off well all the same. There were problems during the shooting: Sam had a heart attack during the production, and his budget was slashed considerably. You can't fight a modern war with just three tanks.

Jim later helped make a documentary on union longshoreman leader Harry Bridges. He died in 2009. After I gave him that critique of his Korean War novel in the Taos Inn, he spent the rest of his life rewriting it. But he couldn't bring himself to cut it, so it went unpublished.

As for Georgie, he died about ten years back at age eighty-three. He suffered a heart attack while walking out of a bank where he went to withdraw money to throw a party for some longshoremen.

21. 8 1/2 Meets
Ride the High Country

Film people are tough. They have to be. And Sam Peckinpah's *Cross of Iron* was one tough shoot. It was based on a novel by Willi Heinrich and told the story of war-weary Germans combating equally war-weary Russians in the winter of 1943. Sam had turned down the opportunity to make both *King Kong* (a flop) and *Superman* (a hit) to shoot *Cross of Iron* in Yugoslavia. The producer was Wolfgang Hartwig, who had become wealthy making porn films in Germany. According to Katy Haber, who was always on the set, nobody liked Wolf. He hung around the set accompanied by his wife, a striking female porn star named Véronique Vendell, to convince himself and others that he was a genuine producer.

As Sam was sometimes prone to do, he would cast unlikely people in film roles in the spur of the moment, and one day he cast Wolf as a German general in a combat scene involving a dugout that was under heavy artillery fire. Somehow the roof to the dugout mysteriously collapsed, covering Wolfgang in dust, dirt, and debris. He emerged coughing, his face, hands, and body covered in dirt, but he was not badly hurt. But that "accident" limited his time on the set from then on, and it was a happier cast and crew. Sam hated Wolf so much that he once stood on the sixth-story balcony of his hotel and pissed down below onto Wolf's pink Cadillac.

Sam had hired James Coburn, James Mason (who had made a beautiful sketch of himself and Sam), David Warner (who had already appeared in two Peckinpah films and who never understood why some people thought Sam was insane), and Maximilian Schell for principal roles. Wolf promised the world and didn't even give Sam the state of Rhode Island, as James Coburn later told David Weddle: "Wolf . . . gave us half, charged us double, and he would disappear every once in a while to get cash from his porn empire, but soon it became obvious that he had enormous problems bringing up the money." The promise of a dozen or so tanks, for instance, whittled down to the reality of three, one of which reportedly did not work.

Sam's son, Matthew, visited the location once. Matthew was beloved by all who knew him. I recall thinking that Matthew, even as a small child, was an independent thinker. As related in David Weddle's biography of Sam, father and son had a private, fierce argument during the shoot that turned into a fistfight, with Matthew responding to Sam's blows with some jabs of his own.

Katy Haber recalled a day on the set when Sam decided to cast Matthew in a small role as a Russian soldier, thinking such a move would encourage Matthew's interest in the film. Matthew felt differently, as evidenced by his refusal to play the part. Sam became enraged and raised his hand to slap his son. Katy, who was almost always right by Sam's side on every production they worked on together, saw this and did the unthinkable: she stepped in between the two men, saying to Sam with quiet force, "No. You mustn't do this, Sam."

Sam stopped, his hand frozen in mid-slap, and glared at Katy. As with all combat, there are moments that occur so quickly that it is all a blur and other moments of such slow motion that time seems to stop. Katy braced for the blow. Sam's eyes filled with anger and a little madness, but at last he dropped his hand as all three breathed again and the normal span of time returned. It was a moment that hardly anyone on the set noticed, but it was a huge, albeit disguised, event for the three participants.

Matthew left to travel Europe and then returned to the states, later going into boot camp with the Marines. Sam was very proud of this move and was present at Matthew's graduation. Katy would leave Sam after his next film, *Convoy*, and move to California as well, where she still helps those in need. As for Sam, he would continue to become a madman among immortals. (He cast a Russian kid in the role intended for Matthew.)

Cross of Iron's cast and crew suffered every inconvenience possible: a difficult location shoot, underfinancing, and Sam's declining health. The cast and crew must have had doubts about even finishing the film as they witnessed Sam dealing with growing chest pains. He tried to ignore the pain until it became so intense that he bent over one day, clutching his chest. Katy again saved Sam's life on that film. She drove Sam to the hospital (as related in chapter 13), recalling that it was the sort of facility you might have seen in pre-war Russia. But her actions helped save his life, the film, and what was left of his career. Sam did return to the set shortly thereafter—his only concession to his health being his willingness to rely on a wheelchair, although he mostly used it as a macabre prop. This was the first of several heart attacks that Sam would suffer—he had two more later on in Montana, and the final, fatal one in Mexico, which killed him. Katy wasn't there for that last one.

Cross of Iron was shot in the spring of 1976. Preproduction began late in 1975, some months after Sam's fiftieth birthday. Following that party, which Katy called a smashing success, she arranged yet another special gift for Sam to be delivered a few days later. She had searched Los Angeles to find cinemas that were screening films by Sam's favorite foreign directors: Ingmar Bergman, Akira Kurosawa, and Federico Fellini. This was during the harvest days of art-house cinema in America. She found a cinema screening Bergman's *Cries and Whispers*, but she couldn't find a Kurosawa or Fellini film anywhere, so she replaced those with Louis Malle's *Murmurs of the Heart* and Bernardo Bertolucci's *Last Tango in Paris*. It had taken her some effort to schedule all three screenings in one day (and night). She said Sam responded with such deep feeling from these Olympian works that he remained in bed in a daze for a week. Sam would later visit in person with some of his filmmaker idols. I know he once traveled to Japan to shoot a commercial with James Coburn with the agreement that the production company would arrange a meeting with Kurosawa, which it did. Sam later met Bergman during a trip to Paris.

And it was during *Cross of Iron* that Sam finally met Fellini, whose *8½* (my favorite film of all time) had lost out to Sam's *Ride the High Country* at the Belgium Film Festival in the early 1960s. During the *Cross of Iron* shoot, the crew members took to burning old tires to create smoke for the battlefield scenes, the most economical method to help bolster the restrained budget. But there was a drawback: the fire could not be extinguished without great difficulty, so the tires burned on and on and on. All the crew members and actors worked without complaint in response to the endless eye-and-lung-burning smoke.

One Friday morning, when a time-consuming set change had to take place, Katy optimistically said to Sam, "Why don't we take a breather and enjoy an extended weekend in Venice?" To her astonishment, Sam agreed, asking James Coburn to accompany them. Katy called ahead and made reservations in a boutique hotel called La Venice. It was a five- or six-hour drive to Venice. There were no burning tires along the way. The trio enjoyed dinner that night in a restaurant where strolling musicians played away. Katy was sure this would instigate trouble with Sam, as music and booze always seemed to contribute to one of his insane all-nighters. Instead, after finishing a bottle of choice wine, Sam gave Katy an unexpected present, suggesting that they all retire early so they could awake refreshed to enjoy Venice the next day. Coburn seemed relieved as well.

The next morning, Katy awoke to bathe and prepare in anticipation of the day as Sam remained in bed. By the time she was ready, Sam was awake but still not out of bed or dressed. He said, "You go on and keep the appointment with Jim. I'm going to stay in and rest." Katy asked if he was sure he didn't want to join them. "No!" he yelled. "Get the hell out of here and have some fun." So she left feeling just fine—noticing that there was a full bottle of whiskey on the table near Sam's bed.

Katy entered the lobby and saw Coburn there shaking hands with a large man in an equally large cape who was wearing a magnificent fedora. It was one of Sam's foreign idols: Federico Fellini. Coburn introduced him to Katy, and she said, "Mr. Fellini, if you follow me, I'll introduce you to a surprise for both for you." Fellini, who obviously thought she was the wife or girlfriend of Coburn, agreed to follow her back to Sam's hotel room.

Katy knocked on the door. "It's Katy, open up!"

"Fuck off!" Sam yelled from within. "I'm not going!"

"Open up," Katy persisted. "I've got a surprise for you."

Sam opened the door, standing there naked as the day he was born.

Katy said, "Mr. Fellini, meet Sam Peckinpah."

Sam said, "Oh my God!" as he disappeared into the embrace of Fellini's giant cape. And then, seemingly unperturbed, Sam said, "Come on in, Mr. Fellini. Would you like a drink?" Sam picked up the bottle of whiskey and plopped back on the rumpled bed, still naked. He motioned to a nearby chair, which Fellini took. Katy closed the door and left the two maestros alone.

Katy and Coburn set out to see the sights of Venice, exploring the waterways and leisurely stopping to shop whenever Coburn wanted to buy some items for his family. (Katy found a gold diamond ring that she knew she could not afford, but she bought it anyway and was always happy that she did, as she eventually sold it to raise funds for the barrio kids she works with in California.) Katy and Coburn ate lunch in the Piazza San Marco. The day had been like a scented rainbow to her. She and Coburn had linked two film icons—it would have been like Shakespeare and Balzac talking shop over a bottle of fine wine, or Leonardo da Vinci and Michelangelo spending an afternoon together to discuss the secrets of making great art. They had given two immortals the respect of a four- or five-hour visit—if, in fact, the visit had lasted that long. Katy and Coburn leisurely strolled back to the hotel, where Katy knocked on the door.

"If that's you, Katy, come in. The door is unlocked," Sam yelled.

She entered. There on the bed, still naked and propped up on the pillows, was Sam. Fellini was still sitting in the chair nearby. The only difference was the bottle of whiskey, now nearly empty.

Shortly thereafter, Sam received a note in the mail from Fellini, translated and transcribed by Katy:

Dear Sam, It was nice and natural to meet you in that way. Life is always nice and natural to meet a friend. I wish you good luck and good work. Thinking to see you again the next week.   —Fellini

And this, as a postscript: "Say 'hello' to James and his charming lady."

The visit with Fellini was the highlight of the *Cross of Iron* shoot. Sam returned to the set to finish the picture, fighting budgetary restraints all the way, and turned out what was his last halfway decent picture. Released in 1977, *Cross of Iron* was a smash in Europe (and one of the highest-grossing films in Germany's box-office history) and a commercial flop in America. When some critics said the film was excessively violent, Sam said, "How the hell can you make a war film that isn't violent?" Still, Sam recalled to the end that another of his cinematic heroes, Orson Welles, wrote him a note saying that *Cross of Iron* was the best antiwar film he had ever seen. None of this would have happened without the dedicated sacrifices made by Katy Haber. She had gifted Sam with a night of life and a day as special as any kid had ever lived.

22. This Play Was Not Meant to Be a Comedy

Every time you saw Sam Peckinpah, there'd be a wreck of some kind. I've mentioned in another chapter how I felt Sam's slide began with the making of *Bring Me the Head of Alfredo Garcia* (1974), but it may have been *Convoy* (1978) that convinced me that he was heading permanently downward.

Sam always had a fondness for Albuquerque, where I have lived since the late 1960s. In the early days of his theater career, he spent time there acting and directing at the Albuquerque Little Theater. Among Sam's friends and colleagues were writer Bill Prevetti and actor Vic Izay. Sam directed two plays that Vic wrote for the theater, and Vic directed two plays that Sam wrote for the theater. When Sam was preparing *The Cincinnati Kid*, he called Vic to come out to Hollywood to coach actress Sharon Tate on the film. She was inexperienced, but Sam had to use her because Martin Ransohoff, an executive at MGM, was stuck on her playing the part. That's how Vic moved to Hollywood. As it turns out, Ann-Margret ended up with the part, while the gorgeous Sharon Tate became the wife of film director Roman Polanski before she was murdered by followers of Charles Manson in the summer of 1969.

Sam would help Vic land some character parts. Sam did cast him, but just in bit roles, which is inexplicable to this day. Sam never gave Vic a shot at a really good part. Vic struggled to make a living out in L.A. He and I talked about all this over a drink at the Lizard Lounge during the shooting of *The Ballad of Cable Hogue*, in which Sam cast him in a tiny part. Later, when I was in Hollywood on some business, I called Vic and his wife and asked them to come to Formosa for lunch. We sat there, the three of us, discussing why in the hell Sam wouldn't give Vic bigger parts. Sam did call Vic in for a reading of *The Cincinnati Kid*, but he didn't cast him. (It didn't matter, of course, since Sam got fired anyway.)

I said, "Let's just go down to that trailer park now and kick something apart and tell Sam you want a really good part." Vic's wife agreed with me, but Vic would never do it. After his wife passed away, he moved back to Albuquerque and became a mainstay at the Albuquerque Little Theater, just as he had been earlier on with Sam.

To be polite, *Convoy* is not a good movie. Sam was already too far gone into booze and drugs to make it work. He had a grandiose idea of introducing people to the world of truckers—cowboys of the pavement—but he didn't have a good script. Sam always believed that he could overcome a mediocre script while shooting. He did that with *The Wild Bunch*, an average script that he rewrote into a great script. He thought that he could do it with *Convoy*, but he couldn't.

Sam hired James Coburn to shoot the second unit on *Convoy*. Coburn may have shot a lot more than is believed. Coburn had acted in Sam's *Pat Garrett and Billy the Kid*, which I think in totality is a magnificent achievement, though it is too slow for today's audiences to properly appreciate. One of the reasons Coburn lasted so long as Sam's friend is that Sam felt he could depend on Coburn in most situations on either side of the camera. Of the creative people in Sam's life, near the end, there was really just me and Coburn left.

Now I know most people believe that it was James Caan who turned Sam onto cocaine during the shooting of *Killer Elite*. But Walter Peter, who had no reason to lie, told me it was Coburn—probably during the making of *Pat Garrett and Billy the Kid*—who introduced Sam to coke. Coburn had a strange control over cocaine that Sam couldn't master. Walter told me that one time he and Coburn were going through customs in Europe, on their way to meet Sam there when he was shooting *Cross of Iron*, and Coburn let it be known that he had a bag of cocaine on him. Walter was sweating bullets and sharp knives, but Coburn wasn't. In those days, customs agents and security guards let movie stars go through without bothering them much.

The first time I saw Sam do cocaine was after he wrapped *Killer Elite* in 1975. He invited Pat and me to the premiere screening in San Francisco, and afterward we all went out to dinner at a restaurant in Chinatown. Sam wanted support. I think he knew that the picture didn't work. He wanted people who were close to him around him. Fern Lea was there along with Walter Peter, Denver Peckinpah and his son David, and Jim and Janna Hamilton. Later, we went back to Sam's hotel, the Biltmore. He took to his bed, holding court from there and drinking and snorting coke. The party went on for two or three days, and Sam was getting crazier and crazier because of the coke.

Two years later, in the summer of 1977, Sam called me to tell me he was coming to New Mexico to shoot *Convoy*. Pat and I invited Sam, Denver, and Frank Kowalski, as well as Katy Haber—the glue and spirit of Sam's life at that time—to our house the very first night they were here. Denver was a brusque, direct man who did not make friends easily, so he made you feel honored if you became his friend. Pat fixed a great enchilada dinner, and we had some barbecued chicken and many other dishes for non-chile eaters. Sam usually ate very little. Everybody would get concerned that he wasn't eating enough, but that night he surprised everyone by eating and eating and loading up his plate with more. We had a wonderful evening, and everyone got along. I remember thinking, "What a beautiful night. No fusses, no fights, no furniture being trashed, and no blood on the carpet. What a great way to start the picture."

Sam and Denver were staying at the Hilton, and Sam told me that everyone was coming in for the shoot: besides Katy and Frank, this entourage included Bobby Visciglia, his prop man. Frank had a wonderful sense of humor, and if he hadn't gotten tied up with Sam, he could have become a marvelous writer-director on his own. His brother, Bernie Kowalski, became a noted television director—I talk more about him in chapter 11.

A few nights after the Peckinpah crew visited us, Katy called to say that Sam wanted us to come see him at the Hilton. He had a whole floor of suites there. Sam was interviewing local actors for small parts in the film (this was the same night Denver told me about his own heart attack and out-of-body experience). Sam invited me into one of the rooms where he auditioned two teenage girls and a boy for small parts. I remember the two girls looked scared. Sam turned to me and said, "Max, I want you to give them a lesson in acting. I want you to play a truck driver who's been puffing on weed all day, and I'll be the cop who pulls you over." I said, "No, I'm going to play the cop. You play the dopehead. That fits us both better."

Sam instantly put on a great act; you believed that he'd been puffing away at the devil weed all day long. You could easily forget what a great actor Sam was because he was acting all the time. Nine out of ten times, when he called me, he would come on like John Wayne or some bum who called me out of the blue, and I wouldn't be able to catch on at first—he'd get me every time.

He never did really test those kids. I felt sorry for them. He treated them with respect, but he probably figured that all they needed to know they could learn by watching him act with me. Sam loved actors, but he would pull all sorts of games on them to get performances out of them. Sam wasn't a method-actor director by any means. I still recall him working with Stella Stevens and Jason Robards Jr. on *The Ballad of Cable Hogue*. Stella was working outside, nude (and God, she was beautiful), in the scene where Jason bathes her. She felt she wasn't getting the scene right, and she broke down and cried. Sam took her aside, sat her down in a chair, gave her a Heineken beer (it was always Heineken with Sam), and talked to her. None of us could hear what he was saying to her, but it must have worked. She got up and did one long, perfect take while he had musician Richard Gilles play "Butterfly Morning," the song she and Jason would sing live. Stella was, underneath the beauty and arrogance, a great actress, but few directors got that out of her. Sam did.

I also recall the trick he played on L.Q. Jones and Strother Martin on that film when the two were caught in the big hole by Robards's Cable Hogue. The scene called for Robards to throw rattlesnakes into the hole to force the two out in the open where he could shoot them. Sam got L.Q. and Strother into the hole and then let them know that the poison had not been removed from the rattlers. Their reactions, caught on film, are genuine. I was happy that Pat was visiting and got to see this action.

Anyway, back to that night at the Hilton. The drink was flowing, and I already had this feeling that madness would erupt. I decided that evening that I was not going to be around the picture, and I did my best to stay away. Inevitably, whenever I'd go out on an errand I'd run into someone who was working on the film, and they'd say, "Sam wants to know why you don't come around to see him." Once he called home when I wasn't there and Pat answered the phone. Sam told her, "I've got to see you. I need some coke." Pat was pretty naïve about those things, so she said, "Well, let me stop by the store and pick some up for you." Sam said, "You can't do that." Sam finally got through to her, and Pat said, "OK," but she took our daughter, Sheryl, a tough bodyguard, along with her—no doubt to Sam's dismay.

I headed over there, too. They were shooting some scenes at the fairgrounds, and there were all these trucks parked around the racetrack. I ran into Katy Haber in the production trailer, and she said Sam was out but he'd be back in about forty-five minutes or so, so I walked around the set. I looked at this huge line of trucks and all the people standing around and thought, "They are throwing away money here faster than they can print it, even in Washington, D.C."—where the money-making process was invented.

Suddenly, somebody walked up behind me. I could feel it. A female voice said to me, very softly: "Do you have anything for me?"

I knew instantly it was someone Sam had sent to me. I saw a pair of cops sitting in a car nearby, acting as security for the production. I said, "Why don't you go ask those men in the car? They'll take care of you." A choked chuckle followed, and then this young woman walked away.

I went back to the production trailer and waited outside. Sure enough, there came Sam. He said, "I need to talk to you about something." I knew instantly that he was up to some nefarious, cockeyed scheme. He led me into the trailer, where I saw Katy talking with her good friend Ali McGraw, who was the female lead in *Convoy*. She was and is a real lady, and one of the few who Sam never made a play for or put down. When I told Ali, years later, that she was the only woman Sam never said one bad thing about, she said, "I'm really glad Sam didn't lust after me." She later called *Convoy* "that ghastly movie." But Ali had that rare honor of Sam's total respect. He loved her as he would his own child—maybe even more. For a time after *Junior Bonner*—where Ali met Steve McQueen—Sam, Steve, Ali, Jason Robards Jr., Katy Haber, and a couple of other people met and had chili and drinks at the Old Place, up Runyon Canyon out of Malibu. It was the Algonquin of the Malibu Hills. One evening, Sam approached McQueen about him and Ali appearing in *The Hi-Lo Country*. Steve said he wasn't ready for another Western, but Ali agreed it was a great idea and said so. Sam was so proud that Ali wanted to do that film that he vowed to respect her for the rest of his life, and he did. I'm sure he lusted for her, but for once he controlled it for good.

Once in the trailer, Sam took me into a back room and turned up the volume on a little portable radio to drown out our conversation. "They've got me bugged everywhere," he said. "Even in my hotel." He was serious. He said there was a bug on his camera and in his car. The culprits were the film's producers, of course.

He pulled out some cocaine, poured out a line, and started snorting. After he took a line, he immediately began acting differently. He stood up, reared back, and stretched. He told me two of the film's producers had just driven in from the airport to talk to him about the delays in production. "I want you to back me up, as usual," he said.

It was beginning to get dark. They had just switched on the fairgrounds lights to shoot. Coburn was there directing. Two producers were sitting nearby, and I already knew this night was not going to be any fun. After all, Sam might want me to smack a producer. I'd already decided not to get involved—sometimes these folks smack back.

The first thing the two suits said to Sam was, "Well, you hired Coburn as the second-unit director, but he's shooting first-unit stuff." Sam said, "Oh yeah, I told him I'd set two days aside for him to do that. He's doing great."

They started asking him questions about the budget—Sam had gone way the hell over budget—and I stepped back. All of a sudden, he said to them, "You sons of bitches can go to hell." Then he turned to me and said, "Let's go, Max." He got his driver to take us to some bar in town that I had never been to. We had a drink, and all he said was, "Thanks for being there."

And then we headed back to the set for the night shoot. Coburn was still directing. I went home.

I later told Pat, "I have no idea what I just did for him, but I hope it helped."

Sometime later, Sam invited me to watch him film a fight scene at a bar called Rafael's midway between Santa Fe and Albuquerque. It's closed down now, but the building is still there, sitting on the side of I-25. Alan "Killer" Keller, Sam's bodyguard, stunt man, and sometimes bit player, was staging the fight. I remember Sam saying, "Come on, you can watch Alan wreck the place." And he was right. He had Alan throw a few guys through some breakaway furniture and against the walls. Sam didn't look at me much at all during the shoot; he was in his element.

Shortly after that, Sam called me at home.

"Max, these producers are plotting against me," he said. He named a litany of charges they had been filing against him—probably all justified.

He said, "I need a guy who can get a tape recorder in their cars and hotel rooms so I can get a recording of them plotting against me. They are trying to wipe me off the face of the earth."

There was some truth to that remark—already I could think of at least three instances where producers had messed up his films.

I pointed out that it was a federal offense to illegally tape record someone, and that it would be a big risk for me and a big risk for Sam.

He said, "I don't care, get me someone."

So I did.

I knew a nice, soft-spoken gentleman-turned-thug in Albuquerque. We will call him Georgie Three Toes. I knew that if there was some sort of recording device like this available in Albuquerque, Georgie would know how to get it. Georgie was a mixed-blood, slightly built man who talked very slow and very smooth. He smiled a lot, and he was very polite. We'd always been on good terms, but we'd never done business together, and one day he gave me his phone number and said that if I needed anything "unusual" done, I should call him at that number and leave word.

I called him. I left word. A few hours later, he called me back.

"How can I help you?" he asked.

"Where can we meet to talk?"

"I can be at El Cid in about an hour," he said. El Cid was an old place on Central Avenue that attracted a lot of somebodies and a lot of nobodies.

We met in a small booth and had a casual drink. I played the music box real loud, and I told him what Sam Peckinpah wanted.

Georgie said, "It'll take me about three days, and it's going to be a little bit expensive."

I said, "I don't want to know anything more about it. I'm gonna give you Sam's phone number, and you can call him in his hotel. I suggest you use a pay phone."

"Of course," Georgie said politely.

I thought I was out of it, but, of course, I was not. Shortly thereafter, I got a call from Georgie Three Toes.

"Max?" he said—slow and smooth.

"Yes?" I said—not so slow and smooth.

He told me he called Sam three times and Sam never answered. "Tell Mr. Peckinpah that he owes me $1,500 cash—and that it would have cost him $5,000 if he had answered the phone," he said to me.

Georgie Three Toes gave me a date, a time, and a place for Sam to bring him the cash. Sam was to put it in an envelope and drop it at his damn feet there. "And then we'll have a cordial drink together," Georgie said.

I called Katy Haber. I told her to make sure Sam called me within thirty minutes. I was pissed. If Sam didn't pay the $1,500, I knew I'd have to pay it.

Sam called me about ten minutes later. I asked him why he didn't answer Georgie's calls.

"I couldn't," he said. There was no further explanation.

I told him what to do and how to do it, and to his credit, he did it. That chickenshit Peckinpah had dropped out of his own plot, but at least he had the guts to face Georgie Three Toes. Georgie told me later that they had a cordial drink together and that Sam paid for the drink, so I thought that showed some style.

Later on, Georgie moved to El Paso. He called me once, and I could tell that he had been drinking. He's never called me since, and I don't know what's become of him.

After that incident, I figured I would not have to deal with Sam again or go back to the *Convoy* set. I was wrong. I got another call from Sam. We met at a Chinese restaurant in town. He said he had assigned Coburn to direct the film while he came to meet me. To my surprise, he ordered a ginger ale.

All of a sudden, he said, "I've got something really heavy that needs to be done. I want those bastard producers hit. I've met some people here who I know you know, and I know you can get those people to do this for me."

I suggested Sam go see a prominent lawyer in town instead. In a rare moment of brilliance on my part, I figured this lawyer would tell Sam how stupid his plot was. I set up an appointment for them and warned Sam that he could not let me down on this meeting or he'd have to answer to me. Sam kept the appointment.

I had already called the lawyer, and it was agreed that he would suggest to Sam that he was boarding the wrong bus. This is what the lawyer later told me: Sam came in and said to him, "Max Evans said you can get me a hit man."

I hadn't said any such thing. The lawyer knew it.

"Mr. Peckinpah, they don't do that kind of thing around here anymore," the lawyer told him. And apparently, that did the trick. They had a polite visit, and that was that. The attorney later told me that he was surprised at Sam's neat appearance—he even sported an ascot.

Now a long time ago, I got to know a young man in the Hi-Lo Country. Our relationship began after I went to a rodeo in Clayton, New Mexico, with my friend Big Boy. I didn't participate, but just came to watch. Up over the border was the tiny town of Kim, Colorado, which produced an incredible amount of national bronco riders for a long time. Some of the Kim contingent were at this Clayton rodeo, where Big Boy took first place in bareback riding, beating out a Kim participant by the last name of Canzoneria. And this guy resented losing.

Big Boy and I were sitting in a restaurant after the rodeo that night, with our pickup parked on the curb outside. We were planning to drive to Des Moines, about forty miles west, after dinner. The table next to us was empty—and then in came six or seven of those Kim cowboys to sit down there next to us. Canzoneria said to Big Boy, "The judges leaned toward you today, you hook-nosed son of a bitch." I could smell it—a storm was comin'.

More words were exchanged, and then the two men got up to go outside to fight. I knew damn well we were going to get the shit kicked out of us. Canzoneria was built like a heavyweight. He hit Big Boy, and Big Boy hit him back. It was a bloody fight. I could sense the other Kim boys wanting to move in for the kill. I don't know what motivated me, but I remembered there was a shovel in our pickup. I jumped up there, grabbed the shovel, and said to those guys, "Don't make a goddamned move to interfere. Let these two work it out." I was as scared as I had been on my first day in Normandy during the war, and that's scared. I thought I was going to have to dirty my Levis.

Big Boy took a lot of punches, but somehow he beat that bastard.

Now there was this little fourteen-year-old kid from the Kim bunch who wanted to get in on the fight. I had to threaten him with the shovel several times. And how could I ever dream that this fight—and that kid—would work its way into my book *The Hi-Lo Country*, and that screenwriter Walon Green would weave it into the movie version? And how would I know that this little kid would move to Albuquerque, where he would become my friend and play a role in one of Sam Peckinpah's plots?

That fourteen-year-old grew up to become a pretty good professional bronco rider. He was just an average-sized guy, but powerfully built. Once, they were repairing a downtown hotel in Albuquerque when some pieces from the ceiling or wall above broke loose and hit this kid in the back. Fred Martin, a wonderful outlaw rancher from Magdalena, New Mexico, adopted this kid. While recuperating there, this young man figured he couldn't go back to cowboying or rodeoing. He started playing with cards. Fred showed him some tricks, and the kid spent six, seven, eight hours a day perfecting his card skills. He moved back to Albuquerque where he became a first-class gambler. There was a real group of high-class thugs up and down Central Avenue in those days, and this kid became one of them. Eventually, he studied how to cheat at cards. He was really good with the cards, but he had a little bit of a temper that could work against him. I met him in one of these Central Avenue spots, and we became friends over time. We'll call him Road Trip.

Road Trip could do more than gamble. It was said that he shot a man up in Trinidad, in a dispute over this other man's girl, and got away with it. The man stupidly called Road Trip to warn him that he was coming to get him at a bar in town. Road Trip had a long-nosed .38 Special, and he went outside of the bar and waited. The guy pulled up in a truck with a shotgun. As the guy got out, Road Trip shot him dead with one bullet between the eyes. After that, nobody wanted to mess with Road Trip. When he came to Albuquerque, he still had that .38—and everyone knew it.

I once asked Road Trip to collect $1,000 some guy owed me in Rio Rancho. This guy was thirty pounds heavier and three inches taller than me. I had loaned him $1,000, and the guy kept lying about when he would pay me back. As a gesture of friendship, I asked Road Trip if he could "pleasant-talk that gentleman to give me my money." Three hours later, that guy showed up to give me my $1,000. I didn't ask Road Trip how he did it, but I gave him $200 for his troubles.

Now Sam was still in Albuquerque shooting *Convoy*, and he said to me one day, "I want to ask you a favor. I want to get even with Jerry Bressler." Sam thought Bressler had ruined what he believed was to be a masterpiece, *Major Dundee* (1965). He said he had an upcoming lunch date with Jerry Bressler at a restaurant on Santa Monica in Hollywood, and he said to me, "I want to have somebody go with me to that lunch, eat lunch with Bressler, and then take him out into the parking lot and break his arm."

Now you would think that Sam's inviting Jerry to come to Mexico during the shooting of *Major Dundee* and meeting him at the airport and ripping his pants down and off his legs in public would have been punishment enough for Bressler. That was humiliating, and all of Hollywood eventually heard that story. But it wasn't enough. Sam wanted his arm broken.

I don't know how I could have been stupid enough to do this, but I told Sam I knew a guy, and I called Road Trip. I told him, "It's $1,500, all expenses paid, a free lunch, a few minutes' work. I want nothing else to do with it."

Road Trip called Sam. Sam said he would get him a plane ticket, a motel reservation, and pick him up at that motel the next morning around 10:30 or so. Sam sent a driver to pick up Road Trip at the airport and take him to his motel. Road Trip expected a really fine hotel for a job like this, but Sam put him in some half-assed dump of a motel. Road Trip was not pleased.

They arranged to meet outside Road Trip's motel, but Road Trip didn't know what Sam looked like. Road Trip walked up and down the sidewalk. Sam parked his car around the corner and walked by Road Trip three times. Road Trip finally said, "Peckinpah?" They shook hands and got into Sam's car.

They drove to the restaurant. Bressler was already there. He stood up. They were all sitting there, but Road Trip couldn't hear a word Sam said because Sam would lower his voice at meetings so you'd have to strain to hear him. This was a game he played.

It backfired on him at least once, when he got me to introduce him to Henry Fonda over lunch. I had given Fonda a copy of *My Pardner*, and he read it and loved it. Sam talked really low during lunch, and Fonda leaned in to hear him and nodded his head a lot, but on the way out Fonda told me he couldn't hear a damn thing Sam said, which was too bad because Peckinpah wanted to talk to Fonda about a movie adaptation of a book, and that book was *My Pardner.* Jesus H. Christmas Christ, with the great Fonda in the film, Sam could have finally gotten it made. All he had to do was ask Fonda so he could hear him. He loved the book.

The lunch with Sam, Road Trip, and Bressler ended. Sam had set it up so that they would go out to the parking lot and wait for the valet to bring their cars. Sam had bribed the valet to tell Bressler that someone had broken into his car, and when Bressler went down to his car, this was when Road Trip was supposed to accompany him and break his arm. But when they stood up from the table, Sam dramatically turned to Bressler and gave him a kiss—the mafia kiss of death. This threw Road Trip. He'd never read any mafia literature or seen one mafia film. He didn't know what to make of it. He thought the kiss was between two lovers.

Sam took off, and Road Trip was mad at him. He felt Sam had not treated him right with that ratty motel and the kiss and all that crap, so instead of breaking Bressler's arm, he asked the valet to get him a cab. He took the taxi to the airport, got a plane out of California, and came back to Albuquerque with $1,500 in cash.

I tried to pretend I had forgotten about the whole damn setup, but all of a sudden I hear this car pulling hard into my half-circled driveway. I heard the car door slamming and footsteps running toward my back door. I opened the door, and it was Road Trip, straight back from the airport. He said to me, "Max, that son of a bitch Peckinpah is a homosexual!" Road Trip had this enormous prejudice against gays.

I said to him, "Well, did you do the job?"

"No. Sam put me in this cheap motel, he didn't know who I was, he didn't even introduce me to Bressler, and he didn't include me in the lunch conversation. But that kiss on the cheek was the last straw!"

I said, "Did you get the money?" He said, "Yeah, up front." And he pulled out the $1,500 in $100 bills. He had no compunction about taking the money and not doing the job. You couldn't really call it dishonor among thieves, but it was close.

Sam did not call me up in a rage demanding to know what happened. Sometime later, when I questioned Sam about the incident, he told the same story that Road Trip told me. Sam was actually lucky that Road Trip didn't decide to work him over instead of Bressler.

How do you figure it all? That fourteen-year-old kid standing on the edge of a brawl on an empty street in Clayton becoming part of not only my life but Sam Peckinpah's madness? And I had it written into Sam's obsession, *The Hi-Lo Country.* Some people are born with a magnet right in the center of their back, and many of these people from different places, different occupations, and different cultures were pulled toward Sam Peckinpah. This all seems to me to be far greater than just coincidence.

Sam—or perhaps James Coburn—completed *Convoy* and left New Mexico. Of the film, Sam told Coburn, "I haven't done one good day's work on this picture." The film ran way over budget and remains a mess, but as many Peckinpah historians have already noted, when released in the summer of 1978 it was his greatest commercial success. Katy Haber, having had enough of Sam's on-the-set unprofessionalism and off-the-set affairs with other women, finally gave up on him and left the set and his life—for a time.

Actor, dialogue director, and sometimes screenwriter Walter Kelley, who helped Sam with the *Cross of Iron* script, also vowed never to work with Sam again after the *Convoy* experience. In a September 1977 letter he wrote to Katy (still in my records), Walter noted, "At present the failure of all of Sam's friends is the reason for the problems on the picture. One fall guy after another." But Sam was the real fall guy on *Convoy.*

As for Road Trip, as of this writing he is still alive. I won't reveal his real name. That guy still has his long-nosed .38—and he lives right down the road from me.

23. Hi-Lo to Hollywood

For years, I wondered if my 1961 novel *The Hi-Lo Country* would ever be made into a film. It finally was, in 1998, but it wasn't Sam Peckinpah who would launch it. About ten years after Sam's death, I was attending an event at the National Cowboy Hall of Fame and Western Heritage Center (now called the National Cowboy and Western Heritage Museum) in Oklahoma City to pick up a Wrangler Award for my novel *Bluefeather Fellini*—which was unusual, to say the least, because there wasn't a cowboy in it, though it was loaded with various southwestern characters and culture. The people at the National Cowboy Hall of Fame treat you beautifully when you are a guest. A lot of my friends, including Glenn Ford, Slim Pickens, and Morgan Woodward, were honored there for their contributions to the entertainment world. You go there, and there never seems to be any sense of jealousy among the writers.

Pat and I were in our hotel room out there, in between banquets or something, when the phone rang. It was one of our twin daughters, Charlotte, calling from Albuquerque. My wife answered, and Charlotte said to her, "There's a call here at home for daddy from Martin Scorsese. It's about *The Hi-Lo Country*." My daughter, a real film fanatic, asked Pat, "Mom, is that *the* Martin Scorsese?" We were headed back to New Mexico the next day, so I figured I'd wait until I got back home to call him back. I called him, and he asked if the rights were available. I said I'd find out about that (it was often impossible to straighten out the rights on that book) and offered to send him a copy. "No," he said, "I'd like to buy a copy"—which I appreciated.

I waited for his response, which came in the form of a letter in February 1995.

That's when Scorsese sent me a note saying that *The Hi-Lo Country* is "a terrific book with some really great characters. No wonder Sam

Peckinpah spent so many years trying to get it made." I still wasn't that excited about the book's prospects. I'd been there so many times before that I was what you might call barely hopeful.

You have to realize that Sam was the first, but not the last, person to option the rights to that book, going way back to the early 1960s. He called me once, after he had made *Major Dundee*, and asked me, "Can you live with Charlton Heston playing Big Boy? I have an appointment to see him tomorrow." I said I'd like to go along, so Sam drove me up to Heston's house. Heston had already read the novel and the script concept that Sam had prepared, and we sat on a couch in his big living room while he got up and started walking around the room acting out the script. It seemed to me that while he was acting it out, he was giving Sam and me direction regarding his concept of how the film should be. Heston had very weak knees. He could hide them on film, but when he walked, he walked sort of bowlegged, and I noticed this. When he finished reading the script and talking out the character, Sam and I left.

Sam turned to me and asked, "Whaddya think of him?"

"He doesn't understand the character at all," I said. "And he can't even walk."

I thought Heston was a stumblebum, but Sam let me know that Heston had bad legs and weak knees. I felt a little guilty knowing this. I appreciated the day, because it proved that it was important for Sam to get me to say, "Heston would probably be OK in the role."

I'm not sorry that Sam never made the film version of *The Hi-Lo Country*. You never really knew what Sam would do to a script once he got on the set and started rewriting it. He would change things to fit his concepts and desires on any given day, or hour. I recently came across his original script, dated 1968, for *The Hi-Lo Country*. It was more than 140 pages long, and it wasn't *Hi-Lo*. The thing I came to realize is that he just couldn't resist going to Mexico and taking all the characters along with him, which is exactly what he did with his first and second draft of *The Hi-Lo Country*. He had Big Boy and his pal Pete head down to Mexico and got them involved with *federales*, and he threw in a big barroom brawl and all sorts of shit that had nothing to do with my book. He saw Big Boy as a giant, and the only way he could make him a giant was to take him to Mexico and turn him into a superhero. I'd just as soon have remained a pauper than to see Sam make that picture with that script. He would probably have extracted a good film from it, but it wasn't *The Hi-Lo Country* I'd lived and written about. Over the years, Sam would option and then re-option the film rights to the book while he talked with several stars about getting it made. He once discussed Brian Keith as Big Boy and Warren Oates as Horse Thief Shorty, and he told me he'd like to use a lot of the character actors he had cast in *Ride the High Country* in supporting parts.

Between different owners and plotters involved with my book, my agent, Bob Goldfarb, called me to say that he had sent a copy to the director George Axelrod. He read it, liked it, and wanted to talk to me about doing a film version. Axelrod had several hit Broadway plays to his credit, including *The Seven Year Itch* and *Will Success Spoil Rock Hunter?* He had just opened a hit movie, too, called *How to Murder Your Wife*, which I didn't think was very funny. He wanted to throw a party in Los Angeles and have a "meet and greet" with me.

I found myself there, staring at a man who was at the top of the entertainment world at that time. Standing by his side was an elegant woman who ran an exclusive Beverly Hills boutique—his wife, Joan. She was tall, blonde, and had pronounced cheekbones. I could imagine her being a model five or ten years before. She had read *The Hi-Lo Country* and had more understanding of the book than I did. She suddenly said, "You may think I'm crazy, but I want to do something for you and a friend of mine *tonight*. Frank Sinatra is a good friend of mine. I want to call him and take you over to meet him tonight. You'd be good for him, and he would be good for you." I had no idea what she was thinking, but she went into the next room, called Sinatra, and told him we were coming over to see him. "He's open to seeing you," she told me.

I said, "Lemme have another drink and think about it." I didn't know what to do—I was floored. In the end, I couldn't do it; I saw it as being impolite. It was that silly old cowboy sense of being polite—I just couldn't bring myself to go meet Frank Sinatra at someone else's insistence. It must have had something to do with my book as a movie, but I couldn't conceive it. Did she think he would act in it? He had huge clout; he could open any door he wanted at that time. It's just as well I didn't meet him.

He would have probably optioned the movie rights, cast himself and Dean Martin in the lead roles, and it would have been a piece of crap.

The rest of the party went well. Axelrod asked me a few questions about the book and the characters, and he and Bob Goldfarb set up a meeting with some executives at Warner Bros. He got Lee Marvin and Steve McQueen lined up, or so he thought. They took this mental package to Warner Bros., where one of the top executives there said to George, "You can't do this. Don't you realize you're trying to do a picture with a fall-down drunk and a madman?" That fall-down drunk was my friend Lee Marvin, and the madman was Steve McQueen. I thought we were all crazy when studios ran off a booming talent in Axelrod.

My agent lived into his eighties and never quit telling that story. We had a good laugh over how ridiculous it all was. And that ended the George Axelrod connection. His career went downhill after that, and he probably would have taken *Hi-Lo* with him. And yet he was right about the casting. Lee won the Oscar for *Cat Ballou* around this time, and McQueen went on to become the top movie star of his generation. So much for judgment—on both the part of Warner Bros. and me.

It was at the Old Place in Runyon Canyon that Sam had a meeting with Ali and Steve about making *The Hi-Lo Country*—around the time that Ali and Steve were making *The Getaway* for Sam. Sam wanted to get a final answer from Steve about his participation. With Steve and Ali on board, Sam could finally get one of his dream books made—if they committed. Steve, no doubt remembering that Warner Bros. executives had once turned him and Lee Marvin down, politely said he did not want to make another Western. Sam never saw *The Hi-Lo Country* as a Western, actually.

There followed what might be called "a pregnant pause" in the careers of a lot of people. Steve suddenly decided against doing the picture, but Ali went ahead and committed right there in front of her husband, to Sam. Sam never forgot that. As mentioned before, he adored and respected her for the rest of his life and later cast her in *Convoy* (well, I'm not so sure that was much of a favor). He treated a lot of women badly, but not Ali McGraw. Ali was the only woman in the world who I never heard Sam say a bad word about. Incidentally, in his never-ending quest to get even with film producers, whom he generally blamed for his artistic problems, Sam told me he wanted to hurt Paramount producer Robert Evans by ruining his marriage to Ali. Early in 1972, Ali traveled to Texas to make *The Getaway* with Sam and Steve. Sam had noticed the immediate chemistry between Steve and Ali when he and Steve went to Evans's Beverly Hills mansion to discuss the film, which was initially supposed to be produced by Paramount. Sam told me he was going to direct Ali into the arms of Steve during the filming, and he did. The film ended up being produced by Steve's First Artists Company, so Evans had no say over the production and was encouraged to not visit the set by both Ali and Sam. By the time the film was over, Ali and Steve were in love, and Evans's marriage to her was crumbling. (Ali remains very underrated and has a brilliant mind, by the way. She and I share a common love and understanding of animals.)

To paraphrase Evans from the documentary about him, *The Kid Stays in the Picture*, he said that he honestly didn't blame Ali for falling in love with Steve. Steve was handsome, a charmer, and had the number-one box office hit in the world. At the time, Evans had become obsessed with the *Godfather* films, and, as he said, he had neglected his family. He was a far better sport than I ever could have been.

The Hi-Lo Country came from me living through that time when the cowboys came back from fighting the war and found that the little ranching outfits couldn't make it. The big guns with lots of pickup trucks were making it work while little guys like me had to go out and work for them for day wages. The West was changing. I didn't have a telephone in the late 1940s. Hardly anybody out there even had a radio. The first television show I ever saw was in a bar in Raton, New Mexico, and I remember thinking, "My God, the world is destroyed."

Martin Scorsese understood that. He had made many memorable films about people in transition, but never a Western. I wasn't sure whether he was going to direct the film himself until I received a seven- or eight-page fax from him outlining his ideas and asking what I thought about Stephen Frears as a director, and whether I was concerned about Frears being British. That was my last concern, because how many American film directors did I know who had really worked as cowboys, gotten into barroom fights, and chased women all in the same day? I'd seen three of Frears's films by that point: *The Grifters*, *My Beautiful Laundrette*, and a forgotten jewel called *The Hit* that he shot in Spain in the mid-1980s. With that film, he took me out of Britain and right into Spain. The actors, costumes, and sets were perfect. I was impressed with that film, even if I did not know the name of its director.

So now the precarious and elusive nature of putting a motion picture together began. I knew it would fall apart at any minute, at any second. Marty's partner, his ex-wife, Barbara De Fina—who coproduced many of Scorsese's films—flew out to New Mexico to meet me, and we started scouting locations for the movie. She brought one of the executive producers, a man named Rudd Simmons, who was smart enough to hire local people to use their skill and ease to gain access to locales around the state. We hooked up with a couple from Cimarron, Rod and Patty Taylor. Rod was a boss of the Philmont Scout Ranch and had been a cowboy on some other big ranches before he married Patty. He was also a musician. He couldn't make time to help us, but Patty could. With her help, Rudd was able to be really thorough while looking at every piece of ground there was in New Mexico. We traveled across ranch roads around Des Moines and Clayton and Raton—the Hi-Lo Country—to find places that could be utilized without much cost. We ran into too many good locations, most of which would be too far away to use because the production company planned to headquarter in Santa Fe.

Somewhere along the way, the screenwriter Walon Green, who helped Sam write *The Wild Bunch* some thirty years before, came out to join us. I was surprised to learn that Frears was considered a writer's director, but I should have known, because here he had the both of us, the novelist and the screenwriter, together in Santa Fe to help shape the project.

Before that, I thought New Mexico was going to lose the film. At that time, it was cheaper to shoot in Canada, and Rudd Simmons took off for there because he had heard of some land that looked like the Hi-Lo Country. He came back, and we made one last trip out to Las Vegas, New Mexico, just the two of us. He just about broke my heart because he said he'd found a place in Canada that may work better for a little less money.

I saw an opening, and I said, "Rudd, Frears is going to have to hire a lot of Hispanics to play local characters, and you're going to have to fly all of those people up to Canada and pay their per diem and lodging and other expenses. Put your pencil to the paper and figure the costs out."

The next day, he decided on New Mexico as the shooting locale.

Word got back that Frears interviewed actress Nicole Kidman to play Mona. She was then working in England on that sex picture, *Eyes Wide Shut*, with her then husband, Tom Cruise, for Stanley Kubrick. They'd been in England a year working and waiting because of their respect for Kubrick, who I always thought was one of the best—and one of the worst—film directors in the world. Kubrick would not give Kidman any time off to come shoot *Hi-Lo Country*. Marty and Frears had even figured out a way to shoot all of her scenes in just two weeks and then get her back to England. And still Kubrick would not let her go, even though *Eyes Wide Shut* was on a month-long break. So Frears chose Patricia Arquette, whom I had seen in some low-budget films and whom I liked and admired.

Frears asked me and Walon to fly to Los Angeles with him to meet actor Sean Penn for the part of Big Boy. I was thinking he'd have to change Big Boy's name, because I'm average sized and Sean Penn is smaller than I am. Big Boy wasn't that big, maybe 6'1" or so, but he was big inside.

Walon had already written a draft, and Penn had read it. We met out there in a room at the Four Seasons Hotel. I'd quit smoking by that time, but Penn was smoking. One thing I already liked about him was that after reading Walon's script, he went back and read my book. That impressed me, because in my experience in Hollywood, I found that most actors don't read the book. We seemed to be getting along, but I thought I'd tell him something just to feel him out. I said to him, "I'm sure you know Sam Peckinpah was interested in this project at one time. Peckinpah liked the friction of transition—that's what attracted him to the book."

Penn looked at me, smiled, rubbed his hands together, and said, "I love transitions." I saw the rubbing of his hands as a sign that he understood the conflict underneath the transition, and I thought to myself, "He's got it. He's gonna be good." We all shook hands and the meeting ended. I figured if Penn had read the book, he understood that a handshake means you have a deal.

Instead, Penn went off to Australia to make that damn war film *The Thin Red Line* for that sometimes pretentious director Terrence Malick.

I was disappointed. In this case, it was obvious that a handshake was meaningless.

Frears went looking for another Big Boy. In the interim, there came the matter of casting big rancher Jim Ed Love, who is taking over the Hi-Lo Country with his trucks and his manpower and his money. Frears wanted L. Q. Jones, who had read the book and always dreamed of acting in it as directed by Sam Peckinpah.

It was L. Q., as I noted before, who actually pitched the book to Martin Scorsese and had gotten this ball rolling. Well, all of a sudden, L. Q. got an offer to act in a movie being shot in Mexico, *The Mask of Zorro*. He played a goofy old miner who comes down the coal chute at one point shooting guns or some shit like that. It was a small role, but he figured he'd be down there shooting for a while and get paid a bunch of money for doing nothing for weeks on end. He was right. He sat down there on his ass for months and made a small fortune. But he missed out on a great part.

I tried not to butt in on this one, but they were not getting anywhere with casting Jim Ed Love. I knew Morgan Woodward had been the first actor to read the book years back, and I suggested to Frears that he interview him. Morgan got all excited. He had recently retired with a ton of money he made from making about 350 movies and TV shows. I think he was killed a record number of times on *Gunsmoke*. Frears went out to interview Morgan, who decided to dress up all western for the event. They visited, Frears treated Morgan real nice, and they said good-bye. Frears never had Morgan read. I don't know why. Morgan said he called him Mr. Frears and described Frears as a charming and fascinating man.

Frears insisted on hiring Katy Jurado as the old witch woman. He flew her up from Mexico City three times to interview her because he had such respect for her work. I suspect he was also paying respect to Sam Peckinpah, who used Katy to great advantage in *Pat Garrett and Billy the Kid*. Frears also gave Penelope Cruz her first part in an American film, as Josepha, Pete's girlfriend. But he still didn't have a Big Boy or a Jim Ed Love.

Then Walon Green called me and told me that Frears had cast Woody Harrelson as Big Boy. A lot of people were dismayed by that, but I wasn't.

They were basing their judgment on Woody's extracurricular activities and not on his acting talent. I recognized him as both an adventurer and a highly skilled actor.

Frears was doing a lot of casting out of Santa Fe, and I remember him calling Pat and me in to look at the film footage from his tests for Little Boy, Big Boy's brother. I had never experienced that kind of treatment from any director in all my years in Hollywood. It sort of amazed me. He screened the tests of three different actors for us. Nobody else was there but Pat and me, and I knew Pat could be coldheartedly honest. I was hoping I would be, too. Both Pat and I picked the same actor out of the three, a guy who is still playing character parts in films today. He's one of those actors who always gets to the verge but never quite passes it. But Frears had taken a liking to Billy Crudup. I was puzzled. I didn't know Crudup or his work, but I came to like him as the shoot progressed. He had no desire to be anything else but a tremendous actor. He did not give one damn about stardom. He just wanted to give to his craft. He craved respect. I remember he went with the same girlfriend for a number of years. I bet he didn't have more than three girlfriends since high school. (I would have had one hundred by his age, under the same circumstances.)

Pat and I came out of the screening room and ran into an old stunt man who said he was in awe of the book *The Rounders*. He wanted to introduce me to another stunt man nearby. And then a tiny miracle happened. This other stunt man had just finished shooting a TV movie with Sam Elliott. Frears was still talking about landing L. Q. Jones, but I knew he wasn't going to do it, so I decided to run three or four names of actors by Frears for the part, and I just dropped "Sam Elliott" in there.

"Sam Elliott! That's it!" Frears said. He ran to the nearest phone, called Sam Elliott's agent, and twenty minutes later had him signed on. There was no interview, no audition.

Sam Elliott didn't play Jim Ed Love the way I envisioned it as I wrote it. He played it his own way. It was his invention and a wonderful interpretation of the part. Sam Elliot was the only actor in the film who was not proud of his work—or so I heard later on. I heard he had so embedded himself in playing Old West Sam Elliott characters that he couldn't fathom changing that portrayal for this story. Everything had to spin around the character of Jim Ed Love. I think Sam Elliott didn't know what he had created, didn't know what he thought about the character or the picture.

Now all the main casting was done, and I went to work on a book called *Faraway Blue*, a historical Western involving the greatest of all Apache warriors, Nana, and the cat-and-mouse game that ensues between him and his men and the Buffalo Soldiers of the 9th Cavalry. I got so involved in my characters that I forgot all about *The Hi-Lo Country* shooting right down the road from me. Sometimes Frears would call me from Santa Fe and ask me about something in the script to see whether I thought it was authentic or not. I'd tell him if it was or wasn't, and he'd run it by Walon, and if he approved of it, he'd use it in the film. Frears called me again, disrupting progress on my novel, and asked if Pat and I could come up and meet all the stars of the film. He had set up a lunch at the Blue Corn Café. He had the entire cast there, except Sam Elliott.

We accepted the offer, and I soon began to enjoy the company of these really keen, creative people. Frears directed everyone to a particular seat. After lunch, Frears rotated the seats so every actor could sit next to Pat and me and ask any questions they wanted to help them play their parts. Patricia Arquette was the most worried. She was very direct with me. She wanted to know how a married woman who was having an affair with a man in that thinly populated country would act, or react. I explained that everyone living in that wide-open space at that time had eyes that were instinctively drawn to movement. If they saw an animal on the horizon, their eyes were drawn to it, and the same was true with people. A woman in that time and place would be scared to death of making an untoward move because everyone around would notice it. For a woman to even wink at her lover would be a risk.

She said, "I get it."

She played it perfectly for that time and place. And three-quarters of the film critics of the major publications knocked her for her performance. That pissed me off. It was a subtle, restrained performance. She knocked it over the back wall. A few critics got her work, including Jon Bowman of the *Santa Fe New Mexican*.

Penelope Cruz is a rare jewel of a human being. She was highly respected in her native country of Spain. The U.S. critics loved her. They put down Patricia and blasted Penelope to stardom. I still think it was unjust to Patricia. She's kept working, including a long stint on the popular TV series *The Medium*, but true stardom has somehow eluded her. She remains a cult figure. Penelope went on to commercial and critical acclaim, becoming the first Spanish actress to win an Oscar for best supporting actress in Woody Allen's *Vicky Cristina Barcelona*.

Woody Harrelson was a hardworking, fun-loving guy. I remember when he first came on board, he asked if his character's saddle could be made out of hemp, so I knew from the start that we were dealing with a really crazy guy. He and I kept talking about going out and getting really drunk, but Rudd Simmons would have none of it. He said, "If you two go out and get drunk, I'll have to do everything in my power to bail you out of jail by morning." Woody later appeared on some TV talk show and called me a cool guy. That's the only time anybody ever called me cool. I took it as a compliment. I happened to be walking by the wardrobe department one day when Woody was trying on hats. I stopped, looked at the one on his head, and said, "That's the right one." And he chose it to wear in the film. It made the character. (Incidentally, I always thought Glenn Ford was the only Western actor who consistently wore the right hat in movies.)

There was one scene in the film I was interested in, a scene Frears called me about. It's the scene where Big Boy, proclaiming his love for Mona, comes into the bar, bangs his pistol down on it, and lets the world know what his feelings are for this woman. It's a scene where you just know somebody is going to get killed. Frears told me that Walon cut the scene down to the bare bones, to where it works in a filmic sense. He said Woody was insisting we put all the dialogue from the book back into the scene. He wanted to play it all.

I said to Frears, "Why don't you give it a try the way Woody wants it? If he pulls it off, you can use it. If not, no harm done."

Frears said, "Done," and hung up on me.

And Woody pulled it off. He worked hard to make it work; he was flawless. It was the crux of the film, this scene, in which Big Boy compares his woman to a horse, the greatest horse he could own and love. He basically challenges all the other men in the bar to contest him, and, of course, they don't.

One day, they were shooting a dance scene out at one of the old Western town sets in New Mexico, the one where they shot *Silverado* back in the 1980s. I had told Frears that near the end of my time in the Hi-Lo Country, there was a popular country song that I truly loved called "San Antonio Rose." Well, he invited Pat and me to the set that day to watch the scene, and to my wonderful surprise he had hired this great old singer, Leon Rausch, who worked with Bob Wills and his Texas Playboys, to perform this song in person to the dance number. They took about five or six takes to get the scene, and I got to hear this beautiful song over and over. Rausch died about six months after making this film.

I was deeply impressed, but that's not all Frears had in mind. He said to me, "The producers are flying in to take a look at a rough cut. I want you and Pat to be there. I want to know what you think, not what the producers think." I remember driving to the screening room with some of the producers, who kept looking out the window at all the big houses up in the hills. All they seemed to be interested in was how much those houses cost.

We watched the rough cut. I was impressed. I thought Patricia underplayed her role beautifully. I was so impressed with Woody's scene in the bar that I was not sure I could do justice to critiquing the rest of the film.

On the way out to the van, the producers began talking about what a great film it was and how they were going to do everything they could to market it. I'd heard that story before.

Frears asked me what I thought of the film. I said, "Don't worry, the producers like it."

He said, "I don't care what the producers think. Did we get the heart and soul of your book?"

I said, "You got it. And I'm very glad you left in the long scene with Woody at the bar." Frears seemed pleased.

Frears wrapped the film on Christmas Eve in 1997. I remember the wrap party very well. There was not the usual madness of a final cast party but a warm sense of accomplishment. Patricia's husband at that time, Nicholas Cage, came, but I didn't visit with him much. I visited with Billy Crudup and realized the truth of what his mother had once told me when she was visiting the set: he wanted to avoid the limelight, learn as he was growing, and give the best performance he could give.

With a few drinks in me, I thought about telling him that with one or two more big pictures he would be a big star, but I decided to keep my stupid mouth shut.

Polygram, who produced the film, held the premiere of *The Hi-Lo Country* in Los Angeles. Fern Lea and Walter Peter showed up for it, as did L. Q. Jones, his pockets full of money from *The Mask of Zorro*. They flew Pat and me out and put us up in the Four Seasons Hotel and sent me out to press screenings. One screening was held for Charles Champlin, who loved the film. He told me he knew about how the company was putting everything behind *Elizabeth*. Everyone knew that they were going to throw away *The Hi-Lo Country*, except Frears, who maintained this strange, wonderful detachment from everything. He once stated, as if totally to himself, "I hope Mr. Peckinpah would like it." I wanted to tell him that I was afraid not—after all, Big Boy didn't go to Mexico. But again, I kept my mouth shut.

What happened was this: Polygram got absorbed by Universal around the time of the picture's release. The company was about to release Shekhar Kapur's *Elizabeth*, starring Cate Blanchett, and it had a choice to put all of its money into one or the other to make it go. Critically and financially, they clearly made the right decision in promoting *Elizabeth*. It won some Oscars and made money. I'm not sure *The Hi-Lo Country* would have made money under the best of circumstances. I know it did well overseas and got good reviews there, just like Sam's *Ride the High Country* did nearly forty years before. Frears even picked up a Silver Bear award at the Berlin International Film Festival, like Sam did with some European film festivals for *Ride the High Country*. But it was at that Los Angeles premiere that I learned the film would be thrown away. It didn't surprise me a damn bit. I never found out if it made its money back. I never asked. Maybe I didn't want to know. I was glad to have finally gotten the option money for the book after all those years. Berkeley Boulevard reprinted the book in paperback form in 1998, before the film was released at the tail end of that year. I wrote the introduction, noting how Sam Peckinpah had long wanted to make the movie version of the book. I wrote, "Although at this writing we have seen only twenty-five minutes of rough cut—which was beautiful and strong—three principals who have seen it put together say it is a very fine film. We are sure it is. If so, maybe it will help our tormented friend Sam Peckinpah rest easier in his grave—or wherever he is."

You can't brood over things that don't go the way you expect them to go. Life is like writing. You give it all you've got, then you let it go and move on to the next page. Lord O'Mighty, ol' Sam and I had used up several tons of energy and at least a barrel of blood before we turned to the next, but last, page for him.

24. The Last Heineken

I still have a photo I took of Sam on the set of *The Ballad of Cable Hogue* in 1970. He's standing alone, out in the Nevada desert, looking off at the lonely frontier around him. I think it says something.

His professional and personal fall has been well documented elsewhere. Suffice it to say that, after his erratic behavior and the critical failure of *Convoy* (despite the film's commercial success), he found it difficult to secure work. Don Siegel hired Sam to work twelve days as second-unit director on the 1981 misfire *Jinxed*, for which Sam was reportedly paid only $25,000. A letter and some production notes I received from Sam's assistant on that film, Barbara Engels, suggest that he was trying his best to prove himself in Siegel's eyes while dealing with producers who would not communicate with him, a tight budget, an even tighter schedule, and working long hours—all while struggling with a heart condition.

His last shot at directing—*The Osterman Weekend* (1983)—is considered one of his worst efforts. Sam himself sadly noted during the production that he didn't really feel like it was one of his films. In early 1984 he directed two music videos for Julian Lennon, but that could not stop the downward slide.

The last time I saw Sam was in his Paradise Cove trailer around Thanksgiving 1984, shortly before his death. I watched as he did a line of coke, enough to stagger a rhinoceros, and became a completely different man in the span of seconds. His eyes widened, and he straightened up. He looked vibrant, alive, a foot taller, yet I knew he was on his way to death.

By this time of his life, Sam no longer held the rights to some of my work but thought he still had the option on *My Pardner*, and I wanted it. I think I could have proved that I owned it, but I just didn't want to use the energy to go through attorneys again. I was willing to pay Sam $2,000 to get the rights back—a stupid deal.

"I can't do it," he told me.

"Why not?"

"I've got to have it as collateral."

We had a Heineken beer. It was always Heineken with Sam.

Other people were coming and going that weekend, including author Joe Bernhard, who discovered *The Rounders* and first got a copy to Sam, as he had also done with *The Hi-Lo Country*. As I left, I looked back at Sam. I knew it would be the last time I would see him. It remains one of the most powerful and sad moments in my life.

After that visit, but before Christmas, Sam called me at my home in Albuquerque. Though he often made prank calls, making out like he was someone else on the phone, this time he was very sweet.

"I'm going to Mexico to meet Begoña and Lupita," he told me. "When I get back, I'll sign over the rights to *My Pardner* to you."

I wished him well. That's the last time I spoke with him. While in Mexico, he had the massive heart attack that eventually killed him after he was flown back to the states.

Many people have recalled Sam's memorial service, held in January 1985 at the Directors Guild Theater in Los Angeles. Burt Kennedy picked Pat and me up from the airport and drove us to the theater. He was a nice guy who brought *The Rounders* to the screen. I've been asked why Burt lasted so long but never made any truly great movies, whereas Sam made some great movies but didn't last long at all. I think it's because Burt preferred to make a lot of friends and keep 'em, whereas Sam made very few friends and lost most of 'em. Burt said to Pat and me, "We should go up in the hills, bring down a really big rock, chisel Sam's name on it, and put it in front of the Directors Guild building." He was right. We should have.

I recall Denver driving up to the memorial service in his pickup truck, parking behind the theater. He would not go in; he preferred to stay outside, drinking whiskey and holding court for whoever happened by. Sam's ex-wife, Marie, came with their kids. Ali McGraw was there, and so was Brian Keith with his wife, Victoria, and Mariette Hartley, who broke down in tears at one point. L. Q. Jones was there and made the now-famous comment that the event was as disorganized as a Sam Peckinpah movie. David Weddle, who drove many of us around as we visited and shared stories of Sam, was also present, perhaps already gaining material for his biography of Sam.

There will always be stories of Sam Peckinpah.

I've heard that Sam hit some women. I do not know if these stories are true, but I have every reason to believe he never physically abused Marie, and I never saw or heard of him abusing or hitting any of his kids. He could be scary. Sam had a left hook that was pretty good for a guy his size. He hit a lot of people. I remember Sam telling Joe Bernhard, "When I get into a fight, I just go for their eyes." He was not mean to his actors—at least not to his stars. He had reverence for them. He respected guys like Joel McCrea and Randolph Scott because he knew they had seen a lot of living. He had a great reverence for Jason Robards Jr. and revived his career with both *Noon Wine* and *The Ballad of Cable Hogue*. At that time, Robards was known as a man of great promise who was throwing his career away for alcohol. Sam defied all logic and cast Robards in both those productions, giving his career a new life. Robards stopped drinking while doing *Cable Hogue* and that was that. Sam could be testy with Stella Stevens, but he was mostly just beautifully kind to her. She gave the performance of her life in *Cable Hogue*.

The Wild Bunch is still revered today as a classic Western of transition. Sam got the absolute essence of men riding out of their time. It took vision to get that done. I'm not sure what clouded that vision later on, but the cocaine certainly contributed. I recall a visit with Sam in an apartment in Los Angeles that Katy Haber set up for him after *The Killer Elite* had been released. He had a lot of writers there, including Jim Hamilton and Joe Bernhard, who wrote the wonderful book *The Ballad of Nonose Valley*. Sam's bodyguard, Allan Keller, was there—he could have whipped all of us—and he was pissed because Sam never invited him into his room, where he was holding court in bed. I remember waiting in the living room of the suite when Katy Haber came out of Sam's room and said, "Sam wants to see you." I went in and there was this East Indian dope peddler from San Francisco snorting a line of coke with Sam. Sam had no idea what I was doing there or why all these writers were outside his room. That dealer was like God delivering heaven to Sam.

And Sam was blowing the money he made from *Killer Elite* on coke; it was almost like he was committing suicide with the last of his money.

Sometime before all this, Chuck Miller, a wild friend of mine who was an insurance adjuster, went with me on a bird-hunting trip down near Roswell, New Mexico. On the ride down, I saw a line of about thirty dead skunks along the road. I told Chuck to stop. I got out, broke off a Yucca stem, maybe six-feet long, and set it up to make it look like I had lined up those skunks and whacked 'em all. Chuck took a photo of this "Max Evans Annual Skunk Round-Up." I had this skunk photo with me when I next visited Sam, and I showed it to him to lighten him up. He just stared at the skunks and didn't say a word. Jim Silke was there, and he asked the dumbest questions in a dead-serious manner about the photo. There was another young Hollywood writer there—I can't remember his name—and he looked at the photo and said, sort of noncommittal, "Isn't that something?" Joe Bernhard was also there, and he broke out laughing and asked a lot of funny questions because he knew the game I was playing. I told them all that skunks have a nerve in their backbone above their tail that freezes them, and if you can line 'em up, you can whack them if they get out of line with you and instantly freeze them. The others all fell for it, or stood silently by, confused. Sam didn't know what to make of it—he just stared wordlessly at this rare photo—he still didn't know why we were there. The whole setup seemed to fit into Sam's mindset at the time: he was creating chaos in his world and not the least bit aware that he was doing it.

Sam called me a few days later, sober. He had a concept to include the story of *The One-Eyed Sky* into his film version of *My Pardner.* The young boy from *My Pardner,* while on this horse drive, would stop, and the old cowboy, Boggs, would tell the young kid the story of *The One-Eyed Sky* along the way. It was a beautiful idea, but it would have made for a four-hour movie. And who would have financed such a wild-ass project when Sam was clearly on his downward trek? He wasn't going to hell—he was going into oblivion. He had already been to hell several times over while trying to put the fire out with whiskey. Then cocaine took him into the deep, dark madness.

One day, long after Sam was dead, Chalo González called me. He said, "I don't know why Sam was so mean to us." I said, "He was mean to everybody. But he did all right by your family." (Chalo wasn't mean back to Sam. I was.) I asked Chalo what happened to Begoña. Chalo said she died just like Sam; she started drinking hard right after Sam's death and, in essence, followed Sam into the dope and decline. Their daughter, Lupita, he told me, was working as a costume/wardrobe mistress in Mexican cinema and doing great.

Sam had tragedies with all the women in his personal life. He hated his mother after she sold the family ranch that he and Denver intended to inherit and live on. I think from that point on, he distrusted women. He thought whores were the only women you could trust. The only one who survived him is Katy Haber. I asked her how she put up with his madness. She told me she felt so blessed to have survived the Holocaust that took her family that she needed a means to give back to the world. "I knew, even with the turmoil within Sam, that there would be moments of genius that would last forever," she told me. There was a great truth in that. Therein lies a hint of the mesmerizing impact Sam Peckinpah had on a whole range of creative people, and I suppose I was one of them. We all thought that at any minute the son of a bitch would do something great, and we wanted to be part of it.

Katy had left Sam's life for good in the late 1970s. She saved his life at least once, maybe twice, if you include the time she took him to the hospital in Yugoslavia during the shooting of *Cross of Iron*. Once Sam was so incredibly sick that she had to drag him into the bathroom. He refused to get back up off the floor or go back to bed. She feared his imminent death, so she called Kris Kristofferson and asked him to come out to the trailer with his guitar. Kris did, and he went into the bathroom and played "Sunday Morning Comin' Down"—one of Sam's favorite songs—so Sam would revive long enough for Katy to get him back to his bedroom, where she force-fed him chicken soup. I witnessed all of this at Sam's famed trailer house—a sort of second home that had turned into a combination hospital, bar, and madhouse for creative people. It took several days, weeks even, but she got Sam back up on his feet. I knew what enormous sacrifices Katy had made for Sam, and this was one time I was there to witness it.

Sam was capable of brilliance—we cannot forget that. I could see what Sam was doing with *The Wild Bunch* and *Cable Hogue*. I used to think,

"But who's going to catch on?" Now they are catching on. Some critics didn't get his work at the time it was released. Sam loved the sparks that flew out of that transition period in the West. John Ford never made a Western like Sam; he made fanciful, good-looking Westerns. Sam was enough of a politician to tell lies when need be, but the only lie I ever heard him utter to further his career was that John Ford was his cinematic hero. That was the political thing to say, but his real heroes were author Robert Ardrey and the American film directors John Huston and Orson Welles, both of whom made stands against the studio system. Huston rarely lost. Welles always did. Sam loved *Touch of Evil* (1958), and when he later saw Welles appearing in television commercials, it broke his heart. Sam's own slide was painful and slow. He couldn't even land a TV commercial as Welles had.

Near the end, he got one last shot at hope for a comeback with a story of mine. Lots of people claim to have introduced Sam to Benny Binion, but it's all bullshit. I introduced Sam to Benny on the set of *Cable Hogue*. About two years before Sam's death, Benny called me to say that Sam was hanging out in Las Vegas. Benny's son-in-law was trying to get into the picture business and they convinced Sam they could produce his film version of *My Pardner*. That's when Sam called me at my home in Albuquerque and asked if I would coauthor the script with him for $75,000. He was pretty excited. He couldn't get work around this time. Somebody told Sam they could get a movie made with him, and he believed them. There was this wonderfully playful, childish tone to Sam's voice when he called me. And obviously it all blew apart. They misled him, and that didn't help his mental or emotional state. His old dream of making another movie was renewed and then destroyed in a flash.

Shortly thereafter, he called me. "I've been invited to the president's palace in Colombia," he said. "I want you to go with me. Those presidents are like kids with big playgrounds. They'll probably give us each a gift, like forty kilos each!"

I nearly swallowed the phone. He knew I didn't use that stuff. There was no point in asking him how we were going to smuggle forty kilos back. I was having more and more trouble flying at that point, and I told him I couldn't go. He was really disappointed. I figured he wouldn't get anyone to go with him on a trip like that unless they were a drug dealer, but then he talked actor Seymour Cassel—who had garnered an Academy Award nomination for best supporting actor for his work in John Cassavetes's 1968 film *Faces*, and who had worked with Sam in *Convoy*—into accompanying him to Colombia. I thought to myself, "That's the end of those two. We'll never hear from either one again." And we damn near didn't. I never quite got the full story of what happened, but I heard secondhand that Sam went crazy and started throwing knives into the doors of the palace when the president came by to talk movies. It turns out that the trip was a dope deal, combined with an attempt to raise some cash to make another movie. According to a brief phone conversation I had with Cassel in 2012, somehow the authorities took Sam's and Seymour's passports, and Sam got his hands on some dope and some cash, and at one point Sam gave Seymour a pistol and said, "Here, you take care of the rough stuff." Somehow Seymour got his passport back and got out of there. "I never thought I'd see Sam alive again," Seymour told me, and he almost didn't. He said the last he heard, Sam had gotten the dope, jumped on a boat with a bunch of whores, and sailed on down the river. I heard rumors that Sam was in danger of being imprisoned down there or might become one of the "disappeared" due to his behavior, but he got back. I had missed another crisis—I would have been stupid and loyally stayed there with Sam to try and keep him out of trouble. But after Seymour told me what happened, I knew why Sam wanted me—it was that pistol. He knew I was a dead shot and dead loyal and that I had been involved with smuggling. He wanted me down there to handle the rough stuff, not for my delightful companionship. I would not have been any use to him in that kind of atmosphere anyway.

When speaking of Sam's madness, I like to think of the tragicomedy in it all. Once, he met me at the old Sands Motel bar, sitting with me in my corner booth, when this big, raw-jawed kid joined us. Sam liked him, and he challenged him to an Indian wrestling contest. I noticed this kid had big hands—the biggest I'd ever seen. That didn't stop Sam. He got up, this kid got up, and they began wrestling. This kid whacked Sam right on the floor. Sam got up and insisted I try the kid. I despise this kind of macho crap, and I'll only get involved if it's for a friend, so I got up, got a helluva grip on this kid, and this guy just about crushed my hand. I knew I was defeated and lamely said, "That was great. You beat me."

It turned out this kid was a pilot, so Sam hired him then and there to be his private pilot, which made no sense because Sam didn't have a plane. The kid left happy, knowing he'd spent the evening with one of Hollywood's greats and gotten hired by him. The kid also worked as a bartender down the strip, and he went around bragging that he was working for Sam Peckinpah as his personal pilot. But when Sam never called the kid to use him, the kid hired a lawyer to chase Sam down and threaten him with a big, expensive lawsuit. Sam called me up. "You have to settle with this kid."

I said, "He can beat me and the best three Hollywood stunt men in a brawl."

Sam said, "I know, but you can do it."

In vast ignorance, I told Sam I would make a run at it, so I got the name of the bar where the kid worked and went down there, and the kid recognized me. I called him over to a table, and I said something like, "Withdraw your lawsuit or you will be withdrawn from the world."

The kid was big, and tough, and obviously trained to handle trouble. He said, "Are you threatening me?"

I said, "No. I am letting you know on behalf of people who do this sort of thing for a living."

The kid glared at me. I thought he was about to pin me to the wall. But he backed down.

It was a bluff on my part. I did once know people who could do that sort of thing, but not in Los Angeles—only in Mexico and New Mexico.

Sam never thanked me. He expected me to do things like that. It was "Did you hear the phone?" all over again.

One evening, Sam drove up from Malibu to take me to dinner some-where. I wasn't staying at the Sands this time, but Sam did pass some time with me at the Sands bar so we could talk with Cliff, the bartender. There was only one other person in the bar that night—I believe it was a Sunday—and the crew was beginning to clean up to prepare for clos-ing. We drank Heinekens. Sam insisted in his low voice that I get Cliff to sell us a case of Heineken for him to take back with him to Malibu because he had run out of the stuff. I said, "It's against the law, but I'll ask."

I asked Cliff. He hesitated, and then checked the storage room. He said, "I don't have a case of Heineken back there, but I can give you a case of another beer." I forget what brand.

We finished our drinks. Cliff closed the bar. We walked out to Sam's car, me carrying the case of beer. Sam opened the trunk of his car and I noticed a pistol in a holster in the trunk. I think it was a .38 automatic. Sam pulled the gun out of the trunk and said, "Let's see what kind of shots we are."

It was about midnight, but everything was quiet on the strip on a Sunday night.

Sam took the pistol out of the holster. He told me to throw a bottle up into the air. I did. He blasted away, and missed of course, and the bottle fell and splattered all over the parking lot.

I was just as stupid as a roll-up man could be. I thought it was funny. I said, "Hell, it's my turn."

So Sam threw one up in the air. I fired, and missed. Another crash followed.

We threw bottles, shot the pistol, and broke glass until the pistol was empty. I hit one bottle. Sam didn't hit any. He claimed to have hit at least two, but he didn't. There was glass and beer all over the place. I don't know why Cliff or any other Sands employee didn't come out to see what the ruckus was about. We were having so much fun that we didn't think about the fact that the police might come by, because they were always patrolling Sunset Boulevard. But they didn't show up.

Sam threw the empty pistol into the trunk and said, "Maybe we should get out of here." We jumped in his car and headed down to his trailer in Malibu. We had a few bottles of beer left in the mostly empty case, so we drank them there. Looking back on it, I can't imagine what we were doing, or why, but we got away with it. We were always pulling stuff like that.

I'd heard stories of Sam shooting recklessly at things out of the back of his trailer. Someone told me he once shot at his own reflection in the mirror there. Everything about Sam was like pulling at a rope that had a little tear in it: you never knew when it was going to break, but you knew it eventually would. He was always pulling that rope in opposite directions.

Here's another gun story: Sam and Denver loved to go camping in the

High Sierras, and sometimes they took me with them. One time Denver rented a fancy four-wheel drive vehicle to take Walter Peter, Sam, and me out on one of these trips. Walter was driving, Sam was sitting next to him, and Denver and I were in the back. We were all drinking and passing a bottle of tequila around. Walter always seemed to be more in control than the rest of us, but he also had the most DWI charges against him. Denver thought Walter and Sam were being careless up front and that Walter was driving too fast. He said, "Hey, you guys, slow down! You're driving too fast."

Sam and Walter were talking about some subject that fascinated them, and they weren't listening to Denver, which was always a mistake. Denver had this briefcase with him, sitting on the back seat between us, and after the third time he told them to slow down, he opened it up, pulled out a .45, and shot the front windshield out in front of Sam and Walter. The car veered into the desert sand on the side of the road and finally came to a stop. Neither Sam nor Walter said a thing to Denver. They knew he had warned them. He was top dog and that pistol kept him top dog.

Denver had to return the car to the rental company in Fresno. I don't know how he explained the damage to the window. Several days later, Sam mentioned to me that his head was still ringing from that gunshot.

I once asked Walter to describe Sam to me in a few words. He called Sam "a chocolate-covered piranha." I wrote that comment down on the back of a red cocktail napkin from the Mikado lounge. I still have the napkin.

Sometimes I get to thinking about the Green's director of entertainment, Chalo González. He was present when the Green was formed and became an instant member, though some misinformed person shortened his title to court jester. If Chalo liked you, he could and would turn your most insane statement into fun. He helped Sam in many ways on *The Wild Bunch* and in playing one of the lead heavies in *Bring Me the Head of Alfredo Garcia*. He also acted in such television programs as *Justified* (2010) and the TV movie *The Second Civil War* (1997), and even starred in the 2006 independent film *Quinceañera*, as Tio Tomas Alvarez. His great contributions to Sam's career are mostly unrecorded. Not only did he bring laughter and friendship to Sam, but it's possible, and probable, that *The Wild Bunch* would not have become the classic it is without Chalo's contribution.

Chalo picked most of the wonderful desert (and other) locations for that film, and he got the musicians together for the touching horseback departure of the Wild Bunch from their idyll with women, wine, and fun before they ride off to their destiny. The music makes this scene the favorite of countless fans worldwide. Jumping forward to the editing of the movie back in Hollywood, it was discovered that the audiotape to this music was lost. Panic ensued. Sam asked the impossible of Chalo: he had to return to Mexico, gather the same talented and in-demand musicians, and tape this magical part of the film score again. Chalo did it. He contributed as much to *The Wild Bunch* as any of its stars. He also played a small acting role, performed endless other chores, and kept everyone around him feeling better no matter what great difficulties were brought about by the madman of film and his infected cast and crew.

Chalo attended the first screening of the film with great anticipation and excitement. When the end credits and titles rolled to black, Chalo asked Sam, "Where am I?" He had received no credit at all for his contributions. Sam just looked at him for a moment. Sam may not have lasted in the rare world of greatness had Chalo, along with Katy Haber and Frank Kowalski, not been present. Sam didn't always understand that.

Late in 2011, I called Fern Lea to ask her to share a personal memory of Sam. She recalled some childhood incidents with him, when they were growing up in and around Fresno. She recalled playing in the barn with other kids when they came across a monster rat. She ran screaming for Sam, who acted as her protector. He grabbed his grandfather's .38 pistol and a flashlight, took Fern Lea's hand, and said, "Come on, Fern Lea—let's get that monster rat!"

They went into the barn, shut the door behind them, and in the dark Sam turned on the flashlight. He said to Fern Lea, "Don't stand in front of me." Sam found the rat, which was hypnotized by the beam from the flashlight, and shot it with the .38. Fern Lea never forgot that moment.

She said Sam had a pony that once tossed him off and banged up his back pretty badly. He had to wear a brace for a while, and she returned the favor of his killing the monster rat by tying his shoelaces for him when he couldn't bend down to do it himself.

Nearby was Bass Lake, and Sam once went down there for days to work on something special. He wouldn't let Fern Lea come down to look. He told her he was building them a ship so they could sail off to explore the world. At last, the grand day arrived. They had a considerable journey to make down the hill to the lake, and she recalled an old drunk stumbling by the lake, drinking and mumbling to himself. Sam made a big show of it all, yelling to Fern Lea, "Run to the boat!" He was already inventing dramatics. She came across a big raft with a pole attached bearing a big white flag with a skull and crossbones and the name "the Black Mariah" painted on it. And Sam took his sister on a great journey across the sea—well, along the shore of Bass Lake, anyway.

There was one other memory she did not witness firsthand. Sam went fishing with his grandfather and came back to the shed to clean the fish they caught. Sam's knife slipped and cut open an artery in his arm. It started pumping blood out like a fountain. Instead of screaming or throwing a fit of any kind, Sam simply moved his head up and down, watching the blood flow out. Here he was experiencing slow-motion blood that early in his life. His grandfather, who later told Fern Lea this story, got the wound fixed up. She said this story got retold in a European newspaper years later, and the writer said it was a sure sign that Sam was born a blood-lusty madman. I see it this way: it's a sign he was born with a theatrical flair for life, which included a fascination for blood, passion, and drama.

As of this writing, Fern Lea lives a serene life with her children and grandchildren in San Diego. She laughs as she tells these stories. She is the epitome of a motto I've always cherished: "All you can do about the ridiculous side of mankind is laugh about it." It was a pleasure to hear her voice enjoying the youthful follies of a certified madman and genius and laughing at his foolishness. She recently told me, "My brother Sam was a son of a bitch, but he had a very tender side to him."

I recently found a letter that Garner Simmons wrote to me in 1986, in which he said of Sam, "If he died of anything, it was overexertion—trying to cram ninety years into sixty. He almost made it." Sam himself told *New York Times* journalist Aljean Harmetz back in 1969, "I suppose it [death] is inevitable. I'm not afraid of it. What I am afraid of is stupid, useless, horrible death—an automobile accident [or] a violent death for no purpose."

Sam had come close to dying several times in his life, and as I've related before, I watched Katy Haber preserve him for at least one more shoot. Journalist Michael Lindsay, in a wonderful 1990 *Hollywood Magazine* piece on Peckinpah, wrote of Sam nearly dying in a swimming pool and being revived via mouth-to-mouth resuscitation. That's when Sam's doctor told him he'd have to give up drinking if he wanted to live. Sam wanted to live, so he gave up alcohol and turned to cocaine and Quaaludes. In his piece, Lindsay paints a typically dark portrait of Sam in decline, finding the caustic humor in Sam's personality when photographer John Bryson invited Sam to dinner to meet British actor Trevor Howard. "Sam went into the back room and sat by himself," Lindsay wrote. "After an hour or so, John came back and found Sam with four lines of coke in front of him and two Quaaludes. John said, 'Sam, you really ought to come into the other room. Trevor Howard drove all this way and he wants to meet you. He's a fan.' Sam looked up, then rolled a dollar bill, snorted the coke, downed the Quaaludes, and said, 'I don't talk to drunks.'"

I don't know that I can top anyone else's final thoughts on Sam, so I'll go back to comments I wrote about him in the *Impact* article in 1985: "I once said in an interview that Sam had the soul of a Mexican general wrapped up in a gringo hide. He was as mean and crazy as a gut-shot javelina and as tender as a windless dawn. His long, ragged race is over. The rest of us will have to get back on our tracks. So it's always been. The end credits are through rolling. The theater is empty and dark. Play it again, Sam."

Now, some thirty years later, I will alter that last comment slightly. As crazy as it sounds, "How I *wish* the whole Broad Beach bunch could play it again, Sam."

Index

Printed in the USA
CPSIA information can be obtained
at www.ICGtesting.com
LVHW041207151223
766489LV00003B/267